LA COCINA MEXICANA

The publisher gratefully acknowledges the generous
support of the Humanities Endowment Fund of the
University of California Press Foundation.

LA COCINA MEXICANA

MANY CULTURES, ONE CUISINE

MARILYN TAUSEND

WITH RICARDO MUÑOZ ZURITA

▪ PHOTOGRAPHS BY IGNACIO URQUIZA ▪

UNIVERSITY OF CALIFORNIA PRESS   Berkeley   Los Angeles   London

University of California Press, one of the most distinguished university presses in the United States, enriches lives around the world by advancing scholarship in the humanities, social sciences, and natural sciences. Its activities are supported by the UC Press Foundation and by philanthropic contributions from individuals and institutions. For more information, visit www.ucpress.edu.

University of California Press
Berkeley and Los Angeles, California

University of California Press, Ltd.
London, England

Design and composition: Claudia Smelser
Text: Miller Text and Benton Gothic
Display: Excelsis and Cg Beton
Index: Thérèse Shere
Map of Mexico: Melanie Ferguson
Printing and binding: Thomson-Shore, Inc.

LIBRARY OF CONGRESS CATALOGING-IN-PUBLICATION DATA

Tausend, Marilyn.
    La cocina mexicana : many cultures, one cuisine / Marilyn Tausend ; with Ricardo Muñoz Zurita ; photographs by Ignacio Urquiza.
        p.   cm.
    In English.
    Includes biographical references and index.
    ISBN 978-0-520-26111-2 (cloth : alk. paper)
    1. Cooking, Mexican.   I. Muñoz Zurita, Ricardo.   II. Title.
    TX716.M4T379   2012
    641.597—dc23

                                                    2012004373

Manufactured in the United States of America

21 20 19 18 17 16 15 14 13 12
10 9 8 7 6 5 4 3 2 1

The paper used in this publication meets the minimum requirements of ANSI/NISO z39.48–1992 (R 2002) *(Permanence of Paper)*.

To the two men in my life without whom this book would not be.

Ed Lewis, my father, introduced me to Mexico as a young child, imbuing me with a curiosity about all foods and a deep respect for those who make feasts out of meager offerings.

Fredric Tausend, my husband, rekindled my love of Mexico, and his influence is shown throughout the book.

And to Cleo, my ancient Siamese cat, who has sat or slept on every page of this book, both drafts and final copy, and in the process edited quite a few of them by shredding.

Contents

MEXICO TODAY

Mexico's thirty-one states and one federal district cover over 761,000 square miles, but only 12 percent are arable. Roughly one-fourth of the land is a mix of highland and tropical forests and the huge Chihuahuan Desert is the largest in North America. There are six mountain chains that bisect the country and three snow-clad volcanoes, with Pico de Orizaba in Veracruz the continent's third-highest mountain. During the twentieth century, nine of Mexico's volcanoes erupted. Rivers and lakes abound, and there are close to six thousand miles of coastline.

The many terrains of Mexico—its jumble of wetlands, mountain slopes, high plateaus, coastal plains, and humid tropical forests—are home to a wide variety of edible native plants and wildlife, some now domesticated, that are used in the regional cuisines of the estimated 111 million people, about 70 percent of whom live in urban areas, the majority of them around Mexico City. While Mexico is the most populous Spanish-speaking country in the world, about half of the over 10 million indigenous people, many of whom live in the more inaccessible regions, still speak their native language.

Preface

When I began to lead culinary trips to Mexico in 1989, I knew it was important that anyone who wanted to learn about Mexican cooking should also know about the people who
raise, prepare, and eat both the daily and the celebratory foods of the country. For me, it
is not enough just to follow the directions in recipes. I believe you must understand the
culture of those who are preparing the dishes. To quote the noted anthropologist Sidney W.
Mintz, "The single most important truth about human beings is the existence of culture. . . .
How could we possibly think about what human beings eat without taking into account
those properties of our species?"

Over the years, I have eaten and cooked with many Mexican families from diverse cultures. Some prepared their food over the lively heat of a wood fire built on the packed-
earth floor of the cooking area, but most had kitchens that mirror those found in typical
homes in the United States. The main differences numbered just two: a traditional basalt
molcajete had the place of pride on the counter and a *comal* was invariably nearby.

During these years, I wrote four Mexican cookbooks. But none of them accomplished
what I hope to do here. Initially I wanted to explore fully the origins and traditions of the
various foods of the country, starting with the basic dishes of the indigenous people, many
of whom still speak only their original native language, and to better understand the pro-
found European influence, especially of the Spanish and the French, which is everywhere
in evidence. Then I became aware of an early third component: the more subtle culinary
contribution of the enslaved Africans brought to the New World by the Spanish. They carried the staple foods of their homeland and the skills and knowledge for growing crops and
raising livestock. I knew that other later influences existed as well, especially those that
traveled along the trade route between the Philippines and the Pacific Coast, but it was the
culture of these first three groups in Mexico that I wanted to know more intimately. All
three cultures came together to provide the basis for the Mexican cooking of today.

Researching and then writing this book was an almost four-year task, and I was fortunate to have the help of Ricardo Muñoz Zurita during much of that time. He appeared in my life about 1991, when Shelley Wiseman, a cooking teacher in Mexico City, told me about an exciting new chef who was doing a brief stint at a very "in" restaurant. Of course, Shelley and I went and there I met Ricardo for the first time. What I remember most from that night, aside from his big smile, was the dish that ended the meal, *encanto de zapote negro*, a wickedly black and irresistible tropical fruit dessert. Ricardo and I bonded that evening and since then we have shared many culinary adventures, having fun along the way. Now, Ricardo is adding his extensive research on the regional foods of Mexico to this book, bringing a truly Mexican perspective to it.

Many of our recipes may be old friends, others quite unfamiliar. You will find dishes of corn, beans, tomatoes, chiles, and herbs and little else that are prepared today in the simple kitchens of some of Mexico's indigenous peoples just as they have been for centuries. You will also discover recipes using these same staples, but transformed by the inclusion of ingredients and cooking techniques from Spain, France, and other parts of Europe and from Africa.

As you go through the pages of this book and learn the history and tradition behind these dishes, Ricardo and I hope you will be encouraged to experience the many tastes and textures of this multifaceted cuisine at your own table.

Introduction

It was a Christmas week in the mid-1980s, and on an unusually clear day, the air crisp and clean, my husband, Fredric, and I left the vast urban sprawl of Mexico City, driving first alongside the magnificent old and new structures at its center and then past the tentacle-like rows of wood-and-tin shacks that climb the surrounding hillsides. We were on our way to spend Christmas with friends in Morelia, Michoacán, one of central Mexico's most beautiful colonial cities. Fredric, a trial attorney, had frequently been there in the past while representing Michoacán in a trial, and I had become became entranced with the hospitality of the people and the different foods that we were served. Up until then, my only experience with many of these dishes was from cooking them out of Diana Kennedy's cookbooks.

The road was winding and quite narrow as it climbed up through pine-forested hills on the way toward the Mil Cumbres, the region of "a thousand mountain peaks." We were so intent on making our way through a series of blind curves that we missed the more direct route to Morelia, and the next thing we knew we were in Zitácuaro. It was midafternoon then, and we still had a long way to go. Zitácuaro is a midsize rural town with a lively commercial center, though not much in the way of interest for visitors. But I remembered that it was near where Diana Kennedy had settled in the mid-1970s, after the death of her husband, Paul. The always intrepid Fredric said we should call her up and see if we could get together, which he proceeded to do from a nearby pay phone. The next thing we knew, Diana had given him directions to the charming Rancho San Cayeteno, a couple of miles away. Here in a cottage next to a continuously humming creek, we were to spend the night and perhaps meet with Diana the next morning. We assumed that she had asked the French Vietnamese manager, André Claude, to check us out, and we must have passed muster, as right after breakfast she arrived in her beloved yellow pickup truck. After questioning, she ascertained that I had binoculars for birding, was knowledgeable about food, birds, plants, and the politics of both our countries, and that Fredric loved opera—all passions she shared—and we spent the morning with Diana at her home.

After that initial get-together with Diana, we visited quite often, and in January 1989, Diana asked if I would consider doing some culinary tours with her. Without thinking I agreed, and that was the beginning of Culinary Adventures, Inc. During the following years we had trips first to Michoacán and soon after to Oaxaca, Yucatán, and Veracruz. I usually did the exploratory research with my then-assistant Carmen Barnard, who was born and raised in Morelia, and sometimes just Diana came along.

It was here in Michoacán, home of the Purépecha people for close to a thousand years, that I first began my long-lasting affection for all things Mexican: the people, their culture and history, and most important, the tastes, textures, and aromas of their foods. For me, these are all intrinsically woven together, connecting the past with the present.

One evening when I was with local friends outside Uruapan, the avocado capital of Mexico, we visited a festival celebrating Purépecha food. No other tourists seemed to be there. It was just us among the happy pandemonium of folks from the surrounding area who were all trying to taste as many different dishes as possible. Strolling musicians and performances of regional dances added to the festive commotion. We were able to try at least twelve different types of tamales. My favorite was made of roughly ground, dusky blue corn filled with mushrooms and shaped into a ball. There were kettles shrouded in steam and bubbling with various aromatic fruit and chocolate *atoles,* and just when I thought I could eat no more, I tried an amazing bowl of thick, pungent greenish stew, which the girl dishing it up for me said was *atápacua de flor de calabaza.* Every state has its own regional specialties, some of which I describe below.

▪ LIFE OF A TRADITIONAL ZAPOTEC FAMILY

When I first started researching the foods in the state of Oaxaca in the early 1990s, I found that there were at least sixteen different indigenous groups living there, many of them still speaking their native languages and practicing their long-standing cultural traditions. The most prominent, the Zapotecs and Mixtecs, were two of the earliest civilizations in Mexico, and impressive structural vestiges of their ancient settlements, such as the archeological site of Monte Albán, now welcome thousands of tourists every year. The more than one hundred thousand descendants of these two groups still inhabit the valleys and mountainsides of Oaxaca and remain an influence in the region, especially through their crafts and their foods.

Early on, as I set out to explore the culinary traditions of the Zapotecs, Patricia Quintana, a noted Mexican chef, convinced me that Abigail Mendoza, who lives in the small weaving village of Teotitlán del Valle, was the ideal person to introduce me to these foods.

I first met Abigail during that time between late afternoon and early evening when the heat of the day rests. Fredric and I were driving down a well-worn but still lumpy cobblestone street in search of the Mendoza family home. "Go past the market, and when the road starts to climb and the street narrows, go left down a narrow dirt road and there will be a gate in a wall, and if you look up, you will see turkeys on the roof" were the directions that had been given to me. As we made our way down the street, a wild-eyed gray bull zigzagged toward our car, followed by a young boy on a burro trying to head him off. When they passed, we parked, and guided by the strident gobbling of the Mendoza family's turkeys, we reached the gate and knocked. When the door opened for me, so did a whole new world. That was over twenty years ago, and although the villagers have since adapted many of the advances of modern technology, such as television and the Internet, the old traditions of Teotitlán have endured.

As Liæ Læn, my Zapotec name, I know that I am blessed for being absorbed into the vibrant Mendoza family: the constantly smiling Abigail, oldest daughter of Clara and Emiliano, her four brothers and five sisters, their wives, husbands, children, and the important *compadres* and *comadres,* the many godparents who are an integral part of the life of this weaving family. That first day, as I was welcomed into the earth-floored large patio, I had no idea that I would share so many of the events that would take place in this home—births, deaths, weddings, and other celebrations.

Food is at the heart of all of these happenings, and Abigail is the one who is now in charge of feeding the family. She told me that when she was seven years old, she was grinding chiles on a small *metate,* a thick, rectangular basalt grinding stone, for *mole amarillo.* When she was eight, she started grinding corn for the large *tlayudas* (or *clayudas*), the tortillas that her mother made daily. At nine, she went early one morning to the home of Tía Zenaida, the sister of her grandfather, to help prepare the traditional chocolate *atole* for her father's birthday celebration. There, she was responsible for grinding all of the special ingredients for the *atole,* including two hundred pounds of cacao beans that had been bleached chalk white in a six-month process that included burying them in clay pots and regularly digging them up and rewashing them. At that time, Tía Zenaida was considered one of the finest cooks in this village of around eight thousand and one of the few women, or *comideras,* who was asked to organize the people preparing the food for this and other fiestas. In Teotitlán, friends and extended family not only attend the fiestas but are also expected to help provide the food and to cook.

Soon Abigail was using her own full-size *metate* and *mano,* a volcanic-rock rolling pin weighing around seven pounds. This is backbreaking work even for an adult, but Abigail quickly became proficient and before long was given additional responsibilities. By the time she was sixteen, Abigail had begun to take over her Tía Zenaida's role in organizing the cooking for many of the family and village festivities. In traditional Zapotec fashion, the technique of preparing the daily and celebratory meals passes from generation to generation, and now Abigail has her first niece, Clarita, grinding chiles on a small *metate.* The dishes seldom vary—they are part of the Zapotec heritage, one that goes back more than three thousand years—with the fiestas now combined with celebrations of the Catholic saints.

Several years later, Ricardo and I walked down the same rutted, rocky road to the Mendoza home for the traditional three-day nonstop wedding *fandango* of Abigail's brother, Jacobo. In preparation for the wedding breakfast, scores of women were kneeling on woven palm mats in a nearby canvas-canopied field, where since dawn they had been grinding masa on their *metates*, pressing it into large *tlayudas*, and quickly cooking the *tlayudas* on their *comales* over small fires.

Nearby was an over-my-head pile of hundreds of chicken and turkey eggshells from eggs cracked for making *higaditos*, or "little livers," a traditional festival dish. The Mendozas often omit the livers when preparing this dish for smaller, less important events, but for this *fandango* the livers from the just-killed chickens and turkeys were included, along with thick shreds of the cooked meat. These meats are folded into eggs and gently mixed into a simmering broth seasoned with garlic and cumin. When the eggs begin to solidify, they are topped with chunks of fresh tomato. Although it sounds simple, it is a challenge, and only the most experienced *comideras* can create this dish.

On this morning, as I passed into the courtyard of the Mendoza home, a row of older women, their hair in ribbon-entwined braids on the tops of their heads, were on their knees, glazed clay bowls in front of them, beating the eggs with long knives. I had often watched Abigail do this, and the sound of the deeply resonant kalump, kalump, kalump as her blade cut through the eggs was impressive. But when that sound was magnified by eight knives, it was like an overture to a culinary symphony. The beaten eggs were then poured into several immense metal cauldrons over a wood fire and stirred with wooden paddles, beginning the alchemy needed to prepare *higaditos* for five hundred guests. Men were sitting around tables, the women on mats, and those few of us who were not from the village were provided tiny chairs. In another part of the patio, other cooks were busily preparing the ceremonial chocolate *atole* that is an important part of this *fandango*. As a brass band played, we were handed bowls of the *atole* crowned with inches of tiny bubbles that created a foam so thick that it is eaten with a *gallito*, a carved, flat wooden implement. Then the brothy eggs were scooped into more bowls, drizzled with a smooth chile salsa, and served with the crisp *tlayudas*, which we broke and used as our utensil for eating the *higaditos*.

For the main dish on the wedding day, the Mendozas served the acclaimed *mole negro*, the king of all moles. My assignment was to spend two hours discouraging large flies attracted to the lush frosting of a multitiered wedding cake. A cluster of turkey feathers was my defense. The next day, the parents of the bride prepared the equally wondrous *mole amarillo*, also with turkey. Firework displays, multiple brass bands, dancing, and endless toasts with *copitas* of *mezcal* all added to the joyous festivities that took place every day and into the night.

UNUSUAL FOODS OF THE MAYAN WORLD

Farther south, the Maya, another ancient and influential civilization, left behind monumental remains of their great settlements, just as the Zapotecs had. I have met their descendants throughout the cities and villages of Yucatán, Campeche, Quintana Roo, Tabasco, and Chiapas, and I am always amazed by the numerous regional dialects I hear and the many traditional dishes that are still prepared. Most of the foods, however, are a blend of indigenous ingredients and techniques with those of the Europeans and Africans who arrived in the sixteenth century. As a result of its geographic isolation, the cuisine that developed on the east coast is quite unlike that in the rest of Mexico. Nowhere else would you find such dishes as *pavo en relleno negro,* which seems right out of medieval literature. The first time I saw this molten black dish being made was in a restaurant kitchen in Mérida. I watched as ground pork seasoned with *recado negro,* the traditional seasoning paste of burnt chiles and spices, was wrapped around several whole hard-boiled eggs, forming a ball, which was then stuffed into a small turkey. Next, the cook simmered the turkey in a broth well seasoned with garlic and more *recado negro.* I later found some home cooks simplified the process by cooking the meatball alongside the turkey. All of the flavors still melded, but the mystique was lost.

It was on one of my first exploratory trips to Yucatán that I began a now-long friendship with Silvio Campos, who has led me through the many intricacies of Mayan cooking. We met when I wanted to sample the traditional *cochinita pibil* (page 149), a whole baby pig that is seasoned and then buried in a pit of coals and left to cook for many hours. To find out who was the expert, my assistant, Carmen, and I asked everyone we could, from businessmen to taxi drivers, and all of them sent us to the village of Tixkokob to find Silvio. The first challenge was to find Tixkokob, but once we did, finding Silvio's home turned out to be easy. We just asked someone in the busy square for the *maestro de cochinita pibil* and soon we were led by several young lads on *tricicletas* (canopied three-wheel bikes) down and around many corners to the Campos home.

In the years that followed, I watched Silvio, truly a master with a knife, slaughter many pigs in his backyard, all in reverence, with most of the meat used for the *cochinita pibil* that he sells at the market or prepares for special events. Little is wasted: the blood is flavored with mint, chives, and *chiles habaneros;* combined with the chopped innards; stuffed into casings of the large intestine; and then simmered to make a tasty sausage similar to the French boudin. The thin layers of pork rind are cut into sheets and hung in the sun for two days before being boiled in oil, snapping and crackling as they turn into crisp *chicharrones.* One time I saw a row of pig's tails hanging to dry on the line, but I was afraid to ask how they would be used. During the days I have spent with Silvio and his wife, Angelica, I also learned how to make an amazing number of other dishes, including the famous *queso relleno* (page 205), a lavishly stuffed Edam cheese smothered in sauces.

Through the years, I have researched and led small groups to other parts of the former Mayan civilization. We have cooked and eaten indigenous foods in the jungles of Chiapas and very Spanish-style dishes in the highlands. I have often traveled through hot and humid Tabasco, where cacao has been cultivated for over fifteen hundred years. Here, one of Ricardo's many *tías* grilled us a number of *pejelagartos,* that primitive freshwater gar that has changed little since the demise of the dinosaur. Its elongated jaw filled with big teeth is similar to the snout of a small, skinny alligator, thus its Spanish name, a contraction of *pez* for "fish" and *lagarto* for "lizard." Now it was slathered with a salsa of the tiny but fierce *chile amaxito* (similar to the fresh *chile piquín*), the heat diluted only by lime juice. This savory fish was eagerly devoured amid such exclamations as, "Oh my God, this is good." It was quite an experience.

Farther south, in Emeliana Zapotá, I sat down at a lovely dining table with the multi-generational family of Ricardo's *tío* Juan for a special *comida* of *tortuga en sangre,* a classic preparation of the river turtle, a dish that Ricardo had long promised me I could try here. (These turtles are not now considered an endangered species, but because they are sought after as a tasty source of food, I have been told that they are growing scarce.) After the turtles are caught, they are kept and fed in a holding pond until the day they are to be cooked. All of the meat from the turtle is slowly simmered with a sauce of pure achiote and the local species of parsley. Peering into the simmering pot, I saw small *bollitos de masa* (masa dumplings) bobbing amid the yellowish immature eggs of the turtle. As I was the honored guest, I was presented, along with Mamá Tona, Juan's ninety-six-year-old mother-in-law, one of these *ganchines,* turtle eggs that looked like Ping-Pong balls. It was quite a challenge to eat, but by picking up cues from watching Mamá Tona, I took my first bite and was surprised at how enjoyable it was.

▤ THE CULTURAL MOSAIC OF VERACRUZ

Veracruz was another early destination for my culinary trips, and from my first planning excursion in June 1998 through my most recent visit in autumn 2011, I have had some of my most exciting and rewarding journeys. The foods of this state reflect its varied topography and its many cultural influences: the Totonacs and Huastecs in the north, the Africans in the central region, the French influence around the small cheese-making community of San Rafael, the culinary remnants of an Italian settlement in the verdant south-central region, and the Spanish throughout the state.

In the bustling port city of Veracruz and the many other coastal towns and villages, seafood dominates the table. With one of my first groups, we traveled south to Tlacotalpan, the former prosperous port town on the banks of the Río Papalaopan (Place of Butterflies).

The facades of the century-old homes are painted muted jelly-bean hues of purple, pink, red, green, and yellow, making it a visual treat just to walk through the streets.

On an earlier trip to Tlacotalpan, I had contacted Pablo Rey Gómez, whose job was to promote this small, lovely town. I learned that he once played baseball in the U.S. minor leagues, and because Fredric was an attorney for the Mariners, a major league team in Seattle, I brought Pablo a Mariners cap on a subsequent trip. He was so excited to receive the cap that he arranged for many of the town's best cooks to serve our first tour group a meal of Tlacotalpan specialties in the town hall's cavernous second floor. It was hot when we all arrived, well into the hundreds, and our small handheld fans, which we discreetly waved, were the only air-conditioning. Our group was not alone. The whole city council, a reporter with a photographer, and Miss Tlacotalpan (Pablo's daughter) and her court all joined us, and only after many welcoming speeches did the extremely tasty food begin to appear. After nibbling on a small gordita lightly filled with black beans permeated with the anise flavor of crumbled avocado leaves, we were served *huevos de lisa*, the mustard yellow egg sacks of a variety of mullet, fried and served with a pungent salsa. Next came a cup of *caldo largo de pescado,* chunks of the same type of fish served in a thin tomato broth seasoned with *chile jalapeño,* all accompanied with an endless procession of tortillas just off of the *comal* and a salsa made from *chiles cuaresmeños,* large red *chiles jalapeños.* Then we were served *chile atole con pollo,* a masa-thickened chicken stew with rounds of fresh corn, little masa dumplings, and the aromatic leaf of *acoyo (hierba santa),* followed by a rice dish tinted a muted green with herbs. By now we were all becoming uncomfortably stuffed, but the local ladies continued to proudly bring us more dishes, ending with plates of Tlacotalpan's famous candies. Although it was too much to consume for all but the heartiest eater, I enjoyed each one of the tastes.

I soon learned that all of my favorite dishes were made by Sra. María Elena Romero, who turned out to be Pablo's mother-in-law, and I convinced her to demonstrate her skills to my future groups. For a number of years, we had classes in her home, which was modest on the inside but sported a rainbow hue of violet on the outside. To reach the kitchen, you had to walk through the small, immaculate living room with almost every flat surface arrayed with treasured small porcelain figures on well-starched crocheted doilies. Of the various dishes that Sra. María Elena demonstrated for us, the most unusual was the *tortitas* (fritters) of *tizmiches,* curious minuscule critters with bulging eyes that turned out to be shrimp larvae skimmed from the river. The most popular dish was *plátanos rellenos* (page 52), cooked and squished plantains filled with the local grated cheese and remade into the shape of a miniature plantain, then crisply fried to shades of golden brown.

One of my most memorable trips to other locations in Veracruz was in 2009, when I and a group of intrepid culinary explorers set out to retrace the route that Cortés and his followers traveled from the sandy coast of what is now the port of Veracruz to present-day

Mexico City. Plagued by clouds of mosquitoes at this first site, they soon headed farther north to near the Totanac center of Quiahuiztlán, which had been sighted by their pilot on an earlier journey, and where the ships would be sheltered by a massive rock island. Cortés's ships ended their journey here, and it was also where Cortés founded the first Villa Rica de la Vera Cruz—"rich town of the true cross."

It was on this same windswept beach off the coast below Quiahuiztlán almost five hundred years later that I flipped off my sandals and walked onto the half-moon of bleached gray sand and then into the shallow water, the silence broken only by the crashing waves and the cry of seabirds that nest on the same island near where the Spanish ships had moored. Standing there, I tried to imagine myself as one of those first seaborne interlopers to this land.

Food anthropologist Yolanda Ramos has a comfortable retreat located directly opposite the rock where Cortés's ships anchored, and she served a meal for us based on her research into the indigenous foods of that time. We started off with a broth made of freshly caught shrimp and with tostadas piled with chunks of the meat of blue crabs and avocados. We feasted on small *mojarras*, unusually tasty fish that received even more flavor from their wrapping of *hierba santa* leaves. And so we would not go away hungry, the fish were followed by bowls of black beans tinged with epazote. All of these dishes were among those that could have been served to the first Spaniards by the indigenous women, if they were so fortunate.

After hearing that the remains of the Spanish fortress encampment were nearby, I set out with my friend Mario Montaño, a cultural anthropologist who teaches at Colorado College, and a local archeologist, who said he thought the remains were in a field higher up. We drove up a steep hill on a road lined with large vacation homes overlooking the Gulf of Mexico and stopped near a rampantly overgrown piece of forgotten land. The three of us, struggling through the vegetation, scared off a small sleeping snake sunning itself coiled on what turned out to be one of the bruised gray stone blocks that had been used as the foundation for this first Spanish settlement in what is now Mexico. For the second time that day, I was experiencing emotions that I had never expected. Looking around, I could see other scarred cubes of stone aligned in rows, probably marking the living quarters and other rooms where one hundred fifty or so Spaniards lived while Cortés and his other men went off to seek the center of Motecuhzoma's empire and its expected treasures.

▮ CELEBRATING THE DAY OF THE DEAD IN TLAXCALA

Tlaxcala, Mexico's smallest state is, unfortunately, often overlooked by tourists. One day while visiting the state capital's small but extraordinary Museo de Artes y Tradicones Populares, Fredric and I became hungry and went next door to a *fonda* that featured *escamoles*, a seasonal regional dish of ant larvae that looked a bit like white rice sautéed in butter with onions, *chiles serranos,* and epazote. It turned out that the person in charge of both the museum and the restaurant was the exuberant, multitalented Yolanda Ramos Galicia. We soon became good friends and she introduced me to many of the ingredients and dishes of her state, including *mixiote de carnero con adobado* (page 162), lamb marinated in chile sauce, wrapped in the thin, outer membrane of the maguey's *pencas* (swordlike leaves), and then cooked in a pit lined with hot coals. Tlaxcala, along with nearby Puebla, quickly became one of my favorite destinations, and over the years, Yolanda has taught numerous classes to my groups in her historic home filled with the arts and crafts of Tlaxcala.

As a young child, Yolanda learned to cook by watching her mother and grandmother in the kitchen. But her life took another direction. After earning a degree in anthropology in Mexico City, she left to continue her studies in Paris, and when she returned, she became a curator at Mexico City's famed National Museum of Anthropology. Later, wanting the simpler life in Tlaxcala, she began studying and preserving the folk art and foods of her state, and today she oversees many of its cultural and historical sites.

I think one of the most moving times that I have ever experienced in Mexico was in Tlaxcala on the Day of the Dead, November 2. In regions of Mexico with a strong indigenous heritage, this date is of great importance, as it is when the spirits of those family members who have died return to reunite with the living they left behind. Each year, a celebration is held in their honor, with a colorfully decorated altar for the *ofrenda* (offering) of favorite dishes of the departed, perhaps some *mezcal,* and a few other familiar items to impart a sense of comfort. My oldest son, Eric, who had suffered a head injury in a car accident, had recently died after years in a nursing home, and Yolanda's mother, who had lived with her, had also just died. It was special for me to share this sad yet celebratory time with Yolanda's family and friends.

Earlier in the day, we had gone to the small local market and brought home huge bundles of *cempasúchitl,* vibrant orange, strong-smelling marigolds whose fragrance and color would guide the spirits back. The altar, a large table, was covered with a sky blue cloth and a mat with red, green, and purple geometric designs and strewn with huge flower garlands. It was laden with candles and with the traditional celebratory foods: fruits and a multitude of small, decorated *pan de muerto* (bread of the dead), complete with bones made of dough crossed on top. There were sugar skulls in all sizes, many labeled with the names of the departed. Yolanda's turkey mole, a favorite of her mother's, was on the altar, along with a *cazuela* filled with tamales and a bottle of *mezcal.*

Reed mats were spread out from the altar through the home and out the front door, and all of us were recruited to strip the petals from the *cempasúchitl* and use them to cover the mats with a profusion of color. We wove other blossoms into an arch over the door to serve as a beacon for Yolanda's mother and other departed relatives searching for their home. Many friends and family members soon began to arrive and continued to appear throughout the afternoon and evening to visit over food and drink. Because Eric had never been here in Tlaxcala, I doubt if his spirit joined us that day, but Yolanda would have certainly welcomed him. At our home in Washington, I have continued to do a much-abbreviated version of this ceremony, one that celebrates life that extends beyond death. Eric's favorite food was spaghetti, not mole, so that is what we eat for dinner, with lots of garlic bread, not tortillas.

SHARING A SIMPLE MEAL WITH A MAZAHUAN FAMILY

I knew that the Otomí people were one of the earliest indigenous groups in Mexico's central highlands, but my first intimate contact with them was the day I went to the small village of Boca de la Cañada, one of the several Mazahuan villages in Michoacán. I was with Celia Carmona Ramoní, who works to preserve the culture of the indigenous Mazahua, an offshoot of the Otomí.

Along both sides of the deeply rutted road to this highland village were hillsides dotted with wood-slab houses. The homes were surrounded by small fields of waist-high corn flanked by spears of agave pointing up to clouds that looked like shards of coagulated egg whites. The pungent odor emanating from the nearby dense stands of cedar and pine filled the air on the cool yet humid day. We were going to the home of Gregoria, where she and Alfreda, her daughter, were going to cook their basic midday meal of tortillas, salsa, and a pot of beans. After we crossed over a wood plank to the foot-trodden earthen courtyard, the family members, all handsome people with pronounced cheekbones, came forward, shook hands, and asked us to sit in small chairs outside their home.

"I don't know how old I am . . . I am alive today. I do not worry about the future," Gregoria told us, and although she has many troubles, she still enjoys the moment. To her, life is beautiful and full. She has her family and her church, and she can still work with her hands doing the embroidery that is such an important part of her Mazahuan culture.

I followed Alfreda into their separate cookhouse, which was a 16-by-16 foot square room with a shelf stacked with unmatched cups and bowls running along one wall. There was a small table covered with an intricately embroidered cloth and on the dirt floor several metal rings with small fires burning inside them. Two small chairs, each one perfect for a three-year-old, were against another wall, with a kitten curled into a tight ball on one of them. I was urged to sit on the other one and watch as Alfreda fanned the fire and added more sticks of wood. Meanwhile, on her knees, Gregoria, who had taken freshly made masa and mixed it with wheat flour to extend the corn, was patting the mixture on the *metate,* rolling the heavy *mano* back and forth with an ease and strength that belied her age. Then she formed the masa into balls, rotating them on the palm of one hand and patting them flat with the other. Alfreda diluted *cal* (calcium hydroxide) in a small amount of water, spread it over the clay *comal,* and placed the *comal* over the crackling fire. After the *cal* dried and was whisked off with a small straw brush, it was time for Gregoria to cook her tortillas and make the salsa. In a *molcajete* placed on the table, she first ground a clove of garlic, then added four *chiles manzanos* and three peeled tomatoes. A big pinch of salt went in next, and after tasting, she added a bit more. Over a smaller fire, Alfreda set a *cazuela* and added some lard. As the lard melted, the room became very smoky and we all started coughing. Unconcerned, Alfreda added a quartered white onion to the lard, and after a few minutes, she spooned in some large cooked beans. This, then, was our meal: thick, hot tortillas made from the corn the family had grown, salsa, and *frijoles.* We had a simple pulque to drink made from the fermented white sap of agave, and a huge bottle of orange *refresco* that most of the children were drinking. I stayed with the pulque, as I love its light, yeasty flavor.

⦙ LA ANTIGUA, WHERE MEXICO'S AFRICAN HISTORY BEGAN

When I am in Veracruz, I often have a leisurely *comida* at a tree-shrouded riverside restaurant in La Antigua, on the banks of the Río Huitzilapán. This is the same spot where in 1525 Cortés, seeking safer moorage for his ships, moved his first Veracruz settlement.

Later, wandering along the dusty streets, I stop at the vine-clad remains of La Casa de Cortés, which served as the Spanish customhouse and until 1600 was the official point of entry on the Gulf Coast. Only after researching the history of the African presence in Mexico did I realize that here in La Antigua I often stood in front of Mexico's first slave market, where thousands of Africans were auctioned off to the highest bidders. The ships carrying their "cargo" of slaves also contained the subsistence staples necessary to keep the slaves alive during the three- to six-week journey, usually only rice, plantains, sorghum, black-eyed peas, and enormous yams.

Many towns and villages in Veracruz echo with the words of Africa. One of my favorite places to eat *arroz a la tumbada* (page 164) and other seafood dishes is in any of the small restaurants in Mandinga, a small fishing village that took its name from a large region in West Africa that now includes Sierra Leone, Gambia, and Ghana. Mocambo, the name of a popular resort area, means "sorrow" in Congo dialect. The large town of Yanga is named for an escaped African slave, Gaspar Yanga, who for thirty years led a band of revolting slaves throughout the mountainous terrain of Veracruz. A statue depicting Yanga breaking out of his chains stands in the town where his people settled—a powerful symbol of this often-overlooked root of Mexican culture.

Owning slaves, which were mainly acquired as a result of Spain's numerous wars, was a way of life for the Spanish upper class, and after the Portuguese began large-scale slave trading between the coasts of Africa and Europe, it became prestigious to have black slaves. These African slaves were baptized as Christians, many becoming household servants who learned Spanish.

Most scholars agree that the first African to set foot in these new lands was a member of Christopher Columbus's second expedition. Twenty years later, one of the first black slaves in Mexico arrived from the West Indies with his master, Hernán Cortés. Tragically, the arrival of the Spanish and African newcomers was accompanied by epidemics of smallpox and other Old World diseases that spread rapidly throughout the indigenous population, killing thousands who had no natural immunity.

In some regions of Veracuz, approximately 80 percent of the total population died, mainly the native born, and over the next century, this decimation continued throughout the country. To the Spaniards, with their seemingly insatiable need for cheap labor, it was only logical to turn to an already familiar source of supply, Africa.

Although the exact number is unknown, it is estimated that between 1580 and 1680, some 150,000 to 200,000 *bozales*—black slaves who had not been baptized—were brought directly from Africa to the colony of New Spain.

Over the next one hundred years, most of the African slaves were freed and absorbed into the fabric of the country's future population. One of the trade's best-known descendants was Vicente Guerrero, a man of mixed indigenous, Spanish, and African blood. A hero in Mexico's War of Independence from Spain, Guerrero went on to become the second president of the Mexican Republic in April 1829 and to have a state named after him. Although his presidency was brief—he was deposed in December of the same year—he was able to execute an unconditional end to Mexican slavery.

Today, what once was the African slave market in La Antigua is a school. Local boys serve as guides for tourists coming to see Cortés's vine-embraced, crumbling residence and the ancient ceiba tree where his ships were supposedly moored. One old cannon is still there and children like to play on it. The history of the little school, however, is never discussed, and probably not even known to these young guides.

One day, I set out with Raquel Torres, a food anthropologist from Xalapa, Veracruz, to visit some of the areas where the Africans first lived and worked. We traveled along a heavily rutted road through a tunnel of sugarcane until we came to Ingenio La Concha, a former large sugarcane hacienda where slaves had planted, harvested, and processed this crop of sweet gold. Growing nearby were rows and rows of malanga (page 232), a close relative of taro. The shaggy-skinned corms, which look like yams, were important in early native Caribbean cooking and later as starchy nutrition for the African slaves.

Eventually we came to a spot where we could see small white buildings perched on the first rise of a series of abruptly rising hills. This was Coyolillo, a town settled by freed black slaves that used to work in former sugarcane fields and mills. Twenty years ago, according to Raquel, there were no roads to this village, just footpaths through the stony cornfields, and no electricity, only wood stoves for cooking. The day we were there, Coyolillo was full of activity. Children were playing in the streets, the women were going to the local market, and the men were working nearby in the fields, their black heritage still evident.

▪ COMIDA WITH AN AFRICAN MEXICAN FAMILY ON THE COSTA CHICA

Nowadays, while the African population of the Gulf Coast is well assimilated, the same cannot be said for the many small black communities on the Costa Chica (the northern Pacific Coast of Oaxaca and adjacent southern Guerrero), which until recently were quite isolated. When I heard that there was a black priest who spoke English in El Ciruelo, one of these *costeño* villages, I set out to find him. Padre Glyn, a Trinidadian, had been there for twenty-three years and would soon be returning home. When we met, he expressed real pleasure that I wanted to write about the culinary traditions of these families who, he emphasized, were "110 percent African," although some had indigenous Chatino, Mixtec, and Amusgo spouses, and others had married mestizos. He emphasized that the *costeño* foods are a combination of all of these cultures.

Soon we were sitting down on a blue cement porch filled with squirming puppies and children and grandchildren of all ages and talking to Antonieta Avila Salinas, who, Padre Glyn implied, was the best cook in El Ciruelo. Over the door to the interior of the house, where some of the children were lying on the rough cement floor watching television, was a picture of the Last Supper. Next to it was a cutout of an American soccer team, and both were incongruently topped with a T square.

Antonieta was born in this village and here with her husband raised her own family. He and his son fish in the nearby lagoon for their daily food and for fish to sell at the market in nearby Pinotepa Nacional. While I was there, one of the older daughters, I think it was María, took some freshly made *nixtamal* in a well-used bucket to the local *molino*, where it was ground into masa for tortillas that she later made and set in a large *jícara* (a hollowed-out dried bottle gourd from a calabash vine) on a flowered oilcloth–covered table. As we ate a tasty meal of *barbacoa de pescado* (page 167), using the tortillas to sop up the spicy sauce cloaking the fish, Antonieta eagerly told us about her other favorite dishes.

When they are in season, she simmers *tichindas*, mussel-like shellfish from the lagoon, in a subtle red chile sauce with garlic and the mintlike herb *pitiona*. They are encased in masa (shells and all) and steamed in dried corn husks or simply served in the broth (page 76).

Another dish her family always asks for is *frijoles negros con jaibas* (page 108), small crabs swimming in a broth of black beans served with a pungent salsa. And when someone is sick, Antonieta makes tamales filled with the meat of an iguana, the large lizard easily caught as it basks in the sun. After killing the iguana, Antonieta burns the skin in hot coals so that she can easily peel it. Then, after cleaning and cutting the meat into pieces, she simmers it with onion and garlic until tender. For her filling, she makes a thick sauce of *chiles guajillo, ancho,* and *puya,* roasted garlic, onion, oregano, and *pitiona* and then mixes in the iguana. It is guaranteed to give the ill back their strength.

During the next days, as we visited many other small villages and larger towns, I found that the black presence was much more evident on the Costa Chica than in Veracruz, although the African-inherited influence on music and dance still plays a major role in the culture on both coasts. In neither region, however, was there an obvious cuisine from Africa, even though the basic African staples had been transported with the slaves and later grown in Mexico.

Melons, plantains, bananas, sesame seeds, *jamaica,* tamarind, yams, coffee, and more originated in Africa and play an important role in the cuisine of contemporary Mexico. But just as important is the role that the early forced labor—backs of the men and hands of the women—played in supplying the foods needed by the expanding population of this newly conquered country.

When you eat Mexican food today, remember that it comes from a well-stirred pot of the foods and cultures of the people from diverse regions of three different continents.

The Basics of Mexican Cooking

The ways in which ingredients are prepared and combined to create the robust tastes and textures characteristic of Mexican cuisine have changed little over the centuries. Yes, in many homes, blenders do the work that was once done by hand in a *molcajete* carved out of volcanic rock, and pressure cookers sometimes replace the large clay pots in which the household's daily beans were simmered for hours. Stoves, some with ovens, are used by most cooks, yet cooking over coals is still the preferred method to prepare certain dishes, such as *pescado tikin xik* (page 174). And for many indigenous families, charcoal is still the only source of cooking fuel. But preparing Mexican food, though not complicated, remains labor-intensive, especially if you want to capture its essential flavors. Luckily, most of the components of the dishes can be prepared in advance, often resulting in even richer and more balanced flavors.

HELPFUL COOKWARE

I have been preparing Mexican food for over thirty-five years, and during that time, I have accumulated a great number of utensils (see Sources). The most valuable of these are my *cazuelas* and *comales*, two *molcajetes*, a well-used tortilla press, and a variety of wooden spoons. I occasionally make use of my pounded-copper *cazuela* from Michoacán for deep-frying small chunks of pork into crispy *carnitas* (page 63) or for making *cajeta* (page 260), rich goat's-milk caramel.

Another pot I regularly use is an olla, a large-bottomed clay vessel with a rather small neck opening. It is perfect for cooking beans, though a heavy metal pot can be substituted. The olla takes longer to heat up, but it holds the heat for a long time and imparts the flavor of history.

Cazuela. Although a heavy cast-iron Dutch oven or pot can be used for cooking moles, *pipianes,* and *adobos,* I encourage you to acquire at least one earthenware *cazuela* for preparing these and other dishes. I have one 10 inches in diameter for moles, *pipianes*, and similar one-pot meals. I also have a smaller, 8-inch *cazuela* that I find useful. *Cazuelas* come in all sizes, shapes, and decorative patterns. Always cure a *cazuela* before using it the first time. Every Mexican cook seems to have a preferred method. I rub the interior with a clove of garlic, fill the pot with water, and then let the water evaporate over low heat. Repeat the process once, rinse, and it is good to go. The United States Food and Drug Administration recommends against storing foods in these pots because the glaze may contain lead (see Sources for unleaded clay cookware). This is especially true of acidic foods.

Comal. In Mexico, a round, flat *comal* of clay or thin metal is used over an open flame for cooking tortillas; roasting fresh chiles, garlic, onions, tomatillos, and tomatoes; and toasting dried ingredients. A griddle or heavy cast-iron skillet can be substituted. I still use the same *comal* I have had since 1951, now encrusted with memories of all the wonderful meals I have ever prepared with it. When using a metal *comal* for the first time, heat it, wipe it lightly with oil, and heat it again, then wipe off any excess oil. The beautiful and very fragile clay ones are difficult to obtain in the United States and are hard to bring back from Mexico in one piece. I have two that I treasure.

Molcajete. I use my volcanic rock three-legged *molcajetes* (mortars) with a *tejolote* (pestle) for making salsas and guacamole and for grinding dried chiles and spices. I have one that is 6 inches in diameter and another that is an inch larger and ideal for preparing guacamole. Look for a *molcajete* in a Mexican market, and always search for one with a fairly smooth surface and very small pores. If water is poured into the bowl, it should never seep through the surface. If it does, it means the surface can flake off when grinding, adding grit to the salsa. Avoid the light gray *molcajetes* often carried in cooking-store catalogs, as they are typically too porous. To ready your *molcajete* for use, grind a handful of uncooked rice to powder with the *tejolote*. Rinse, dry, and repeat two or three more times until no grit is in the rice. Today blenders, or *licuadoras,* are found in many Mexican kitchens, but if you use a blender rather than a *molcajete* for making salsas, the texture will not be the same.

Spice grinder. An electric spice grinder or an electric coffee grinder dedicated to spices is invaluable for grinding larger quantities of spices.

Tamalera. If you plan to make tamales often, I suggest you purchase a *tamalera,* a specially designed pot for steaming tamales, at a Mexican market. It will have a perforated rack for suspending the tamales above the steaming water, a divider for holding the tamales vertically, and, if you're lucky, a small opening in the lower part of the pot for adding more water, if needed. For me, a *tamalera* that is about 18 inches high and a little less across is perfect. Don't worry if you do not have an authentic Mexican steamer for tamales, however; any big pot with a tight-fitting lid will work. You will need a perforated rack that can be propped up 3 inches or so above the bottom of the pot so that the simmering water underneath can surround the tamales with steam. For smaller amounts, or for resteaming, a Chinese bamboo steamer works well.

Tortilla press. I have watched in awe as manually dexterous women from Yucatán and other regions quickly rotate and flatten a lump of masa into a perfect tortilla with their hands. But most cooks rely on a tortilla press to achieve a similar result. The press, usually of heavy metal, consists of two flat plates, each 6 to 7 inches in diameter, hinged together so that the top one can be lifted and then lowered to flatten a small ball of masa. The presses are available in Mexican markets, many specialty food stores, and online.

▌ TECHNIQUES—ROASTING, TOASTING, AND SEARING

These three techniques are used when preparing chiles, onions, garlic, tomatoes, and tomatillos for most salsas and sauced dishes.

ROASTING AND PEELING FRESH CHILES

Use chiles with few indentations in the body so that the surface will char as evenly as possible. If you have a gas stove, place the chiles on the stove top directly in or over the flame and, using tongs, turn them often until the skin is well blistered and the flesh is just beginning to soften, 2 to 4 minutes. The aroma that the roasting chiles emit is the very essence of Mexican cooking. An equally satisfying method is to follow the centuries-old practice of Mexican cooks, roasting the chiles directly over white-hot coals on a small grill. If you plan to stuff the chiles, always prepare a few extra in case some tear.

Chiles can also be lightly brushed with oil, placed under a preheated broiler, and roasted, with frequent turning, until blackened on all sides, 5 to 8 minutes. Chiles prepared this way are usually too soft for stuffing but are satisfactory for cutting into *rajas,* or strips. If you are roasting more than a dozen chiles, Ricardo suggests pouring oil to a depth of several inches into a heavy pot, heating it until it begins to shimmer, and then submerging the chiles, a few at a time, into the hot oil and turning them frequently with a perforated spoon until they are totally blistered, 2 to 3 minutes. The moment they are ready, scoop them out with the spoon and immediately plunge them into cold water to stop the cooking.

Peeling roasted fresh chiles: Immediately put the just-roasted chiles in a heavy plastic or paper bag, close the bag, and let them sweat for about 10 minutes, or less if you want the flesh to be quite firm. If you have used the oil method, this step is not necessary.

Pick off the skin, then rub off any remaining rebellious bits from the chiles with a damp cloth. It is best to peel and stuff chiles the same day, but they may be placed on a paper towel–lined plate, covered, and refrigerated for up to 2 days before stuffing. If preparing the chiles for stuffing, with the tip of a sharp knife, cut each chile lengthwise from ½ inch below the stem area to within ¼ inch of the bottom and open gently. Remove all of the seeds and membranes with your fingers or a spoon and wipe the inside with a damp cloth, making sure that the inside surface is clean. Pat dry and salt lightly. The chiles are now ready for stuffing. If you are cutting the chile into *rajas*, cut off the stem end, slit the chile lengthwise, and remove the seeds and membranes as directed, then cut into long, narrow strips.

ROASTING ONIONS, GARLIC, TOMATOES, AND TOMATILLOS

Roast onion quarters or slices on a hot *comal*, in an ungreased heavy skillet, or on a griddle over medium heat, turning as needed, until slightly charred, 10 to 15 minutes. You may want to line the surface of the utensil with aluminum foil so the onion does not stick. Unpeeled garlic cloves can be roasted the same way until the papery skins blacken, which usually takes about 10 minutes.

I follow the same procedure with tomatoes and with tomatillos with their husks removed, roasting them on an aluminum foil–lined *comal* or skillet just until the tomatoes begin to blister and blacken and the skin of the tomatillos is spotted with brown. Depending on their size and how ripe they are, the tomatoes and tomatillos may need less time than onions and garlic. Cool the tomatoes in a bowl, then slip off the skins, letting any juices fall into the bowl. Any stubborn pieces of charred skin that remain will just add to the rustic flavor. The tomatillos do not need to be peeled.

TOASTING DRIED CHILES

Toasting brings out the flavor of dried chiles, though not all dishes that call for dried chiles require this step. Stem the chiles, cut them open, scrape out the seeds and membranes, and tear into large pieces. Heat a *comal*, heavy skillet, or griddle over medium heat until quite hot, then place the chile pieces, skin side down, on the hot surface and press down quickly but firmly with a spatula for barely a second. Flip the pieces over and press down again. The pieces will blister, change color, and emit an intense odor of chile. The whole process should only take a few seconds.

TOASTING SESAME SEEDS, PUMPKIN SEEDS, SPICES, AND HERBS

In Mexican cooking, unhulled sesame seeds are the best type to use. Look for them in Mexican markets and in health-foods stores. To toast sesame seeds and pumpkin seeds, heat a small, heavy skillet over medium heat, add the seeds, and stir them constantly so they don't burn. The sesame seeds will lightly toast in about 4 minutes, the pumpkin seeds in 5 to 8 minutes. Toast cloves, allspice, cinnamon, and other spices and dried herbs the same way, leaving them on the heat for several seconds or so, just until the aroma intensifies.

SEARING SAUCES

The concept of searing sauces in very hot oil is anathema to cooks used to long-simmered Italian sauces. What it does is meld the disparate flavors of the puréed ingredients into balance, sweetening and concentrating the flavors. I have included directions for this step in all of the pertinent recipes. Keep in mind that the sauce will spatter and spew as the ingredients blend together.

OTHER TECHNIQUES

PREPARING CORN TORTILLAS

When tortillas will be part of your Mexican meal, if possible, make your own and serve them hot. Although store-bought tortillas (preferably thin ones made from white corn) can be warmed and served, there is no excuse not to make them yourself for special occasions. If you are a novice, practice a few times before you invite friends to dinner.

Most Mexican markets sell freshly made masa for tortillas, which comes in 5- to 10-pound plastic bags. (It is also sometimes available frozen.) Use what you need, divide the remainder into smaller portions, and freeze in plastic freezer bags. If you cannot buy fresh masa, look for masa harina, or dried corn flour (not cornmeal, an entirely different product), which can be made into masa with the addition of water. Maseca is the most popular brand, but 90 percent of the corn they use is grown from genetically modified seeds.

To make 14 to 15 fresh corn tortillas, use 1 pound freshly prepared masa or 1¾ cups masa harina for tortillas. If you are using prepared masa, put it in a large bowl and knead it with your hands until it has a consistency similar to cookie dough. Add just a few drops of warm water if needed to achieve the correct consistency. It should be soft but not sticky.

If you are using masa harina, put it in a large bowl and gradually pour in 1 cup quite warm water, mixing it in with your hands as you add it. Knead the dough briefly until it is soft and smooth but not sticky, adding up to ¼ cup more warm water, a little at a time, if the dough is too dry.

Cover the masa with plastic wrap or a slightly damp towel and set aside for about 10 minutes. If the dough becomes too dry before you return to it, just knead in a sprinkle of water before using.

Using one or more heavy plastic bags, cut out two squares, each large enough to cover the plates of your tortilla press. Put one on the top plate and one on the bottom plate of the open press.

Heat an ungreased *comal,* large, flat griddle, or heavy skillet over medium-low heat until hot. With your hands, take out a lump of masa and roll it into a 1¼-inch ball (a ball this size will yield a tortilla 5 to 6 inches in diameter). Put the ball in the center of the sheet of plastic on the lower plate and gently flatten it with your hand. Cover with the other piece of plastic and firmly, but not with too much force, press down with the top plate of the press. Lift the top of the press, rotate the circle of dough 180 degrees, and press again to ensure the tortilla is of even thickness. The tortilla should be about 1⁄16 inch thick.

Open the press and carefully peel off the top sheet of plastic. Lift off the tortilla from the lower plate with the bottom sheet, flip the tortilla onto the fingers and upper part of one hand, and peel away the second piece of plastic with the other hand. If the tortilla is less than perfect, just roll it into another ball and start again.

The next step is when most beginning tortilla makers have problems. Slowly tip your hand with the palm up near the center of the hot *comal* and gently slide the tortilla off of your hand, angling your hand slightly (about 45 degrees) so that the tortilla falls flat onto the hot surface. Resist the temptation to flip it over. Cook for a count of 20 seconds; the underside should be just freckled. Turn the tortilla over with your fingers or a spatula and cook for another 30 seconds. You may want to flip the tortilla back onto its first side for several seconds before removing it from the hot surface. Ideally, the tortilla will puff up a bit, which is helped by lightly pressing down on it with your fingers or a cloth after the final turn.

As the tortillas are cooked, wrap them in a kitchen towel to keep them "warm and lazy." Serve the wrapped tortillas in a towel-lined basket, making sure that the remaining tortillas are always re-covered after guests help themselves.

REHEATING TORTILLAS

If you will not be eating freshly cooked tortillas right away, wrap them in a kitchen towel and then in aluminum foil and keep them warm in a 200°F oven. If you have made the tortillas earlier in the day, let them cool, seal them in a plastic bag, and refrigerate. To reheat, wrap a small stack in aluminum foil and place in a preheated 300°F oven until warm, about 20 minutes.

FRYING TORTILLA CHIPS AND TOSTADAS

Yes, you can buy a big sack of tortilla chips for nibbling at your local store, but if you make them yourself, the texture is much crispier than store-bought and they are a perfect way to use up any unused corn tortillas in your refrigerator. Tortilla chips, or *totopos*, make ideal scoops for Guacamole Clásico (page 43), Ensalada de Papas Glaceados con Queso (page 54), or a salsa such as Salsa de Cuaresmeños (page 32). Any extras can be used in *chilaquiles* (page 100) for a casual brunch with friends. Tostadas, crisp-fried whole tortillas, are a convenient way to serve any of your favorite toppings or taco fillings. I especially like to spread *carne apache* (page 57) or scoops of ceviche (page 53) on these crisp "plates."

TOTOPOS Y TOSTADAS
Crispy Corn Tortilla Chips and Edible Plates

To make tortilla chips or tostadas, you will need a heavy pot or skillet 6 to 8 inches in diameter and at least 3 inches deep.

Makes about 5 cups *totopos*, enough for 6 to 8 people, or 12 tostadas . . . .

12 (4½- to 5-inch) store-bought very thin white corn tortillas, preferably without preservatives

Peanut or sunflower oil for deep-frying

Sea salt

For *totopos*, stack 4 tortillas in a neat pile, cut the pile in half, and then cut each half into 3 triangles. You should have 6 triangles from each tortilla. Repeat with the remaining tortillas. For tostadas, leave the tortillas whole.

Spread the whole tortillas or the tortilla pieces in a single layer on 1 or more baking sheets, cover with a thin kitchen towel, and let dry at room temperature for about 2 hours or even overnight.

Heat the oven to 200°F. Pour the oil to a depth of ¾ inch into a wide, heavy pot or skillet and heat to 375°F on a deep-frying thermometer. The oil should be shimmering but not smoking, and a tortilla triangle dropped into it should become crispy quickly. Adjust the temperature as needed.

To fry the *totopos*, scatter a couple of handfuls of the triangles into the hot oil and toss them with a slotted spoon until they are crispy and lightly golden on both sides, about

1 minute. Using the spoon, quickly lift them out of the oil (which should have stopped sizzling), allowing any excess oil to drip off, then drain on absorbent paper. Discard any that have darkened too much as they will be bitter. Sprinkle the *totopos* with salt while they are still hot, if you like.

To fry the tostadas, follow the directions for heating the oil. Add 1 whole tortilla at a time and quickly fry on both sides, flipping once, until the color deepens and the tortilla is crisp, about 1 minute. Transfer to absorbent paper to drain.

Always allow the oil to return to 375°F, or until it is shimmering, before frying the next batch of *totopos* or another tostada. Cover the *totopos* or tostadas with a dry kitchen towel and keep them warm in the oven for up to 30 minutes. If the oil has not taken on a burned flavor, it can be cooled, strained, and reused on another day.

Although it is best to make *totopos* and tostadas right before they are served, they can be made several hours or even 1 day ahead. Let them cool completely, transfer them to an airtight plastic bag or container, and recrisp them in a 250°F oven for a few minutes before serving.

VARIATION: CRISPY TORTILLA GARNISHES

Cut the tortillas into ¼-by-1-inch strips or ½-inch squares and fry in the same manner as for the *totopos*. Use as garnishes for soups, salads, or other dishes.

SOFTENING CORN HUSKS AND BANANA LEAVES

Corn husks: Packages of dried corn husks (*totomoxtles*) can be found in most supermarkets, but for the best wrappings, shop at a Mexican market where you are more likely to find husks with their cupped ends intact, which are easier to use. They should be as large as possible, at least 5 inches across at the top. If not, you will have to overlap two or more before using. Separate the husks and put them in a large bowl or pot. Pour boiling water over them, then submerge them by weighting them down with a small plate. Soak them for several hours until they are pliable, then drain and pat dry before using.

Banana leaves: You will usually find packages of banana leaves in the freezer section of a Mexican or Asian market. Thaw the leaves overnight in the refrigerator or 2 minutes in the microwave, unfold, and cut out any thick veins. Cut the leaf into unbroken segments of the desired size, reserving the trimmed portions for making long, narrow ties and for lining the steamer. To soften the cut banana leaves, one at a time, pass them slowly over a gas burner until they darken and change texture. Alternatively, loosely roll them, stand them vertically in a steamer, and steam until quite flexible, about 30 minutes.

MAKING MEXICAN CREMA

Most of the *crema*, a rich, thick, slightly soured cream, sold in U.S. grocery stores includes additives to extend its shelf life. So plan ahead and make your own—it's easy, although it can take a couple of days. If you are in a hurry, a good-quality crème fraîche, available in most well-stocked grocery stores, can be substituted.

To make 1 cup *crema*, in a glass container, mix 2 cups heavy cream (not ultrapasteurized) with 1 tablespoon buttermilk or good-quality plain yogurt with active cultures. Cover with plastic wrap, poke a few holes in the wrap, and place in a warm spot (about 80°F) until the cream sets and is quite thick, 8 to 24 hours. Uncover, stir, re-cover with new plastic wrap, and put in the refrigerator for 6 hours until well chilled and firm. If the *crema* becomes too thick, thin it with a little whole milk or half-and-half.

PREPARING NOPALES

The nopal, or prickly pear cactus, *Opuntia ficus-indica*, plays a dual role in the life of Mexicans. It is a prized food source, especially rich in vitamins C and D, and it is a historic symbol, representing the beginning of the Aztec empire. Today, the Mexican flag includes an eagle perched on a prickly pear cactus with a snake in its talons, depicting the legend of the arrival of the Mexicas (Aztecs) at the site of present day Mexico City.

Both the young, tender paddles, or nopales, and the fruits, or *tunas*, of the nopal cactus are consumed in Mexico, particularly in the central part of the country. Buy the smallest and crispiest paddles you can find; around 6 inches long is ideal. If you do not have a Mexican market nearby and your local grocery store does not carry them, ask the produce manager at the store to order them. They are available year-round. To prepare the nopales, use a small, sharp knife or a vegetable peeler and, holding the base of the paddle, scrape off any stickers and their bulging eyes, moving away from the base. Trim off the thick base and all of the edges and cut the paddle into pieces the size and shape called for in the recipe.

Fill a saucepan with salted water and bring to a boil. Add the cactus pieces and a handful of green onion tops, cover, and cook over medium heat, stirring occasionally, until tender, 8 to 10 minutes. Using a slotted spoon or wire skimmer, scoop the pieces out of the water into a sieve or colander and rinse off any remaining viscous residue under cold running water. Drain well before using.

Grilling is my other favorite way to prepare nopales, especially for tacos of grilled meats. After removing the thorns, make five slits from the top edge down to within about 2 inches of the base. The paddle will resemble a green hand but with longer fingers. Place the nopales on a lightly oiled grill rack directly over a medium fire and grill until they turn a lighter color with some slightly browned areas, about 4 minutes. Then turn and cook the second side for about 3 minutes. Remove from the grill and use as desired. They are especially good chopped and added to beef tacos, a specialty of the east-central state of Tlaxcala, or used as a variation for Ensalada Clásica de Nopales (page 235).

PREPARING PORK LARD

Oh, how I love the distinctive taste of *manteca,* Mexico's rich pork lard. In Mexican cooking, it is essential for making most tamales and for flavoring beans.

Although many cooks still consider lard the culinary equivalent of poison, if you put butter on your toast every morning, you can use lard in your refried beans. According to the United States Department of Agriculture, butter has more than twice the cholesterol of lard (60 milligrams per ounce for butter versus 27 milligrams per ounce for lard). I'm lucky that I can buy plastic containers of pale caramel–colored freshly made lard from my local Mexican markets. I store a few containers in my freezer, where they keep for up to a year, and at least one in the refrigerator, where it will stay fresh for several months. Don't even think about substituting those tasteless hydrogenated shelf-stable bricks of waxy fat called lard found in supermarkets.

If you cannot buy flavorful lard, it is not difficult to make your own, which I often do. Unfortunately, most supermarket meat departments now receive pork that is mostly fat free, but maybe you can convince your local butcher to sell you several pounds of pork fat and to grind it for you too. If not, every time you buy pork with excess fat, cut the fat off and freeze it until you have enough to render. Then, when you are ready to render the fat, chop it rather fine in a food processor or with a sharp knife.

I have used various methods for rendering fat, and although many are effective, this is now my favorite method. Heat the oven to 325°F. Spread the fat in a large roasting pan, place in the oven, and heat, stirring occasionally, until much of the fat has melted, about 25 minutes. Carefully spoon off any of the melted fat that can be easily removed, then lower the heat to 275°F and continue to let the fat melt in the oven for about 1½ hours longer. At this point, the pan should be full of melted fat with small brown bits of pork meat. Remove the pan from the oven and set aside to cool briefly. Strain the contents of the pan into a heatproof container and refrigerate or freeze for use in recipes calling for lard. (I try to keep one small container of lard with the cracklings, or *asiento,* in it. This is a specialty of Oaxaca, where it is spread on freshly made tortillas. Think of the taste of buttered toast with bacon.)

If you will be using oil for frying over high heat, use peanut or sunflower oil refined for this purpose. For other uses, you may substitute canola or safflower oil for the lard.

PREPARING CHICKEN BROTH

The starting point for preparing many of Mexico's soups, as well as countless other dishes, is often *caldo de pollo*, a light, aromatic chicken broth. A canned broth can be used, and some are quite flavorful and without additives. But if you make your own broth, you will be able to use up those seldom eaten parts of the chicken you may have, such as the backs, wing tips, and necks. I just cut them off and freeze them to use later. It takes more time to make your own broth, but the results are worth it, and the meat from the meaty chicken parts can be shredded and used in soups, tacos, or enchiladas. Although this recipe may more accurately be termed a stock, as the liquid simmers for a long time with lots of bones after the meaty parts have been removed, I have stayed with the term *broth*. It can also be easily doubled to yield 3 quarts broth, using either a very large pot or two pots.

CALDO DE POLLO
Chicken Broth

Makes about 6 cups

2 pounds chicken parts, preferably some
    drumsticks and thighs

1 small white onion, quartered

2 cloves garlic, sliced

2 bay leaves

1 teaspoon dried oregano, preferably Mexican

10 black peppercorns

1 large sprig fresh cilantro

1 teaspoon sea salt

In a stockpot or other large pot, bring 3 quarts water to a boil over medium-high heat. Add the chicken pieces and bring back to a gentle bubble, skimming off any foam that rises to the surface. Add the onion, garlic, bay leaves, oregano, peppercorns, and cilantro, lower the heat to a simmer, cover partially, and cook until the meatier chicken parts are tender, about 20 minutes. Remove the meatier parts, let cool until they can be handled, and then pull off the skin and discard. Pull the meat off the bones, shred it, and save to use in soups, tacos, or enchiladas. It will keep covered and refrigerated for several days.

Return the bones to the broth, re-cover partially, and continue to simmer until the liquid is reduced by about half and the broth is flavorful, 2 to 3 hours. If the chicken is not covered by liquid at any time, add a cup or so more water until it is. Stir in the salt, then taste and add more salt if needed. Remove from the heat.

Let cool, remove and discard the bones, and strain the broth through a fine-mesh sieve into a large container. Alternatively, line a colander with several layers of damp cheesecloth and pour or ladle the broth through the cloth, trapping any sediment.

For an even tastier broth, put the whole covered pot, bones and all, in the refrigerator and let it sit overnight. The next day, remove the congealed surface fat with a spoon. Bring the broth back to a boil, then cool and strain.

The broth can be refrigerated for up to 5 days. Scrape off any fat solidified on the surface before using. It can also be frozen in 1- or 2-cup containers or in ice-cube trays for convenience. If using trays, pop the cubes free, put them into freezer bags, and store in the freezer to use whenever small quantities are needed.

VARIATION: CALDO DE RES (BEEF BROTH)

To make a flavorful beef broth, follow the directions for chicken broth, but substitute 2 pounds meaty beef bones, preferably some with marrow, for the chicken parts. I like to make a dark beef broth, so I always roast the bones first in a 400°F oven for about 1½ hours, then I pour off any fat before transferring the bones to the stockpot.

PREPARING A BITTER ORANGE JUICE SUBSTITUTE

The juice of the aromatic bitter orange (*Citrus aurantium*) is prized in the southern states of Mexico, especially on the Yucatán Peninsula, where it is mixed with achiote and other spices for making a seasoning paste for chicken, pork, and fish dishes. Native to southern China, the bitter orange was brought to Mexico by the Spanish in the sixteenth century. Today it is primarily grown in Yucatán, Chiapas, Tabasco, and Veracruz.

The fruit, which has a thick, wrinkled greenish yellow skin, is similar to the Seville orange used for making marmalade. Bitter oranges occasionally show up in markets in Florida and the Southwest. If you can find Seville oranges, their juice can be substituted for bitter orange juice (*jugo de naranja agria*). I also have found that some cooks from other regions of Mexico use a mild vinegar instead of the bitter orange juice.

You also can approximate the juice by mixing together fresh orange juice and fresh lime juice, preferably from the tiny Key lime. To make 1 cup juice, mix together 7 tablespoons freshly squeezed orange juice (from about 2 large oranges) and ½ cup plus 1 tablespoon freshly squeezed Key lime juice (from 12 or 13 limes). The juice can be covered and refrigerated for up to 4 days. Or, if you need only a small amount, make just what you need using these same proportions.

SALSAS Y ENCURTIDOS

Salsas and Condiments

Recipes can be assembled in many different ways for a cookbook. I chose to begin with the indispensable salsas, as bowls of different salsas are the first thing you find on every table when you sit down to eat. They may be red with tomatoes or green and tangy with tomatillos, and there is usually a variety from which to choose. The salsas may be made with only raw ingredients, simmered, or sometimes just quickly fried. All but a few will include chiles, fresh or dried. Intense flavor is essential to a salsa, and the ability of the chile to bite back is what infuses a salsa with spirit. Some salsas, such as the incendiary Salsa de Chile Habanero (page 39), are even made with just chiles, their heat untempered by tomatoes or tomatillos.

Although now many cooks in Mexico use a blender to prepare their salsas, the *molcajete* is still favored for rustic salsas with a rough, chunky texture and for guacamole.

You will also find a handful of important condiments here, accompaniments to some of Mexico's traditional dishes. For example, it is hard to imagine eating the Yucatán's *cochinita pibil* (page 149) without shredded marinated cabbage, or quesadillas (page 58) without guacamole.

Chiles

When asked what ingredient distinguishes Mexican food from other cuisines, the hot, spicy chile is invariably mentioned first. Although it is true that some chiles are quite incendiary, the heat may be muted in others. Indeed, chiles vary widely not only in their pungency, aroma, and flavor but also in their color and size. A subtle flavor difference is usually the reason a cook will select one chile over another or a combination of several different chiles to arrive at the desired *sazón*, or taste. Thai, Indian, and Asian dishes can also be extremely fiery, but they are prepared with a relatively limited array of different chiles, usually Asian cultivars of Mexican chiles.

Chiles cross-pollinate liberally, and many growers are now producing, either by design or by chance, chiles with different characteristics. I especially see and taste this with *jalapeños,* which most consumers apparently prefer big and with muted heat.

It is also perplexing to discover that the same chiles may have different names depending on the region in Mexico where they are found. This same situation often exists in the United States. For example, the Mexican grower of *chiles poblanos* on the West Coast may be from a family in Michoacán where the same chile is routinely called a *pasilla.* This can be confusing for a shopper looking for a fresh, fat green chile at the local supermarket and finding a skinny, almost-black dried chile with the same name. My suggestion is to go by the characteristic description of the chile, not the label.

COMMON FRESH CHILES

CHILACA This long, narrow brownish green chile with a rounded, blunt end from central Mexico has a slightly fruity flavor and may be quite *picante.* It is the fresh form of the chile *pasilla* and is seldom found in U.S. markets.

GÜERO Any relatively long, light-colored chile, usually pale yellow or pale green, may be called a *güero,* or "blond" chile. The name most commonly refers to a chile about 5 inches long and 1 inch wide, with a pointed end. It can vary from mild to quite hot, depending on the cultivar. The yellow banana or Fresno chile in the United States is a good choice in recipes calling for *güero.*

HABANERO A cultivar of *Capsicum chinense,* this small, green, lantern-shaped chile is extremely hot, has a distinctive flavor, and turns orange and red as it matures. Considered native to Cuba and the Yucatán Peninsula, it is now found in markets throughout Mexico and the United States.

JALAPEÑO This short (2 to 3 inches long), rather plump green chile, named for Xalapa, the capital of Veracruz, is used primarily in salsas or pickled (*en* *escabeche)* and occasionally stuffed. These chiles can be quite hot, though they have been interbred so much that the zing is vanishing, especially in the larger chiles. Mature red peppers *(cuaresmeños)* are sometimes available, though most of them are smoke-dried for marketing as *chiles chipotles*.

MANZANO An unusual small, fleshy green chile (a cultivar of *C. pubescens*) with large ebony seeds that may turn red or on some plants yellow-orange when mature. It has an explosive heat but with a balancing fruity flavor that is addictive to people living in the cool highlands of Mexico where it grows.

PIQUÍN Sometimes spelled *pequín,* this very tiny chile packs a great deal of heat. There are at least twenty-two different varieties of these orange-red chiles, with almost as many names: usually *max* or *amaxito* in Yucatán and in Tabasco, *chiltepín* in the northern border states, and variations of these names throughout the rest of the country. The dried chiles are usually ground and used as a seasoning.

POBLANO This large, roughly triangular blackish green chile, named for the state of Puebla, has a delicious flavor that varies in heat. It is the most common chile for stuffing and is often cut into strips, or *rajas*.

SERRANO Small, bright, and shiny, this green chile with a somewhat pointed tip has a grasslike flavor and is quite *picante*. It is commonly used in salsas or pickled *(en escabeche)*.

COMMON DRIED CHILES

ANCHO A household staple, this wide-shouldered, wrinkled chile is the dried form of the *poblano*. Deep reddish brown and about 5 inches long, it smells a bit like prunes and has a rather fruity taste that can vary in heat. The *ancho* is widely used in sauces and for stuffing.

ÁRBOL Although its name means "tree," this short (about 3 inches long), skinny reddish orange chile is not grown on a tree. Because of its fiery flavor, it is typically used in salsas or ground into a powder for a condiment.

CASCABEL When this small, round, shiny red chile is shaken, it sounds like a rattle, or *cascabel*. Its nutty, rather hot flavor makes it a favorite for table salsas.

CHIPOTLE MECO This leathery, short (about 2½ inches long) reddish tan chipotle is the smoked-dried form of the ripened *jalapeño*. It is very versatile and can be pickled, stuffed, and used to flavor cooked sauces for such dishes as shrimp and meatballs.

CHIPOTLE ROJO A small, deep red chile with a distinctive smoky fragrance, this chipotle is usually canned, either in adobo sauce *(en adobo)* or in vinegar *(en vinagre)*. It is commonly used in salsas and is sometimes stuffed.

GUAJILLO This long, pointed brick red chile is sometimes referred to as the "mischievous chile," as its heat can vary widely, though it always carries a tangy bite. Along with the *ancho*, it is one of the most commonly used dried chiles. Its sharp flavor is often detected in enchiladas.

MORA In some regions, this small, very hot smoke-dried *jalapeño* is called simply *chipotle*, or more often *chipotle mora* for its deep mulberry color. It is often canned in adobo sauce as *chiles chipotles en adobo*.

MORITA Usually quite *picante*, these small, typically triangular-shaped smoke-dried chiles are said to be the last picking of ripe *jalapeños*.

MULATO The dark version of the *chile ancho*, the *mulato* has deep, almost-black skin and a hint of chocolate flavor. If you tear the chile open and hold a piece of the skin up to the light, you should not see any red color. It is prized as an ingredient in dark moles, such as *mole poblano*.

PASILLA This is the dried form of the *chile chilaca*, and like the *chilaca*, it is long and narrow. It has puckered brownish black skin and a complex, rich flavor that can be quite *picante*. It is primarily used in moles, *adobos*, and other cooked sauces, and sometimes for salsas or in strips *(rajas)* as a garnish. It is called *pasilla de México* in Oaxaca and *chile negro* in Michoacán, Baja California, and in some western states of the United States.

PUYA This smaller, thinner variety of the *chile guajillo* is often combined with the *guajillo* in cooked sauces for extra heat.

SALSA VERDE CRUDA
Raw Green Tomatillo Salsa

While salsas made from red tomatoes are often on the table, especially in central Mexico, it is the green salsas made with *tomates verdes*, the smaller, papery husk–wrapped tomatillos of the same nightshade family, that predominate in most of the country. This simple salsa with its tart chile flavor is a surprising accent for any grilled meat.

Makes about 1½ cups

½ pound tomatillos (about 5 or 6), husked, well rinsed, and roughly chopped

2 chiles serranos, stemmed and roughly chopped, including seeds

2 tablespoons roughly chopped white onion

1 teaspoon roughly chopped garlic

¼ cup chopped fresh cilantro, thick stem ends removed

¾ teaspoon fine sea salt, or to taste

Starting with the tomatillos, put all of the ingredients in a blender or food processor, then process to a smooth consistency. The salsa should be quite thick, so don't be tempted to add water to thin it. It is best when served right away, but it will keep in the refrigerator for up to 1 day.

SALSA VERDE COCIDA CON AGUACATE
Cooked Green Chile and Tomatillo Salsa with Avocado

My first taste of this vibrant tomatillo salsa subdued with creamy chunks of avocado and a whiff of garlic was at a small street stand in Santa Clara de Cobre in Michoacán. The few tables on the side of the street were crammed with locals eating tacos filled with *carnitas estilo Michoacán* (page 63), crispy pieces of pork. When I finally got my *carnitas*, I did as everyone else did and slathered it with this salsa, a perfect pairing. I find it is equally good with almost any taco or *antojito*.

1 pound tomatillos (about 9 or 10), husked and well rinsed

1 clove garlic, roasted (page 18), then peeled

3 chiles serranos, roasted (page 17), then stemmed

¼ cup finely chopped white onion

¼ cup loosely packed, roughly chopped fresh cilantro, thick stem ends removed

1 teaspoon sea salt

1 large or 2 small ripe Hass avocados, halved, pitted, peeled, and cubed

Put the tomatillos in a saucepan with water to cover and bring to a boil over high heat. Lower the heat to a gentle simmer and cook until quite soft but not falling apart, 5 to 10 minutes. Drain the tomatillos, reserving the water.

Put the tomatillos, garlic, and ⅓ cup of the reserved water in a blender and blend briefly to break up the tomatillos. Add the chiles, seeds and all, and pulse just until the mixture is chunky. Add the onion, cilantro, and salt and pulse just until well blended with a textured consistency. Taste and add more salt if needed.

Pour into a small bowl and stir in the avocado. This salsa will keep in the refrigerator for up to 3 days; add the avocado just before serving.

SALSA DE CUARESMEÑOS
Red Jalapeño Chile Salsa

During the forty days of Lent, crimson red *chiles jalapeños* are so sought after by Catholic worshippers in Mexico City and the surrounding states that they are called the Lenten chiles, or *cuaresmeños*.

In San Felipe del Progreso, a poor rural village in the state of Mexico, the local Mazahua (a branch of the Otomí people) families work the land year-round raising beans, corn, fava beans, tomatillos, and *chiles jalapeños*, which they allow to turn red ripe before they harvest them. María Máxima Martínez López told Ricardo that throughout the year, except in the summer rainy season, food is usually difficult to obtain, and freshly made corn tortillas, this salsa, and perhaps a bowl of beans are often the main midday meal. Because there is no nearby mill for grinding the corn for the many tortillas needed for her large family, María grinds it by hand on her *metate*.

This salsa is unusual not only because it calls for red *jalapeños* but also because the common final step of frying everything together is skipped and the salsa is served with most of the ingredients raw. If you cannot find red *jalapeños*, green ones can provide a similar flavor. I often serve the salsa alongside Quesadillas con Queso (page 58) or tacos.

Makes about 2 cups . . . .

1 pound tomatillos (about 9 or 10), husked and well rinsed

2 large red chiles jalapeños

¼ cup roughly chopped white onion

1 large clove garlic

1½ teaspoons sea salt

¼ cup finely chopped fresh cilantro, thick stem ends removed

Put the tomatillos, chiles, and onion in a saucepan with water to cover and bring to a boil over medium heat. Reduce the heat to a simmer and cook until the tomatillos are soft when touched, 5 to 10 minutes. Drain the tomatillos, chiles, and onion. When the chiles are cool enough to handle, remove the stems and use a spoon to scrape out the seeds and membranes, then dice finely.

Grind the tomatillos, chiles, onion, garlic, and salt in a *molcajete* as María does, or use a blender and blend just until mixed, leaving some texture. Pour into a small serving bowl and stir in the cilantro. Taste and add more salt if needed. This salsa is much better eaten on the day it is made, but it can be kept for a second day in the refrigerator.

SALSA DE CHILES COSTEÑOS
Coastal Oaxacan Salsa

The small, burnished copper–skinned *chiles costeños* from the Costa Chica of northern Oaxaca and southern Guerrero are the favorite for making the rustic, tangy salsa of the region. In the small village of El Ciruelo on the coast of Oaxaca, Antonieta Avila Salinas makes it daily from the chiles her husband grows. Both the dried red *costeños* and an even smaller bronzy yellow variety, *costeño amarillo*, can be quite incendiary, so use sparingly. I usually buy these chiles in markets in Oaxaca, but I have seen them in the United States in areas with a sizable concentration of Oaxacan immigrants and online (see Sources).

Chile puya, the smaller form of the *chile guajillo*, can be substituted. It is equally *picante* but has a different flavor.

½ pound tomatillos (about 5 or 6), husked and well rinsed

2 or 3 chiles costeños or chiles puyas, stems, seeds, and membranes removed, then toasted (page 17)

1 clove garlic, cut in half

¼ cup finely chopped white onion

¼ cup finely chopped fresh cilantro, thick stem ends removed

½ teaspoon sea salt

Put the tomatillos and chiles in a small saucepan with water to cover and bring to a boil over high heat. Lower the heat to a simmer and cook until the tomatillos are very soft, at least 10 minutes. Drain the tomatillos and chiles, reserving the water.

Put the tomatillos and chiles in a blender, add the garlic and ¼ cup of the reserved water, and blend until smooth. Pour into a serving bowl and mix in the onion, cilantro, and salt. Taste and add more salt if needed. This salsa can sit for several hours before serving, or it can be kept in the refrigerator for another day. Bring to room temperature before serving.

SALSA DE PICO DE GALLO
Fresh Tomato Salsa

Wherever you eat in Mexico, this chunky fresh salsa will usually be found on the counter or on your table. It may be called *salsa mexicana, salsa fresca,* or *pico de gallo,* depending on where you are in the country. The name *pico de gallo,* or "rooster beak salsa," is descriptive of the way the tomatoes are chopped at sharp angles and, I suppose, of the bite of the chile. If you are in or around Guadalajara, however, *pico de gallo* will not be a salsa at all, but a typical street vendor's snack of jícama, cucumber, melon, or pineapple sprinkled with ground chile.

The salsa is quick and easy to make and can be added to a wide variety of dishes in need of a lift. I have even been known to spoon my *pico de gallo* on hamburgers, and it is a spirited addition to fried or scrambled eggs.

It is important that the tomatoes be red ripe but still quite firm. The best tomatoes will be the ones you grow yourself or buy from local farmers.

¾ pound ripe tomatoes (about 2 medium or
  6 plum)

⅓ cup finely chopped white onion

¼ cup finely chopped fresh cilantro, thick stem
  ends removed

2 tablespoons finely chopped chile serrano
  (about 1 chile), including seeds

2 tablespoons freshly squeezed lime juice

¾ teaspoon sea salt

Slice the tomatoes in half vertically and, if you want, scoop out the seeds. (I like the rustic texture of the seeds and leave them in.) Dice into roughly ¼-inch pieces. Scoop into a serving bowl and stir in the onion, cilantro, chile, lime juice, and salt. Taste and add more chile, lime juice, and salt if needed. Let the salsa rest for up to 30 minutes before serving so the flavors will mingle. If keeping for a few hours longer, cover and refrigerate, then drain off any liquid and give the salsa a final toss just before serving.

SALSA COCIDA DE JITOMATE
Cooked Tomato Salsa

Commonly called *salsa ranchera*, Mexico's spunky, earthy cooked red tomato salsa has many variations. It is often served for people to enjoy with bread or *totopos* (page 21) while they await their meal. It is also an integral part of such dishes as *huevos rancheros*, in which fried eggs are liberally doused with the spirited, rather sweet salsa.

In the coastal southeastern states, it is typically served with *antojitos,* and on the Yucatán Peninsula, a similar but smoother salsa called *chiltomate* is drizzled over *codzitos* (page 66), crispy rolled tacos, and served with other local dishes.

This version is one of the most common and will keep for up to 2 days in the refrigerator. Bring to room temperature before serving.

Makes about 2 cups

1 pound ripe tomatoes (about 8 plum or
  3 medium)

2 large chiles serranos, stemmed and halved
  lengthwise

Bring 4 cups water to a boil in a saucepan over high heat. Add the tomatoes, chiles, onion, and garlic, lower the heat, and simmer until the tomatoes are well cooked

¼ medium white onion

2 small cloves garlic

2 tablespoons canola or safflower oil

¾ teaspoon sea salt

but not falling apart, 8 to 10 minutes. Remove from the heat. Using a slotted spoon, lift the tomatoes, chiles, onion, and garlic out onto a plate and let cool. Set the cooking liquid aside.

Quarter the tomatoes and put in a blender. Add the chiles, onion, and garlic and blend at high speed for 30 seconds. The sauce should be silky smooth and hardly any bits should remain when it is poured through a fine-mesh sieve.

Heat the oil in a small saucepan over medium heat until quite hot. Pour in the sauce, stir, and when it begins to boil, lower the heat and add the salt and ⅓ cup of the reserved cooking liquid. Bring to a boil again and then lower the heat and simmer, stirring occasionally, for about 5 minutes to thicken. Transfer to a serving bowl and serve at room temperature.

SALSA XNIPEC

Picante "Dog's Nose" Salsa

Why this Mayan salsa has such an unappealing name in translation I have no idea, but I assume it is because it is so smoldering hot that it would heat up even the usually cool nose of a dog. On the Yucatán Peninsula, it is served with seafood dishes and also with eggs and beans.

Makes about 1¾ cups

1 cup finely chopped ripe tomato (about 1 large)

½ cup finely chopped red onion

½ cup finely chopped fresh cilantro, thick stem ends removed

½ cup chopped red radishes

1 to 2 chiles habaneros, according to tolerance, seeds and membranes removed, finely chopped

⅔ cup freshly squeezed bitter orange juice (page 26)

½ teaspoon sea salt

Toss together the tomato, onion, cilantro, radishes, and chiles in a bowl. Mix in the citrus juice and salt, then taste and add more salt if needed.

Serve the salsa the same day, if possible. It will keep overnight in the refrigerator, but the heat tends to ratchet up if it is kept too long.

SALSA ROJA DULCE
Sweet Red Tomato Salsa

In Guadalajara, this rich cooked tomato salsa is traditionally used as a counterpoint to the fiery *salsa de chiles de árbol* (page 37) that drenches *tortas ahogadas* (page 74). As a sauce it also adds flavor and color to a side dish of steamed chayote or zucchini.

Makes about 2 cups

3 medium, ripe tomatoes, roughly chopped, or 1½ cups drained diced canned tomatoes

3 tablespoons roughly chopped white onion

2 cloves garlic, roughly chopped

½ teaspoon sea salt

¼ heaping teaspoon dried marjoram

¼ teaspoon ground cumin

1 tablespoon canola or safflower oil

Put the tomatoes, onion, garlic, salt, marjoram, and cumin in a blender and blend until very smooth.

Heat the oil in a heavy skillet or saucepan over medium-high heat until shimmering but not smoking. Pour in the tomato mixture, reduce the heat to a gentle simmer, and cook, stirring frequently, for 5 minutes. It will sputter and deepen in color.

Remove from the heat, let cool slightly, and pour through a medium-mesh sieve into a serving bowl. Serve slightly warm or at room temperature. If making in advance, the sauce can be covered and refrigerated for a few days.

SALSA DE CHILES DE ÁRBOL
Árbol Chile Salsa

Made with mouth-searing *chiles de árbol*, this is the fiery half of the salsa duo used to flavor Guadalajara's famous sandwich, *torta ahogada* (page 74). Formerly made with peanuts, today the salsa is usually prepared with sesame seeds. I love it either way. If you are not planning on making the *torta* or have leftover salsa, its tang also enhances grilled meats and seafood.

Makes about 2 cups

2 ounces chiles de árbol (about 50—yes, 50 chiles), stemmed and toasted (page 18)

1 tablespoon mild white vinegar such as vinagre de piña or diluted unseasoned rice vinegar (page 50)

1 tablespoon unhulled sesame seeds, toasted (page 19)

2 whole cloves, toasted (page 18)

1 clove garlic, roasted (page 18), then peeled

½-inch-thick slice white onion, roughly chopped

1½ teaspoons fresh marjoram leaves

1½ teaspoons sea salt

Put the chiles in a small saucepan with water to cover, place over medium heat, cover, and cook until quite soft, about 30 minutes. Drain and let cool.

Put the chiles and vinegar in a blender and add the sesame seeds, cloves, garlic, onion, marjoram, and salt and blend until the spices break down and the salsa is very smooth. If coarse bits remain, scrape the salsa through a fine-mesh sieve. Taste and add more salt if needed.

Transfer to a serving dish and serve at room temperature. The taste improves if the flavors are allowed to mingle for at least a few hours. The salsa will keep, covered, in the refrigerator for up to 5 days. Bring to room temperature before serving.

SALSA DE TRES CHILES
Three-Chile Salsa

In northern Veracruz, this aromatic table salsa is used for spicing up soups or tacos or for lathering on grilled meat. Each of the three chiles adds a different taste counterpoint. If the deep red dried *chiles chipotles* are difficult to locate, canned *chiles chipotles en adobo* can be substituted.

Makes about 3 cups

3 small chiles pasillas, stems, seeds, and membranes removed, then toasted (page 18)

3 chiles guajillos, stems, seeds, and membranes removed, then toasted (page 18)

3 large chiles chipotles, stems, seeds, and membranes removed, then toasted (page 18)

½ pound ripe plum tomatoes (about 4 large), roasted and peeled (page 17)

Soak the dried chiles in a bowl in hot water to cover until soft, about 30 minutes. Remove the chiles, reserving the water.

Put the chiles, tomatoes, garlic, and salt in a blender and blend just until you have a very textured sauce, using just enough of the reserved water as needed to release the blades. Transfer the salsa to a serving

3 large cloves garlic, roasted (page 18), then peeled

1 tablespoon sea salt

bowl and serve warm or at room temperature. It can be made up to several hours in advance.

SALSA DE CHILE HABANERO
Habanero Chile Salsa

This tongue-blistering salsa is traditionally served with *cochinita pibil* (page 151), the famed steam-roasted pork of Yucatán. The salsa is so fiery that you need to dribble only the smallest amount on top for that needed fillip. It is also an excellent accent on Chilpachole de Yuca con Camarones (page 91).

Chiles habaneros pack such intense heat that I suggest wearing rubber gloves when handling, or covering your hands with small plastic bags. Be careful not to rub your eyes or other sensitive parts of your body.

Makes about 1 cup

10 chiles habaneros, stems, seeds, and membranes removed and cut into small pieces

2 teaspoons sea salt

½ cup freshly squeezed lime juice, preferably Key lime

Put the chiles and salt in a *molcajete* and grind to a rough paste. Add the lime juice and continue grinding until quite smooth. This salsa can also be prepared in a blender, in which case you can just cut the chiles in quarters. This salsa is much better eaten on the same day it is made but it can be kept for another day in the refrigerator.

SALSA PURÉPECHA DE CHILES PUYAS
Purépecha Salsa of Puya Chiles

Francisca and Esther de la Cruz, two Purépecha sisters from Michoacán, showed Ricardo how to make this traditional salsa when he was in their village of San Francisco Uricho, near the shores of Lake Pátzcuaro. The salsa, which uses a combination of the smaller, but more potent, *chile puya* and its larger relative, the *guajillo*, is important because it is one of the few remaining testimonies to the Purépecha foods of this village, for only about twenty-five Purépecha women remain here to pass their knowledge on to their children. I've shared meals in Purépecha homes in other parts of Michoacán, and although many of their salsas used *chiles guajillos* enlivened with *chiles puyas*, the toasting of the garlic adds complexity to this version.

Serve the salsa with corn tortillas (page 19) and eggs, grilled meats, or chicken.

Makes about 2 cups

4 chiles puyas, stems, seeds, and membranes removed, then toasted (page 18)

2 chiles guajillos, stems, seeds, and membranes removed, then toasted (page 18)

¾ pound tomatillos (about 7 or 8), husked and well rinsed

2 cloves garlic, roasted (page 18), then peeled

1¼ teaspoons sea salt

1 pound plum tomatoes (8 or 9), coarsely chopped

Soak the chiles in a bowl in very hot water to cover until soft, about 30 minutes. Drain, tear into smaller pieces, and set aside.

Put the tomatillos in a saucepan with water to cover and bring to a boil over high heat. Lower the heat and simmer until tender, about 15 minutes. Drain and let cool slightly.

While the tomatillos are cooking, put the garlic and salt in a *molcajete* and grind to a paste. Add the chiles and grind until pulverized. Add the tomatillos and tomatoes to the garlic-chile mixture and continue crushing until you have a coarsely textured salsa. Or, if you like, grind to a finer texture. (This can also be done in a blender, adding the tomatillos and tomatoes at the same time as the garlic, salt, and chiles.) Taste and add more salt if needed. Serve in the *molcajete* or transfer to a serving bowl. This salsa will keep, covered, in the refrigerator for up to 4 days.

SALSA NEGRA CON CHIPOTLES
Black Salsa with Chipotles

M any times I have watched the exuberant Veracruzana Carmen Ramírez Degollado prepare this remarkable spicy, sweet salsa using the deep red, smoke-dried *chiles chipotles* or the smaller, darker red *chiles mora*. Do not use the leathery brown *chipotles* known as *chiles meco*, and definitely do not use canned *chipotles en adobo*. Carmen serves the salsa with *gorditas de frijoles* (page 68) and also lavishes it on sautéed shrimp. Following her lead, I smear it on chicken before grilling.

Makes about 1 cup . . . .

2 (1-ounce) piloncillo cones (page 42), 2 ounces from a softened 1 (9-ounce) piloncillo cone, or ¼ cup azúcar morena or other unrefined brown cane sugar or firmly packed dark brown sugar

1½ to 2 cups canola or safflower oil

3½ ounces chiles chipotles or chiles mora (about 40), stemmed

2 cloves garlic

½ teaspoon sea salt

Bring 1 cup water to a boil in a medium saucepan, add the sugar, and stir until dissolved. Remove from the heat and set aside.

Pour the oil to a depth of ¼ inch into a heavy 8- to 9-inch skillet and heat over medium heat until the oil is rippling hot. Stir in a couple of handfuls of the chiles and fry until darkened, about 2 minutes. Using a slotted spoon, lift out the chiles, letting the excess oil drip off, and add them to the sugar water. Repeat with the remaining chiles.

Fry the garlic in the same oil over medium heat, stirring until a deep yellow. Using the slotted spoon, transfer the garlic to a blender. Add the chiles and sugar water to the blender and blend until smooth.

Pour off all but a thin layer of the oil remaining in the skillet and return the pan to medium heat. When the pan is hot, add the chile mixture, lower the heat to medium-low, and let bubble until almost black, at least 15 minutes. Stir in the salt, remove from the heat, and let cool.

Pour into a small serving bowl and serve at room temperature. The salsa will also keep in a tightly covered container in the refrigerator for up to 1 month. You may need to add a little water before serving as it will thicken in the refrigerator.

Piloncillo
Unrefined Sugar Cones

Wherever I drive through the Veracruz countryside, I always seem to be wedged between large trucks piled high with long stalks of sugarcane. Grown in the surrounding fields, the cane is transported to sugar mills, where it is crushed, the juice extracted and then boiled until thick. I once visited a mill outside of Martínez La Torres and watched as this earthy, caramel-colored syrup was poured into cone-shaped molds of various sizes, from ¾ ounce to 9 ounces, where it crystallized as it cooled. The sweet smell was almost overpowering.

These cones of unrefined sugar, with the pronounced taste of molasses, are the ones you will find in most Mexican markets and well-stocked grocery stores in the United States. Buy the darkest cones available, as the flavor will be richer. The cones are quite solid, so either chop off what you need with a serrated knife or grate it on a box grater. To make working with the cones easier, I often soften them very briefly in a microwave.

In parts of Mexico, this same sugar is formed into mahogany brown blocks and sold as *panela*. If you are in a market in Guerrero or Michoacán, you might find the sugar in irregular roundish shapes called *panocha*. These rough disks are coarsely textured and strongly flavored and have usually been made in small family-operated mills.

Piloncillo is essential for making Café de Olla (page 280) and is used in many dishes, especially desserts. If you cannot find *piloncillo*, *azúcar morena*, a Mexican unrefined finely granulated cane sugar, is the best substitute. It can be found in Mexican grocery stores or the Mexican foods section of well-stocked supermarkets or ordered online. Other unrefined brown cane sugars or even dark brown sugar can also be substituted.

GUACAMOLE CLÁSICO
Classic Guacamole

The avocado, with its thick, creamy texture, is native to Mexico and is the essential ingredient in guacamole. There are many different ways to prepare guacamole, chunky or smooth, combined with other ingredients, or like this typical version, which is one of my favorites. In Mexico, guacamole is more than just a dip. It is an accompaniment to tacos, egg dishes, and grilled meats. If you do not have seasonal ripe tomatoes on hand, omit the tomatoes, which I often do.

I recommend that guacamole be made right before serving, although the tomatoes, onions, chile, and cilantro can be crushed in advance. If necessary, it can be made up to 1 hour ahead, covered with plastic wrap pressed directly on the surface, and then stirred just before serving, though it tastes much better when freshly made. Serve as a dip with *totopos* (page 21) or cut-up raw vegetables, or as a condiment on tacos, *tortas*, or grilled meat. I love its buttery flavor over Arroz Blanco (page 223).

Makes about 2 cups, enough for 2 or 3 servings

1 soft-ripe tomato, finely chopped (optional)

¼ cup finely chopped white onion

2 chiles serranos, stemmed and finely chopped, or to taste

2 tablespoons plus 1 teaspoon finely chopped fresh cilantro, thick stem ends removed

3 ripe Hass avocados

½ teaspoon sea salt

If you have a *molcajete* and a *tecolote*, use them. If not, use a bowl and a fork. Put the tomato (if using), onion, chiles, and 2 tablespoons of the cilantro in the *molcajete* or bowl, toss well, and roughly mash with the pestle or fork. Halve each avocado, remove the pit, and scoop the flesh into the tomato mixture. Smash the avocados with the tomato mixture, either leaving some chunky pieces of avocado or mashing them all smoothly—this is a personal preference. Mix in the salt, then taste and season with more chile and salt if needed.

Serve in the *molcajete* or transfer to a bowl. Sprinkle the remaining 1 teaspoon cilantro over the top and serve right away.

ADEREZO DE CHIPOTLE
Chipotle Condiment

This modern, quite *picante* accompaniment for Tacos de Pescado (page 64) also becomes a tasty dip for *totopos* (page 21) or raw vegetables. Ricardo tells me that in Baja California canned tuna fish is often added to the mixture if serving with *totopos*.

Makes 1½ cups, enough for 12 tacos

1 cup mayonnaise

4 chiles chipotles en adobo, finely chopped

1½ teaspoons sherry vinegar

1 (3-ounce) can chunk tuna, drained (optional)

Whisk together all of the ingredients until a creamy sauce forms. Transfer to small bowls for serving.

SALSA DE RÁBANOS
Radish Salsa

The women from the isolated Yucatecan village of Yaxunah traditionally serve this crispy radish salsa alongside platters of tacos filled with succulent *cochinita pibil* (page 151) and mounds of freshly made tortillas. Ricardo was a grateful guest on the day that the men steam-roasted the domestic pig and the native *pecarí*, and watched as the women prepared this condiment. I was lucky enough to share a similar meal with Ricardo later and am now addicted to the biting flavor of this salsa. I serve it with a variety of other pork and even fish dishes.

Makes about 2 cups, enough for 12 to 14 tacos

1 cup red radishes, cut into ⅛-inch cubes

¾ cup freshly squeezed bitter orange juice (page 26)

½ cup chopped fresh cilantro, thick stem ends removed

1 cup finely minced red onion

Mix together all of the ingredients. Transfer to small bowls for serving.

CEBOLLA MORADA CURADA
Pickled Red Onions

Pickled red onions, a constant in Yucatecan kitchens, are used as a topping for many dishes. In any market where the regional *panuchos,* tacos, and *salbutes* are served, you will find these crunchy red onions. This is Ricardo's version, which makes a savory addition to any grilled fish.

Makes about 2 cups . . . .

2 cups thinly sliced red onion (about 2 large onions)

¼-inch-thick sliver roasted chile habanero (page 17)

¼ cup freshly squeezed bitter orange juice (page 26)

1 teaspoon sea salt

Put the onion and chile in a large bowl, add the orange juice and salt, and toss well. Cover tightly and place in the refrigerator for at least 2 hours, stirring two or three times. The marinating process will turn the onions from red to an intense pink. Before serving, taste and add more salt if needed. They often need a sprinkle more. Serve at room temperature.

The onions can be served immediately but they are best if prepared in advance and refrigerated for 1 to 3 days before serving. They will keep for up to 8 days in the refrigerator; after that they will no longer be as crunchy.

ENSALADA DE COL ESTILO YAXUNAH

Cabbage Slaw

This simple shredded cabbage condiment provides crunchy texture to tacos filled with *cochinita pibil* (page 149).

Makes about 2 cups, enough for 12 to 14 tacos

2 cups finely shredded cabbage (about ½ small head)

½ cup freshly squeezed bitter orange juice (page 26)

1 teaspoon sea salt

Mix together all of the ingredients in a bowl, cover, and set aside for about 1 hour to allow the flavors to mingle. Transfer to small bowls for serving.

BOTANAS, ENTREMESÉS Y ANTOJITOS

Snacks, Appetizers, and Quick Bites

I n Mexico whenever friends gather for a drink, enticing small bites, or *botanas*, will be on the table as a sign of hospitality. They may be as simple as toasted nuts flavored with garlic and chiles, bite-size pieces of cheese, or a bowl of pickled vegetables. *Entremesés*, on the other hand, are more apt to be served as the first course of a more formal meal, and *antojitos* are served just to sustain you until you are ready to really eat, perhaps many hours later.

The world of *antojitos* is diverse and varies depending on where you are in the country. There are quesadillas, soft or crispy tacos with a great variety of regional fillings, and crunchy tostadas with savory toppings. In Nuevo León, you will find *cazuelitas*, miniature flat-bottom masa bowls stuffed with bits of fried potatoes and Chihuahua cheese. *Tlacoyos*, oval masa cakes plump with beans, are typical of central Mexico; puffy gorditas, masa infused with black bean puree, are popular in Veracruz; the similar *sopes*, filled with chorizo, are eaten in the small state of Colima on the central Pacific coast; and small, tapered fried *molotes*, masa encasing chorizo and potatoes, smashed beans, or favas, are traditional in Oaxaca. They all are wonderful, tasty treats, and there are many more to seek out as you explore Mexico.

You will find that little or no demarcation exists between *botanas, entremesés,* and those sometimes heftier masa *antojitos*. There are no rules. It's all about enticing flavors and textures shared with family and friends, and any of them can be enjoyed anytime.

I enjoy them all but I must admit when I am asked what my favorite is, I usually answer *tortas*, hefty sandwiches of layered meats, cheese, vegetables, herbs, and salsas in a crusty roll. I crave the messy *tortas ahogadas* (page 74) smothered in sauce from the street vendors in Guadalajara. But my very favorite version of a *torta*, which is sold only in the *mercados* of Puebla, is the wonderful *cemita* (page 73) flavored with *chile chipotle* and the pungent herb known as *pápalo*.

NUECES Y PEPITAS CON AJO Y CHILE
Nuts and Seeds with Garlic and Chile

As pecans and pumpkin seeds are native to Mexico and peanuts from South America found another home in Mexico centuries before the Spanish arrived, it should be no surprise that some version of this quite natural combination is now a popular snack.

Makes 3 cups

1 tablespoon peanut oil

10 cloves garlic

1 cup skinned raw peanuts

1 cup pecan halves

1 cup hulled raw pumpkin seeds

1 teaspoon sea salt

¼ teaspoon ground chile piquín or cayenne, or to taste

Heat the oven to 275°F.

Warm the oil in a heavy skillet over low heat. Add the garlic and sauté, stirring often, until it turns yellow, about 2 minutes. Stir in the nuts and seeds, coating them with the oil. Sprinkle with the salt and stir in the ground chile, a pinch at a time, until the mixture has the right pungency for you; ¼ teaspoon is usually enough.

Remove from the heat and spread the mixture out in a single layer on a baking sheet. Bake, stirring occasionally, for 20 to 25 minutes. When all of the nuts and seeds are lightly toasted and are giving off a rich aroma, scoop the mixture into a paper bag and add more salt if needed. Keep the bag open as the mixture cools.

Serve at room temperature. The mixture will last in a sealed container at room temperature for several weeks.

SIKIL-PAK CON NARANJA AGRIA
Pumpkin Seed Dip with Bitter Orange Juice

Isla Mujeres (Island of Women), just off the shore from Cancun in the state of Quintana Roo, is now a laid-back, small resort community with a population of only fifteen thousand inhabitants. Few of them, however, are native Maya, even though the island once served as the sanctuary for Ixchel, the Mayan goddess of the moon, fertility, and medicine.

Ricardo spent hours sitting in the doorway of the home of Julia Magaña, a member of a local Mayan family, talking with her about her many regional dishes. Among them was *sikil-pak*, the name of which is a combination of the Mayan words for pumpkin seeds and tomatoes. She told him that she always serves it as a prelude to a special meal of the grilled fish known as *tikin xik* (page 174). Be aware that the *chiles habaneros* are extremely hot. I strongly recommend wearing latex gloves if you have particularly sensitive skin and to be very careful not to rub your eyes or touch other vulnerable parts of your body.

Serve the dip at room temperature with crispy *totopos* (page 21).

Makes about 2 cups

1½ cups small unhulled raw pumpkin seeds

1 pound ripe tomatoes (about 3 medium), roasted and peeled (page 18), then roughly chopped, or 1 (14½-ounce) can fire-roasted tomatoes, drained

1 chile habanero, stem, seeds, and membranes removed and roughly chopped

½ medium white onion, roasted (page 18) and roughly chopped (about ¼ cup)

¼ cup freshly squeezed bitter orange juice (page 26)

½ teaspoon sea salt

¼ cup finely chopped fresh cilantro, thick stem ends removed

Heat a heavy skillet over medium-low heat. Pour in the pumpkin seeds and heat, stirring constantly, until they begin to puff up and start to pop. Do not let them turn brown. Pour the seeds onto a plate and let cool, then grind finely in a spice grinder or coffee grinder.

Put the tomatoes, chile, onion, orange juice, and salt in a blender or food processor and process or pulse until a smooth sauce forms. Pour into a small bowl and stir in the ground seeds and most of the cilantro. Taste and add more salt if needed. Let sit for about 30 minutes before serving to allow the flavors to meld. Sprinkle on the remaining cilantro just before serving.

Vinagre de Piña

Pineapple Vinegar

This is not a quick way to have mild, flavorful vinegar on hand. It takes several months to make this vinegar, but the result is well worth the wait. The very first time that I walked into Diana Kennedy's home in Zitácuaro, Michoacán, I saw in her sunlit window a large jar of nearly opaque liquid with fermenting pineapple peels bubbling around in it. I soon learned that this was the foamy start of this fruit vinegar. She also makes one from very ripe plantains that I have yet to try. In Mexico, you can sometimes buy these fruit vinegars from market vendors.

The next time you buy a pineapple, rinse it well, then cut off the lumpy peel and put it in a large container such as a gallon jar. Add 4 heaping tablespoons dark brown sugar or *azúcar morena*—in Mexico, you would use broken-up or shaved *piloncillo* (page 42)—and 6 cups water, cover lightly, and set in a warm place. I put mine on a shelf over my stove, but a sunny window also works well. Soon the mixture will begin to ferment, and over the next month or so, it will turn a lovely amber. In another month, a white gelatinous layer will form on top. This is the "mother" and its appearance is the signal that the vinegar is ready to use. Just scoop out the mother and set it aside in a clean container. Strain the vinegar through a fine-mesh sieve into a clean jar or bottle and cap it. You can use the mother to start another batch of vinegar by returning it to the large container and adding the same amount of sugar, water, and pineapple peels. Or better yet, start fresh. My favorite motto is TTT—Things Take Time—and making this vinegar exemplifies it.

The most widely used white vinegar sold in Mexico has 2 percent acidity, and the distilled white vinegar most commonly available in the United States has 5 percent acidity. That means to re-create Mexican dishes that call for vinegar, you may want to dilute the U.S. vinegar by half with water. Unseasoned rice vinegar can also be used, and although it is somewhat milder, it should still be diluted the same way.

BETABELES EN ESCABECHE
Pickled Beets

When I was on an early scouting trip to Mérida with Diana Kennedy, our taxi driver, on learning that we were interested in regional Yucatecan foods, drove us to his favorite *botanero,* La Reina—unfortunately, now closed—where we had endless small dishes of appetizers, all for the cost of a couple of glasses of tequila. These deep red pickled beets were one of my favorites, along with similar versions of Ensalada de Papas Glaceadas con Queso (page 54) and crispy Codzitos (page 66).

Serves 6 to 8

4 red beets, with some stem attached, well scrubbed

1 red onion, thinly sliced

¾ cup mild white vinegar such as vinagre de piña or diluted unseasoned rice vinegar (page 50)

¾ cup freshly squeezed orange juice

¼ cup Spanish dry (fino) sherry

¼ cup freshly squeezed lime juice

1 teaspoon sea salt

½ teaspoon black peppercorns

½ teaspoon whole allspice

¾ teaspoon dried oregano, preferably Mexican

¼ teaspoon ground coriander

1 teaspoon brown sugar

4 narrow strips scrubbed orange peel, white pith removed

1 tablespoon extra virgin olive oil

Freshly ground black pepper

Heat the oven to 325°F.

Put the beets in a small baking dish, sprinkle them with ¼ cup water, and cover the dish with aluminum foil. Bake until soft when lightly squeezed, about 1 hour. If they are not quite soft, continue to bake for another 15 to 20 minutes. The timing will vary depending on the age and size of the beets.

Remove the beets from the oven, drop them into a bowl of ice-cold water to cover, and let cool until they can be handled. Retrieve them from the water and peel away the skins. Cut the beets vertically into ¼-inch-thick rounds. If you have used large rather than medium beets, cut the slices in half. Place the slices in a glass bowl.

Using only the center rings of the onion, none larger in diameter than the beet slices, measure out about ½ cup and reserve the remaining slices for another use. Add the ½ cup onion rings to the beets and pour in the vinegar, orange juice, sherry, and lime juice. Lightly stir in the salt, peppercorns, and allspice. Rub the oregano between your fingers until broken up and stir into the beets along with the coriander, sugar, and orange peel.

Toss gently but thoroughly to mix well. Cover and refrigerate, stirring from time to time, for at least 3 hours before serving. The beets will keep refrigerated for up to 6 months.

When ready to serve, bring to room temperature, drain, and put in a small bowl. Just before serving, stir in the olive oil, then season to taste with salt and pepper.

PLÁTANOS RELLENOS CON FRIJOLES NEGROS
Plantain Fritters Stuffed with Black Beans

Plantains are prepared in many ways by cooks throughout the state of Veracruz. In one of the favorite versions, they are made into fritters plump with beans or a variety of other fillings.

In Tlacotalpan, a small riverside town about an hour's drive south of the port of Veracruz, the fritters Sra. María Elena Romero serves are lush with a filling of almost-melted cheese. I have often enjoyed them accompanied with a cold glass of *horchata con coco* (page 275) while sitting on a balcony overlooking the river and watching the small fishing boats drift by, a very sensory experience.

Ricardo serves the fritters hot with Salsa Verde Cocida con Aguacate (page 31) or Salsa Cocida de Jitomate (page 35), and María Elena tops hers with *crema* (page 23).

Serves 6

2 mottled black–ripe plantains (page 103)

¼ cup sugar

¼ cup all-purpose flour

1 egg, slightly beaten

½ teaspoon sea salt

½ cup fine dried bread crumbs, if needed

Peanut or sunflower oil for oiling and frying

About ½ cup Frijoles Refritos (page 217), made with black beans

Cut off the ends of each plantain, then cut in half crosswise through the peel. Put the halves in a large saucepan, add water to cover, and bring to a low boil. Lower the heat until the water is just simmering and cook until the plantains are soft enough to mash (the tip of a sharp knife should slide easily into a plantain), about 1 hour. Drain the plantains and let cool until they can be handled, then peel off the skin, removing any tough fibers from the flesh.

Put the plantains in a large bowl and smash into a fairly smooth consistency with a potato masher. Add the sugar, flour, egg, and salt and mix until well combined and a rather firm dough forms. If the dough remains too soggy to shape, add some of the bread crumbs as needed to absorb the excess moisture.

Lightly oil a baking sheet. Divide the dough into 6 equal portions. Dampen your palms and roll each dough portion into a ball about the size of a tennis ball. Using your fingers, make a large hollow in the center of each ball, tamp in 1 to 1½ tablespoons of the beans, and then close the dough over the beans. Form each ball into an oblong, like an elongated miniature football, and place on the prepared baking sheet. Cover the baking sheet with a damp towel and set aside for 30 minutes.

Pour the oil to a depth of about 1 inch into a *cazuela* or a heavy skillet and heat over medium-high heat to 275°F on a deep-frying thermometer or until the oil starts to shimmer. If the oil gets too hot, turn down the heat or the outsides of the fritters will cook too fast and the insides will be mushy. Working in two batches if necessary to avoid crowding, add the fritters to the hot oil and fry, turning frequently, until golden on all sides, 5 to 10 minutes. Using two slotted spoons or spatulas, carefully remove and drain on absorbent paper. Repeat with the remaining fritters.

Serve the fritters while they are still hot. I have occasionally reheated leftover fritters in a 325°F oven, but they are just not as good.

CEVICHE DE DZILAM DE BRAVO
Seafood "Cooked" in Lime Juice

Most coastal village cooks on the Yucatán Peninsula have their own way of preparing ceviche. This version from Manuel Nadal Marufo is from his village of Dzilam de Bravo. Just as the ingredients and methods can differ from place to place, so too can the spellings. Ceviche, *cebiche,* and seviche are all names used for this popular way of preparing seafood not with heat but by almost pickling it in lime juice. Most authorities agree that knowledge of this method of cooking arrived in Mexico long ago after contact with the indigenous people of Peru, where it has been used for many centuries.

Ricardo uses very fresh, lean meaty fish, such as *corvina* (croaker) or *mero* (grouper). I often use snapper or even tuna, and I sometimes add salmon for color contrast, a handful of tiny cooked shrimp, or a few quartered sea scallops—use your imagination.

In Yucatán, most of the chiles used, with the exception of the *habanero*, are quite bland. The *chile xcatic* (*xcatic* means "blond" in Mayan) can be replaced with Anaheim, Fresno, or other similar long, light-skinned chiles. *Chile dulce* is a small, bell-shaped green sweet pepper that is a miniature look-alike for the U.S. bell pepper. Both chiles are colorful additions to Manuel's ceviche.

Serve the ceviche scooped onto a tostada as a refreshing starter for a casual gathering of friends on a warm day. Or, spoon it into chilled cocktail glasses or small deep bowls and serve as a prelude to a more formal meal featuring rich, saucy Pipián Verde (page 189). With both meals I often serve a glass of Mexican beer or a crisp Oregon Pinot Gris.

Makes 4 cups; serves 6 to 8

1 pound very fresh fish fillets such as croaker, grouper, red snapper, sierra, or sea bass

2 tablespoons diced chile xcatic or similar chile, seeds and membranes removed

1 cup freshly squeezed lime juice (about 3 large limes), plus more for serving if needed

½ tablespoon sea salt

½ cup chopped ripe tomato

½ cup finely chopped white onion

½ cup finely chopped green chile dulce or green bell pepper

¼ cup minced fresh cilantro leaves, thick stem ends removed

Run your fingertips along the edges of the fish fillets and tweeze out any pin bones you find. Cut the fish into ½-inch cubes. Mix together the fish, *chile xcatic*, lime juice, and salt in a bowl. Cover and refrigerate until the fish is opaque, 1 to 2 hours.

Drain off any excess lime juice in the bowl. Add the tomato, onion, *chile dulce*, and cilantro and mix together gently. Taste and sprinkle on additional lime juice if needed.

ENSALADA DE PAPAS GLACEADAS CON QUESO
Potato Salad Glazed with Cheese

Some time ago, Ricardo discovered Manuel Nadal Marufo's little seaside restaurant at the end of a road on the northern coast of the Yucatán Peninsula. On one of our culinary trips there, Manuel was serving his popular potato salad as an appetizer. He stressed that the large amount of the regional sweet pepper he used in the salad was important because it accentuated the subtle flavors of the dish. (I have found that the early-ripening Red Knight bell pepper variety is easy to grow and quite similar.) I consumed way more than my share of the salad, even though I am not usually a fan of sweet peppers. If using *manchego* cheese, it should be Mexican, not Spanish, which is quite different.

A cold beer is usually welcomed with this dish, and Manuel next brings to the table a large platter of Pescado Tixin Xik (page 174), achiote-seasoned grilled fish.

Serves 8 to 10

2 pounds small Yukon Gold potatoes (14 to 18, depending on the size)

3 teaspoons sea salt

½ cup freshly shelled or thawed frozen green peas (optional)

1 pound Mexican manchego or Monterey Jack cheese

2 cups Mexican crema (page 23), crème fraîche, or thick sour cream thinned with 1 tablespoon whole milk

2 cups finely chopped green or red bell peppers (about 2 large)

1 teaspoon freshly ground black pepper

Totopos (page 21)

Put the potatoes and 2 teaspoons of the salt in a large pot three-fourths full of water and bring to a boil. Reduce the heat and simmer, uncovered, until the potatoes are fork-tender, 15 to 20 minutes. Using a slotted spoon, transfer the potatoes to a colander and rinse under cold running water until cool enough to handle. If using the peas, add them to the same boiling water and cook just until tender, about 5 minutes. Drain into a sieve and rinse under cold running water until cool.

While the peas are cooking, peel the potatoes and cut into ¼-inch cubes. Place in a bowl. When the peas are cool, drain them well and add to the potatoes.

Heat the oven to 350°F.

Divide the cheese in half. Cut half of the cheese into ¼-inch cubes. Shred the remaining half of the cheese. Add the cubed cheese, *crema*, bell peppers, black pepper, and the remaining 1 teaspoon salt to the potatoes and peas and mix gently. Taste and adjust with more salt if needed.

Spoon the potato mixture into a large, shallow baking dish or smaller individual baking dishes. Cover the surface evenly with the shredded cheese. Bake until the cheese is melted but not browned, about 20 minutes.

Serve an abundance of *totopos* for scooping up the hot potato and cheese mixture.

GAZPACHO DE MORELIA
Fruit Gazpacho of Morelia

When I lived in Spain, I was enamored of the refreshing cold tomato gazpacho of Andalusia, with its vinegar, cucumber, and green pepper overtones. I was also taken with other versions with no tomatoes at all, including one with ground almonds and grapes. Then in Morelia, the capital of Michoacán, I heard of yet another gazpacho that was not that usual cold soup, but instead much more like a portable fruit salad. There is a small place near the center of the city that is a magnet for anyone wanting a light snack during the day, and I soon understood why. Four apron-clad men were busy slicing jícama, mango, pineapple, and other fruits. At the same time, customers in a rather free-for-all line placed their orders for either the usual gazpacho or the gazpacho with the addition of cucumber or of watermelon, which I loved. All of the ingredients were prepared to order, with some customers asking for large, rectangular chunks of fruit instead of the usual smaller pieces. The combined fruits were served in large paper cups with plastic spoons, and everyone, order in hand, exited as I did, with smiles on their faces. Other locally available fruits can be substituted, but it is essential to have a medley of colors and textures.

I find this dish an ideal start for a casual brunch buffet, as everyone can mingle while eating.

Serves 4 to 6

2 mangos, peeled, pitted, and cubed (page 249; about 1 cup)

⅓ ripe pineapple, peeled, cored, and cubed (about 1 cup)

1 small jícama (¼ pound), peeled and cubed (about 1 cup)

1 small cucumber (¼ pound), seeded and cubed (about 1 cup)

1 slice watermelon, seeded and cubed (about 1 cup)

½ cup freshly squeezed orange juice

2 tablespoons freshly squeezed lime juice

2 tablespoons crumbled queso fresco

1 teaspoon ground chiles de árbol or cayenne

Bottled salsa such as Salsa Valentina (optional)

Toss together the mangos, pineapple, jícama, cucumber, and watermelon in a large bowl. Add the orange and lime juices and mix gently to coat evenly.

To serve, spoon the fruit mixture into large paper or plastic cups, or for a more formal presentation, use tall glasses, like soda or milk shake glasses. Top with the cheese and ground chile. If you like, pass the salsa for those who want to add an extra spark to their gazpacho.

CARNE APACHE CON TOSTADAS
Mexican Steak Tartare with Tostadas

Michoacán's version of steak tartare is one of the specialties that keep locals lined up around my friend Chavo's cart, which stands in its traditional spot every afternoon in front of a skinny walkway squeezed between two rows of buildings leading to his home in Pátzcuaro. I have eaten this dish throughout Michoacán, but Chavo's is, by far, my favorite version.

I first met Chavo many Christmases ago when my husband, Fredric, and I were walking down one of the winding streets of Pátzcuaro. Through a very narrow passage we saw people of all ages sitting on benches interspersed with *anafres*, traditional portable heat sources for cooking, though in this case the hot coals were only for keeping the chill away. At the far end, on a rope strung across the passageway, hung a piñata, a colorful tissue paper–clothed clay figure of a mermaid stuffed with edible surprises. We watched as blindfolded children, one by one, were whirled around, handed a big stick, and struck away in all directions, in an attempt to break the piñata and release the bounty of small jícamas, mandarins, and candies for all to grab. As we watched, a hefty man with a kind face came toward us and asked us to join his friends and family, which we eagerly did, and that was the beginning of my friendship with Chavo. Since that time, his wife of many years has died of cancer and he has remarried and is raising a second family, supporting them by selling various tostadas from his cart.

It is essential that you use high-quality lean beef for this dish of finely chopped, highly seasoned raw meat and that it be eaten right away to ward off any threat of harmful bacteria invading the dish before it is consumed. Chavo uses the regional *chiles manzanos* to spark up the tartare, but since they are seldom available in the United States, *chiles habaneros* can be substituted, providing a different flavor but a similar sizzle.

Serves 6

½ pound boneless beef tenderloin, top round, or sirloin, all fat and membranes removed and cut into ½-inch cubes

¼ cup freshly squeezed lime juice, preferably Key lime

½ teaspoon dried oregano, preferably Mexican

½ teaspoon sea salt

Put the meat in a food processor and pulse until coarsely ground (about ⅛-inch pieces). Add the lime juice, oregano, and salt and pulse briefly to combine.

Transfer to a bowl and stir in the *chile manzano*, onion, tomato, ¼ cup of the cilantro, and oil. Add the *chile chipotle*

1 teaspoon seeded and minced chile manzano, or ½ teaspoon seeded and minced chile habanero

⅓ cup minced white onion

⅓ cup finely chopped tomato

¼ cup finely chopped fresh cilantro, thick stem ends removed, plus 2 tablespoons for garnish

2 tablespoons olive oil

About ½ chile chipotle en adobo, finely chopped, with a little of the sauce

1 teaspoon capers, rinsed and minced (optional)

6 tostadas (page 21)

to taste and the capers (if using), then taste and add more salt if needed. Spread thickly on the tostadas and sprinkle a bit of cilantro on top.

QUESADILLAS CON QUESO
Quesadillas Filled with Cheese

Fold one just-made tortilla around some cheese and a leaf or two of pungent epazote, grill on a hot surface, and you will have made the traditional quesadilla. Many different fillings exist, however, such as *tinga* (shredded pork; page 147) or shredded chicken (page 25) with cubes of avocado and maybe tiny slices of *chiles chipotles en adobo* or *chiles jalapeños en escabeche* or even a meager amount of *frijoles refritos* (page 217). The possibilities go on and on, so use your imagination. Nowadays, quesadillas are often quickly fried until crispy, and in the northern states are made with small flour tortillas. However they are made, whatever filling is used, and even no matter what they are called—sometimes they are dubbed empanadas—they provide an easy and tasty way to have a quick bite.

Quesadillas accompanied with Guacamole Clásico (page 43), Salsa Verde Cruda (page 31), or Salsa de Pico de Gallo (page 34) are ideal to pass around with drinks. Or, you can serve them alongside a bowl of Sopa de Hongos (page 79) for a satisfying supper.

Makes 14 quesadillas

1 pound freshly made masa for corn tortillas (page 19), rolled into fourteen 1¼-inch balls

Line a large platter or tray with plastic wrap. To make each quesadilla, using a

2 cups shredded Monterey Jack or Muenster cheese

14 fresh epazote leaves (optional)

1 chile poblano, roasted, peeled, seeds and membranes removed, and cut lengthwise into narrow strips (page 17), or 2 chiles jalapeños, thinly sliced lengthwise

tortilla press and a ball of masa, make a 4- to 6-inch tortilla as directed on page 19. Remove the upper piece of plastic and put a little of the cheese, an epazote leaf (if using), and some chile across the center of one-half of the tortilla, leaving a ½-inch border uncovered. Using the bottom piece of plastic, bring up the uncovered half of the tortilla and fold it over the filling to form a half-circle, then press the edges with your fingertips. Lift the plastic and invert the quesadilla onto the platter, peeling away the plastic wrap. Cover the quesadilla lightly with another piece of plastic wrap. Repeat to make the remaining quesadillas, adding them to the platter. They can be assembled several hours in advance, covered tightly with plastic wrap, and refrigerated.

When ready to serve, heat the oven to 200°F. Heat a *comal*, griddle, or large, heavy skillet over medium heat. When hot, working in batches, quickly place the quesadillas on the hot surface and cook, turning once, until speckled brown on both sides, 3 to 4 minutes on each side. If the folded edge of the quesadilla is still soft, hold it firmly on the hot *comal*. Transfer to a heatproof plate and place in the oven to keep warm until all of the quesadillas are ready. Serve right away.

VARIATION: CRISPY-FRIED QUESADILLAS

Pour canola or safflower oil to a depth of ½ inch into a heavy skillet and heat over medium-high heat until shimmering but not smoking. Working in batches to avoid crowding, fry the quesadillas, flipping them over once, until crispy and golden brown on both sides, 2 to 3 minutes total. Using a slotted spatula, transfer to absorbent paper to drain. Serve hot from the pan or keep warm on a heatproof platter in the oven until all are ready.

VARIATION: QUICKLY MADE QUESADILLAS

This simple version of a quesadilla is a fast way to have something to eat with lunch, maybe along with a bowl of soup. Use store-bought thin corn or small flour tortillas. Heat a *comal*, heavy skillet, or griddle over medium heat for several minutes. When the surface is hot, lay a tortilla on it. As it heats, add shredded cheese and other ingredients to half of the tortilla. Fold the tortilla over the filling and flip the quesadilla over until lightly speckled brown on both sides and the cheese is melted. You may have to flip it over one more time. My favorite combination is made by brushing a little piquant sauce from a can of *chiles chipotles en adobo* on the tortilla and topping with some cheese and then with a strip of avocado and maybe some shredded cabbage.

TLACOYOS
Oval Masa Turnovers

Throughout Mexico City and the surrounding states, people in all walks of life—bankers in suits and ties, college kids in T-shirts and jeans, women cradling babies—cluster around the *tlacoyo* vendor who makes their favorite version of this miniature football-shaped masa snack. Most are made with ordinary white or yellow corn, but a few vendors still serve *tlacoyos* made from the scarce blue-black corn.

One day on the way from Mexico City to the popular getaway of Tepoztlán, Ricardo took me on a back road that was virtually enveloped on both sides by fields of nopal cactus. In this area, known as Milpa Alta, the *tlacoyos* are typically topped with a green salsa and nopales, and not surprisingly, we stopped for a quick, tasty snack. For a more colorful variation, add a contrasting tomato red salsa on half of each *tlacoyo*.

Makes 12 tlacoyos; serves 6

▌FOR THE TLACOYOS
1 pound freshly made masa for corn tortillas, or 1¾ cups masa harina for tortillas reconstituted with 1 cup plus 2 tablespoons quite warm water (page 19)

¼ cup freshly rendered pork lard (page 24)

1 teaspoon sea salt

About ¾ cup Frijoles Refritos (page 217)

▌FOR FRYING THE TLACOYOS
½ cup freshly rendered pork lard (page 24) or canola or safflower oil

▌FOR THE TOPPING
2 cups Salsa Verde Cruda (page 31), or 1 cup each Salsa Verde Cruda and Salsa Cocida de Jitomate (page 35)

½ cup finely chopped white onion

1 cup crumbled queso fresco or queso panela

About 2 cups cooked, diced nopales (page 23), from about 1 pound paddles (optional)

FOR THE TLACOYOS: Put the fresh masa or the reconstituted masa harina in a large bowl, add the lard and salt, and mix with your hands until a smooth dough forms. A little warm water may have to be added to the masa mixture to achieve the correct consistency. Divide the dough into 12 equal portions and shape each portion into a 1½-inch ball. Flatten each ball lightly with your hands to form a thick tortilla about 3 inches in diameter and ⅛ inch thick, or use a tortilla press (see directions on page 20), pressing down rather lightly so the masa is ⅛ inch thick.

Press a hollow in the center of a tortilla large enough for 1 tablespoon of beans. Add the beans to the hollow and close the tortilla, forming it into a ball. Flatten the ball between your hands to form a football-shaped turnover about 5½ inches

¼ cup chopped fresh cilantro, thick stem ends removed

10 red radishes, julienned (optional)

long, 2¾ inches across at its widest part, and ½ inch thick. Repeat with the remaining masa balls.

Heat the oven to 200°F. Place a large, heavy skillet or a griddle over low heat. Add as many *tlacoyos* as will fit without crowding and cook, turning often, until the masa is cooked through and the *tlacoyos* are slightly charred on both sides, about 10 minutes. Lightly cover and set aside while you cook the remaining *tlacoyos*. (This step may be done up to a day ahead. Let cool, cover with plastic wrap, and refrigerate.)

FOR FRYING: Heat the lard over medium heat just until sizzling hot. Working in batches to prevent crowding, add the *tlacoyos* and fry on one side only, spooning the hot oil over the top until golden, 30 to 60 seconds. Using a slotted spatula, lift the *tlacoyos*, allowing any excess fat to drip off, and drain on absorbent paper. Keep warm on a heatproof platter in the oven until all are fried.

Drench each *tlacoyo* with a spoonful of the Salsa Verde Cruda. If using both salsas, spoon them on opposite ends. Sprinkle each *tlacoyo* with a little onion, some *queso fresco*, about 2 tablespoons of the cooked nopales (if using), and some cilantro and radishes (if using) and serve hot. *Tlacoyos* must have hungry people waiting to eat them on the spot.

TACOS DE BERROS
Watercress Tacos

Tangy watercress is a popular salad green throughout Mexico. It was, however, a revelation to me when Emelia Cabrera, a friend in Oaxaca, combined the peppery green with the fiery bite of the regional *chile de agua* to make a filling for our tacos. I have substituted a *chile jalapeño* for the difficult-to-find *chile de agua*. Emelia paired the tacos with a dish of *frijolones con costilla de puerco* (page 106), so we could dunk each taco into our bowls of beans before taking a bite.

Makes 6 tacos

1 bunch watercress, stemmed and finely chopped

1 chile jalapeño, seeded and finely chopped

¼ white onion, finely chopped

Put the watercress, chile, onion, and radishes in a bowl and toss together with the lime juice and salt.

3 red radishes, chopped

1 tablespoon freshly squeezed lime juice, preferably Key lime

2 pinches of sea salt

6 small corn tortillas, freshly made (page 19) or store-bought

Reheat the tortillas if not freshly made. Spoon 1 heaping tablespoon of the watercress mixture into the center of each warm tortilla and roll up the tortilla. Serve right away.

TACOS DE RAJAS DE CHILES POBLANOS CON ELOTE

Tacos of Poblano Chile Strips with Corn

Ricardo's simple taco filling of creamy *chiles poblanos* and corn is popular in Mexico City and throughout central Mexico and makes an out-of-the-ordinary vegetarian taco filling. I also find this chile and corn mixture a tasty garnish for grilled meat or topping for Arroz Blanco (page 223).

Serves 4 to 6

2 tablespoons olive oil

⅓ cup finely chopped white onion

1 clove garlic, minced

4 chiles poblanos, roasted, peeled, seeds and membranes removed, and cut lengthwise into narrow strips (page 17)

½ cup cooked or frozen corn kernels

¼ cup Mexican crema (page 23), crème fraîche, or thick sour cream thinned with 1 tablespoon whole milk

½ teaspoon sea salt

6 small corn tortillas, freshly made (page 19) or store-bought

Heat the oil in a *cazuela* or heavy skillet over medium heat until just shimmering. Add the onion and cook, stirring often, until it turns pale yellow, about 2 minutes. Lower the heat to low, add the garlic, and stir for a few seconds, then stir in the poblano strips, cover, and cook for about 4 minutes to meld the flavors.

Stir in the corn, *crema*, and salt and cook, stirring occasionally, for 2 minutes to heat through. Do not allow the *crema* to curdle. Remove from the heat and taste and add more salt if needed.

Reheat the tortillas if not freshly made. Spoon an equal amount of the hot chile mixture into the center of each warm tortilla, fold over, and serve immediately.

TACOS CON CARNITAS ESTILO MICHOACÁN
Tacos with Crispy Pork Cooked Michoacán Style

On street corners and roadsides throughout Michoacán and other parts of central Mexico, if you are hungry and in luck, you will find little *carnitas* stands selling crispy, small chunks of pork that are surprisingly moist and tender inside. They have been "fry-boiled" in lard, which bubbles away in enormous copper cauldrons made in the village of Santa Clara de Cobre, widely known for its beautiful copperware. Here, every afternoon on one corner of the square, people line up for their *carnitas*, which they fold into tortillas that are often first smeared with refried beans, adding a scoop of guacamole and a dribble of extremely hot salsa made from the local *chile manzano*.

Here is a somewhat less formidable way to make your own *carnitas*.

Serves 6 to 8

3 pounds boneless, rather fatty country-style ribs or pork shoulder, cut into 2-by-1-inch pieces

½ white onion, quartered

4 cloves garlic

1 tablespoon sea salt

½ cup freshly squeezed orange juice

Peel of ½ scrubbed orange, white pith removed, cut into narrow 1-inch-long strips

2 tablespoons freshly rendered pork lard (page 24) or canola or safflower oil

½ teaspoon dried oregano, preferably Mexican

12 to 16 small corn tortillas, freshly made (page 19) or store-bought

Guacamole Clásico (page 43)

Salsa de Cuaresmeños (page 32) or your favorite salsa

Frijoles Refritos (optional; page 217)

Put the pork, onion, and garlic in a large, heavy skillet or Dutch oven. Add water to cover by ½ inch and the salt and bring to a boil over medium-high heat, skimming off any foam that rises to the surface. Lower the heat to medium-low and add the orange juice, orange peel, lard, and oregano. Cover partially and simmer until the meat is tender and all of the liquid has evaporated and the pork begins to fry in its own fat, about 1½ hours.

Reduce the heat to low and cook, stirring often, until the pork just starts to become crispy and brown, about 10 minutes longer, being careful not to let it scorch. If the meat does not have enough fat in it, add a bit more lard.

Reheat the tortillas if not freshly made. Scoop the *carnitas* into a warmed serving dish. Wrap the warm tortillas in a cloth and set out with the guacamole, salsa, and refried beans (if using) for making tacos.

TACOS DE PESCADO
Fish Tacos

For some time, Federico López, a Mexican chef, traveled along both coasts of northern and southern Baja in search of the "ultimate" fish taco—almost these states' official dish. This was his favorite, and without a doubt, one of the best Ricardo or I have ever tasted. It is a good idea to have an extra pair of hands to help with the assembly.

A frosty glass of Michelada (page 268) or lemonade made with a splash of sparkling water always adds to my enjoyment.

Serves 6

6 ounces cabbage, finely sliced

2 cups Pico de Gallo Salsa (page 34)

1⅔ cups all-purpose flour

1½ teaspoons dried oregano, preferably Mexican

1 teaspoon sea salt

Freshly ground black pepper

1 quart dark Mexican beer

1½ pounds skinless fish fillets such as grouper, porgy, sea bass, or red snapper

Canola or safflower oil for frying

12 small corn tortillas, freshly made (page 21) or store-bought

1½ cups Aderezo de Chipotle (page 44)

2 limes, quartered

Mix the cabbage and salsa together in a bowl and set aside.

Stir together the flour, oregano, salt, and a few grinds of pepper, then slowly whisk in the beer to make a thin batter. Let the batter sit for 10 minutes.

Cut the fish into 4-by-1-inch strips and tweeze out any pin bones you find. You should have 12 strips.

Pour the oil to a depth of ¾ inch into a large, heavy skillet over medium-high heat and heat just until rippling. Dip each fish strip into the batter, slip it into the hot oil, and fry, turning once, until golden, about 1 minute on each side. Using a slotted spatula, lift out the fish strip, allowing any excess oil to drip off, and drain on absorbent paper. Repeat with the remaining fish strips. Meanwhile, reheat the tortillas if not freshly made.

Spread some of the chipotle seasoning on each warm tortilla, place a strip of fish in the center, and add a layer of the cabbage mixture. Fold the tortilla over and serve immediately. Serve the tacos with small bowls of the limes and the remaining chipotle condiment and cabbage mixture for those who want to add more flavor or texture to their tacos.

TACOS DE COCHITO AL HORNO
Soft Pork Tacos

Although most tourists arriving in Chiapas head immediately to the highland regions surrounding San Cristóbal de las Casas, it is in the capital city of Tuxtla Gutiérrez and nearby Chiapa de Corzo where I find the most interesting regional dishes. One of the most famous is *cochito al horno,* or "baked" little pig.

Alty Orantes de Fernández, who was a long-time professional cook in Tuxtla, now prepares this succulent pork in her kitchen, selling it by the kilo or in tacos adorned with only crunchy pickled onions, with a small mound of *frijoles refritos* alongside. Hungry locals flock to her home to eat at one of the two outside tables, accompanying their meal with a cold beer or a thirst-quenching glass of *horchata con coco* (page 275) to drink. Both the onions and the meat are best started a day in advance.

Serve the pork with bowls of shredded lettuce, pickled onions, and lots of hot corn tortillas. Sra. Orantes heaps the omnipresent *frijoles refritos* (page 217) on a platter for folks to help themselves.

Serves 4 to 6

¼ pound chiles guajillos (about 14), stems, seeds, and membranes removed, then toasted (page 18)

¼ pound chiles anchos (about 6), stems, seeds and membranes removed, then toasted (page 18)

6 whole cloves, lightly toasted (page 19)

10 whole allspice, lightly toasted (page 19)

8 black peppercorns, lightly toasted (page 19)

2 bay leaves, lightly toasted (page 19)

4 cloves garlic, roasted (page 18), then peeled and coarsely chopped

½ cup mild white vinegar such as vinagre de piña or diluted unseasoned rice vinegar (page 50)

Soak the chiles in a bowl of very hot water to cover until soft, about 30 minutes. Drain, tear into smaller pieces, and put in a blender.

Coarsely grind the cloves, allspice, black pepper, and bay leaf in a spice grinder or coffee grinder. Add the spices to the blender along with the garlic. Pour in the vinegar and process until a smooth paste forms, adding up to 1 cup water if needed to release the blades. Transfer to a large bowl.

Add all of the pork to the chile mixture and mix well, making certain that every piece is thoroughly coated. Cover and marinate in the refrigerator for at least several hours or preferably overnight.

2 pounds boneless pork shoulder, trimmed of excess fat and cut into 1-inch cubes (do save the fat to make lard, page 24)

2 pounds boneless country-style pork ribs, trimmed of excess fat and cut into 1-inch pieces

1 tablespoon sea salt

12 to 18 small corn tortillas, freshly made (page 19) or store-bought

3 sprigs fresh cilantro, thick stem ends removed and chopped

2 cups Cebolla Morada Curada (page 45)

1½ cups finely shredded romaine lettuce or cabbage

Heat the oven to 350°F.

Put the meat in a large *cazuela* or Dutch oven and sprinkle with the salt. Cover and bake, turning the meat occasionally and scooping up any pieces stuck to the bottom of the pot, for 1 hour. Add 1 cup hot water and continue to bake, stirring occasionally, until the meat is almost falling apart, about 30 minutes longer.

Reheat the tortillas if not freshly made. Spoon the meat and any sauce onto a warmed deep platter and sprinkle with the cilantro. Set the pork out with the tortillas and with bowls of the onions and lettuce for making the tacos.

CODZITOS
Crispy Rolled Little Tacos

In the state of Yucatán, the law requires that food be served with drinks, so midafternoon in Mérida often finds me at one of the city's unusual *botaneros*, where one side is a bar exclusively for men and the other is set aside for families. On both sides, you buy your beverages but plates of delicious *botanas* keep appearing free of charge as long as you keep drinking. I once counted over thirty different kinds served. Crispy *codzitos* stuffed with shredded chicken were one of my favorites. I often serve them for a casual get-together of friends, along with other *botanas* and *antojitos*.

Serves 4 to 6

FOR THE OPTIONAL CHICKEN FILLING

2 tablespoons canola or safflower oil

3 tablespoons finely chopped white onion

½ pound tomatoes (about 1 large or 2 small), chopped

FOR THE OPTIONAL CHICKEN FILLING: Heat the 2 tablespoons oil in a skillet over medium-low heat. Stir in the onion, tomatoes, and chiles and fry until all are softened, about 5 minutes. Add the

2 chiles serranos, stemmed and coarsely chopped

2 cups shredded cooked chicken (page 25)

½ teaspoon sea salt

⫶ FOR THE CODZITOS
12 corn tortillas (page 19), about 4 inches in diameter, reheated if not freshly made

¼ cup canola or safflower oil, plus more if needed

1 cup Salsa Cocida de Jitomate (page 35)

½ cup crumbled queso fresco or shredded Monterey Jack cheese

chicken and salt and continue cooking for several more minutes until the mixture is almost dry. The filling must be warm when it is wrapped in the tortillas, so if not using immediately, reheat just before using.

FOR THE CODZITOS: Spoon a line of the chicken mixture, if using, down the center of each warm tortilla, roll up the tortilla, and then slide a toothpick horizontally into the roll to secure in place.

If making unstuffed *codzitos*, simply roll up each tortilla as tightly as possible and slide a toothpick horizontally into the roll to secure it in place. It is important to do this while the tortillas are warm or they will break apart.

Heat the oven to 200°F. Heat the ¼ cup oil in a large, heavy skillet over medium-high heat. Add half of the rolled tortillas to the hot oil and fry, spooning the hot oil over the tortillas so they color evenly, until crispy, less than 1 minute. Using a slotted spatula or tongs, lift out the *codzitos* onto absorbent paper and pat off any excess oil. Remove the toothpicks. Keep the *codzitos* warm on a heatproof platter in the oven while you fry the second half. Add more oil to the skillet if needed.

Pile the *codzitos* on several small plates. Drizzle them with the salsa, sprinkle with the cheese, and serve immediately.

GORDITAS DE FRIJOLES NEGROS
Puffy Masa Cakes with Black Beans

The term *gordita* means "little fat tortilla" and all gorditas are made from masa, but what you are served when you order a gordita will vary depending on where you are in Mexico. For example, in Mexico City, the gordita may be a little masa drum filled with ground *chicharrón*, while in Aguascalientes, the puffy masa cake is partially split in half like a pocket and stuffed with all sorts of different fillings. And in Veracruz, a rather sweet gordita flavored with anise is a specialty.

Here in this port city, I also discovered my favorite version of the gordita, at La Casa de Tío Teno, run by Atenogio and his wife, Sara. Each morning they served *gorditas de frijoles negros*, the masa dark with ground black beans, along with the puffier, plain *gorditas blancas*. Unfortunately, Atenogio sold his little place, but similar gorditas are served by Carmen Ramírez Degollado in her El Bajío restaurants in Mexico City. What makes Carmen's version unusual is the smoky black but potent, rather sweet *salsa negra* made with *chiles chipotles*, which is cautiously dribbled on top to create an amazing flavor contrast to the mild-natured gorditas.

Makes 15 gorditas; serves 6 . . . .

1 cup drained Frijoles de la Olla (page 214), made with black beans, or canned black beans, plus ½ cup black bean broth or liquid from can

½ pound freshly made masa for corn tortillas, or ¾ cup plus 1½ tablespoons masa harina for tortillas reconstituted with ⅔ cup quite warm water (page 19)

1 cup all-purpose flour

1 teaspoon sea salt

Peanut or sunflower oil for frying

6 to 8 tablespoons Salsa Negra con Chipotles (page 41) or Salsa de Jitomate Cocida (page 35)

½ cup crumbled queso fresco or queso añejo

Put the beans and bean broth in a blender and process until the mixture is thick and satiny smooth. In a bowl, combine the fresh masa or reconstituted masa harina, bean puree, flour, and salt and mix with your hands until a soft but not sticky, quite blackish dough forms. Divide the dough into 15 equal portions and shape each portion into a ball the size of a Ping-Pong ball. Cover the balls with plastic wrap.

Heat the oven to 200°F (in the hot climate of Veracruz or anywhere else if the kitchen is warm, this is not necessary). Pour the oil to a depth of ¾ to 1 inch into a large, heavy skillet and heat to 375°F on a deep-frying thermometer. To make each gordita, using a tortilla press lined with plastic sheets (see directions on page 19), gently press each masa ball into a 4-inch round about ¼ inch thick. Using the bottom plastic sheet, remove the tortilla from the press and immediately slip it into the hot oil. Fry the tortilla, using a spoon to splash hot oil onto its top surface, until it puffs up for just a second. Flip it over immediately, leave for just a moment, then use a slotted spoon to remove to absorbent paper. Transfer to a heatproof plate and keep warm in the oven until all are ready. Repeat with the remaining masa balls.

Serve right away on a warmed platter or individual plates with bowls of the salsa and the cheese.

Tortillas de Harina
Wheat-Flour Tortillas

From the beginning, corn tortillas sustained the peoples of the pre-Columbian civilizations living in southern and central Mexico. But when the Spanish expanded throughout Mexico, they found no such culinary traditions to draw on in northern Mexico, as the few native groups in the area were primarily nomadic or seminomadic.

Because bread was almost as essential to the Spanish as corn tortillas were to Mexico's native population, wheat was soon cultivated, and in the north, the compromise, flour tortillas, were used in many of the same ways.

Enchiladas in the border states are made with giant paper-thin tortillas, up to eighteen inches across, as are the burritos and the deep-fried *chimichangas*. Equally versatile smaller flour tortillas are served in the other northern states.

I seldom make my own flour tortillas, but when I do prepare them, I use a stubby wooden rolling pin with no handles to roll them out thinly. It was given to me by Dora Chávez, who lives in Santa Fe, New Mexico, and has made about fifty flour tortillas a day for her large family over the last four decades.

As much as I love flour tortillas, I find it curious that in these health-conscious times flour tortillas containing oil, shortening, or lard outsell the more nutritious corn tortillas.

BURRITOS CON CHILORIO
Spicy Shredded Pork Burritos

*C*hilorio, shredded chile-seasoned pork, is a regional specialty of the northwestern state of Sinaloa. If you are into the popular music of the people of northern Mexico, Sinaloa's brassy *banda* and balladic *corrido* traditions will give you a good idea of what this dish is all about: a gritty honesty of flavor with heat that is sometimes explosive. Alma Cervantes Cota, who grew up in Sinaloa, strongly believes that this classic preparation, typically served wrapped in a flour tortilla as a burrito, should be more widely known. I agree.

For a memorable light meal, serve with Ensalada de Jícama, Melón y Pepino (page 240) and Frijoles Charros (page 220). Any leftover *chilorio* can be mixed into Frijoles Chinos o Fritos (page 216) made with light red beans and scooped up with *totopos* (page 21) as a tasty snack, accompanied with cold beer.

Serves 8 to 10

▋ FOR THE CHILORIO

- ¼ cup plus 1½ teaspoons freshly rendered lard (page 24) or canola or safflower oil
- 2 pounds boneless pork shoulder, with some fat, cut into 2-inch pieces and patted dry
- 2 teaspoons sea salt
- 1 cup freshly squeezed orange juice
- 2 chiles pasillas, stems, seeds, and membranes removed
- 6 chiles anchos, stems, seeds, and membranes removed
- 5 small cloves garlic, roughly chopped
- 1 teaspoon dried oregano, preferably Mexican
- 1 teaspoon ground cumin, preferably freshly ground
- 1 teaspoon freshly ground black pepper
- ⅓ cup cider vinegar

FOR THE CHILORIO: Heat ¼ cup of the lard in a *cazuela* or Dutch oven over medium-high heat. Sprinkle the pork all over with the salt. Add half of the meat to the hot oil and fry, turning as needed, until lightly browned on all sides, about 5 minutes. Then, using a slotted spoon, take out and set aside. Repeat with the remaining pork. When all of the pork has been browned, return it to the pot, add 7 cups hot water and the orange juice, and bring to a boil. Lower the heat to medium-low, cover partially, and cook until the liquid is reduced and the meat is fork-tender, about 50 minutes.

Remove the pork from the cooking liquid. Pour off the broth remaining in the pot and set aside to cool. When the pork is cool enough to handle, finely shred it with your fingers or two forks and reserve.

FOR THE BURRITOS

8 to 10 flour tortillas, 8 to 10 inches in diameter

1 tablespoon canola or safflower oil

2 Anaheim or Hatch chiles, roughly chopped

½ red onion, chopped

3 ripe tomatoes, chopped

2 cups chilorio

1 cup Mexican crema (page 23), crème fraîche, or thick sour cream thinned with 1 tablespoon whole milk (optional)

1 ripe Hass avocado, halved, pitted, peeled, and sliced (optional)

While the pork is cooking, soak the chiles in a bowl of very hot water to cover until soft, about 30 minutes. Drain, tear into smaller pieces, and put in a blender. Add the garlic, oregano, cumin, pepper, and vinegar and process until smooth, adding ½ cup or more of the reserved pork broth as needed to help release the blades.

Wipe out the pot, add the remaining 1½ teaspoons lard, and heat over medium-high heat until shimmering. Pour in the chile mixture, and when it begins to sputter, lower the heat to a gentle simmer. Add the shredded pork and simmer, stirring occasionally, until it is well seasoned and begins to dry, about 15 minutes. Remove from the heat.

FOR THE BURRITOS: Heat the oven to 300°F. Wrap the tortillas in aluminum foil and warm in the oven for about 20 minutes.

Heat the oil in a heavy skillet over medium heat. Add the chiles and fry for a few minutes until they begin to soften. Add the onion and continue to cook, stirring, until it begins to turn golden, a few minutes longer. Stir in the tomatoes and *chilorio*, lower the heat, and cook, stirring occasionally. When the tomatoes have released their juices, cover and simmer for 5 minutes to blend the flavors. Remove from the heat.

Place a warmed tortilla on a plate and spoon a generous amount of the *chilorio* mixture (about 3 large spoonfuls) onto the tortilla. I like to top the pork with some *crema* and avocado to round out the flavor. Roll up the tortilla snuggly and place it seam side down on the plate. Repeat with the remaining tortillas and *chilorio*. Serve right away.

TORTAS DE MILANESA
Hefty Steak Sandwiches

If I am in Mexico City and the midday sun and my stomach are telling me it is time to eat, Fredric and I usually head to La Perla for *tortas* to bring back and enjoy in the garden of our hotel. Hanging on the walls of La Perla and other *torterías* are lists of various fillings for these hefty, multilayered sandwiches crammed with a kaleidoscope of flavors and textures. Although there are many fillings from which to choose—chicken, pork, ham, cheese—without a doubt, the *milanesa*, a breaded and fried thin, boneless beef steak, is everyone's all-time favorite, including mine. It is a complete meal by itself.

The first record of this style of meat preparation was the inclusion of *lombolos con panitio* (breaded veal scallops) on the menu of a banquet for the head cleric of a cathedral in Milan in 1134. Because Milan and Vienna are only about two hundred miles apart and the Duchy of Milan was part of the Austro-Hungarian Empire from 1815 to 1866, it is not surprising that a similar dish appeared in Vienna, where it was known as *Wiener schnitzel* by 1862. Instead of veal, it is now often made with pork, and in Mexico with thin slices of beef.

The flat-iron steak from the shoulder of the chuck roast or the top round is a good cut to use. In Mexico, the sandwiches are made with *teleras*, round, soft-crusted rolls, or with *bolillos*, crustier, torpedo-shaped rolls.

Serves 4 hungry people . . . .

2 eggs

1½ cups fine dried bread crumbs

1 teaspoon sea salt

¼ teaspoon freshly ground black pepper

4 boneless beef steaks, each about 3 by 4 inches and a scant ⅓ inch thick, trimmed of excess fat

2 tablespoons peanut or olive oil

4 teleras, bolillos, or large, soft, crusty French rolls, split horizontally and a slight indentation pinched out of the bottom half

4 tablespoons Frijoles Refritos (page 217), made with pinto beans, warmed

Have all of the ingredients set out and ready to assemble.

Break the eggs into a wide, shallow bowl and beat lightly. Stir together the bread crumbs, salt, and pepper in a separate shallow bowl. Put 1 steak between 2 sheets of waxed or parchment paper, or place it inside a plastic bag. Using the heel of your hand or a small rolling pin, pound gently to flatten it even thinner. Repeat with the remaining steaks.

Heat the oil in a large, heavy skillet over medium-high heat. Dip a steak first into

4 tablespoons mayonnaise, Mexican crema (page 23), crème fraîche, or thick sour cream thinned with 1 tablespoon whole milk

4 small romaine lettuce leaves, roughly shredded

8 slices ripe tomato, ¼ inch thick

8 thin slices white onion

4 chiles chipotles en adobo, coarsely chopped, or chiles jalapeños en escabeche, cut lengthwise into ¼-inch-wide strips

1 ripe Hass avocado, halved, pitted, peeled, and cut into 8 slices

½ cup shredded quesillo de Oaxaca or Monterey Jack cheese

the beaten egg, allowing the excess to drip off, and then into the crumbs, coating evenly. When the oil is rippling hot but not smoking, add the steaks as each is breaded. Sauté the steaks on one side until golden brown, about 2 minutes. Using tongs, carefully turn over the meat so that the breading does not pull away, and then sauté on the other side. Using the tongs, lift the steaks out of the oil, allowing the excess oil to drip off, and drain on absorbent paper.

Put the halves of each roll cut side up and side by side. Spread 1 tablespoon of the beans on the bottom half of each roll and spread 1 tablespoon mayonnaise on the top half. Layer one-fourth of the lettuce, 2 tomato slices, 2 onion slices, and one-fourth of the chiles on the bottom half of each roll, then lay a steak on the chiles. Top each steak with 2 avocado slices, smashing them gently onto the meat, and then sprinkle with 2 tablespoons of the cheese. Put the top on each *torta* and press the top and bottom together firmly.

Serve immediately. You will need both hands to eat your *torta*, and make sure you have lots of napkins. It's a satisfying if sometimes messy culinary experience.

▌VARIATION: CEMITAS DE PUEBLA (PUEBLA'S SPECIAL SANDWICHES)

As the saying goes, "When in Rome, do as the Romans do," so whenever I am in Puebla, I go to the small Mercado Carranza, which is packed with hungry Poblanos heading for one of the *fondas* specializing in *cemitas*. The term *cemita* is used for the name of both the round sesame seed–topped roll and the *torta*, which is plumped with layers of just about any filling you can imagine, even pig's feet. My favorite *fonda* is El As de Oro, where Rebecca, the longtime matriarch of *cemitas*, always seems to remember me and my love for the highly aromatic herb *pápalo*, a leaf or two of which is traditionally served in these *tortas*.

Although *cemitas* are not widely available in the United States, a similar *torta* can be made by preparing the Tortas de Milanesa and tossing a handful each of whole watercress and cilantro leaves together in a small bowl to use as a much less pungent substitute for *pápalo*. Add a hefty sprinkle on the last layer of fillings you are using, maybe substituting a thick slice of chicken or other meat for the *milanesa* if you like.

TORTAS AHOGADAS

Salsa-Smothered Sandwiches
Layered with Beans and Pork

The magic behind this pork-filled *torta* is the *birote*, a special flattish *bolillo* (elongated bread roll) made in Jalisco with a particularly crunchy crust that can absorb the very incendiary salsa without falling apart. The name *ahogadas* comes from the fact that the *torta* is "drenched" with mouth-sizzling *salsa de chiles de árbol,* and sometimes to subdue the heat, a tomato salsa with no chiles at all is added. At small street stands in Guadalajara, both salsas are offered and most eaters seem to have worked out a favorite combination. Then there are those who happily suffer as they eat their *torta* drenched in only the hot salsa. I do half and half.

Have the beans, *carnitas,* and salsas made in advance and the condiments at hand before you begin.

Serves 6 . . . .

6 crusty French rolls, about 5 inches long, split horizontally and a shallow depression pinched out of the bottom half

6 tablespoons Frijoles Refritos (page 217), made with any brick-colored beans, warmed

2½ to 3 cups Carnitas Estilo Michoacán (page 63)

2 ripe Hass avocados, halved, pitted, peeled, and sliced (optional)

¼ head iceberg lettuce, shredded (optional)

1½ cups Salsa de Chiles de Árbol (page 37)

1½ cups Salsa Roja Dulce (page 37)

2 limes, quartered

Spread the cut side of the bottom half of each roll with 1 tablespoon of the beans. Stuff with the pork, and if you want the avocado and lettuce, divide them evenly among the *tortas.*

Put small pitchers or bowls with the two salsas on the table along with a plate of the limes. Put each *torta* on a plate (I usually use thick paper plates) and encourage everyone to drench the *tortas* with the salsas and to squirt on some lime juice to bring out even more flavor. Be sure to have lots of napkins on hand.

CALDOS Y SOPAS

Broths and Soups

Soups are an almost indispensable part of any Mexican's daily diet, and it is not even unusual to start the day with a bowl of soup, as is common in Asia and many other parts of the world. One of my early-morning breakfast delights in the port of Veracruz is to prop myself up on a stool at one of the brightly painted seafood bars that are nestled right outside the frenetic fish market and slurp down a bowl of spicy crab or fish soup.

When the Spaniards brought their tradition of eating long-simmered, rib-sticking soups to Mexico they were quick to include the native corn, tomatoes, beans, pungent chiles, and herbs. These robust soups provide a nourishing and satisfying meal in a pot, especially when meat and other vegetables are added.

Light soups or broths serve as a prelude to more elaborate meals, reflecting the tastes of Austrian archduke Ferdinand Maximilian and his wife, Princess Charlotte of Belgium. Selected by Napoleon III of France, they reigned as emperor and empress of Mexico for only three years in the late nineteenth century, but their influence on Mexican cuisine is still apparent. Many soups include rice or pasta and creamy soups are often served for special occasions. All of these soups are comforting and bring back memories of past family meals that are now nurturing a new generation.

CALDO DE TICHINDAS
Mussel Broth

This shellfish soup is from El Ciruelo, an isolated village on Oaxaca's northern Costa Chica populated primarily by descendants of African slaves. It calls for *tichindas,* which look like very small mussels, and *pitiona,* an aromatic herb, both of which can be difficult to find outside the region. But small mussels or even clams can be substituted for the *tichindas* and mint or epazote (or a combination of the two) can be used for the *pitiona.*

Antonieta Avila Salinas, one of the women I met in El Ciruelo, always has a bowl of *salsa de chiles costeños* (page 33) on her table when serving this soup for those wanting an additional fiery kick.

Serves 4 to 6 as a main course, or 6 to 8 as a first course

2 pounds small mussels

10 chiles puyas, stems, seeds, and membranes removed, then toasted (page 18)

4 cloves garlic, roughly chopped

10 fresh pitiona, mint, or epazote leaves or equal parts mint and epazote leaves, roughly chopped

½ cup masa harina (page 19)

2 teaspoons sea salt

Salsa Purépecha de Chiles Puyas (page 39)

2 or 3 limes, preferably Key lime, quartered

Scrub the mussels well under cold running water. Remove the "beard" from each shell and set aside.

Soak the chiles in a bowl with 3 cups very hot water until soft, about 10 minutes. Remove the chiles, reserving the water, and tear into smaller pieces. Put the chile pieces, soaking water, garlic, and *pitiona* in a blender and process until smooth. Pour into a large *cazuela* or Dutch oven and bring to a simmer over medium-low heat.

In a bowl, stir the masa harina into 2 cups cold water until thoroughly combined, then slowly add to the simmering chile mixture while stirring constantly. Raise the heat to medium-high, add 3 more cups water and the salt, and bring to a boil. Add the mussels, lower the heat, and simmer just until they open, usually within a few seconds but no more than a couple of minutes.

Remove from the heat and throw away any mussels that failed to open. Ladle the soup into warmed bowls. Put on the table with bowls of the salsa and of the limes to squeeze on for their essential sour flavor.

CALDO DE SHUTI

Seasoned Tomato River Snail or Clam Broth

In New York City, this flavorful soup might be considered a spicy version of Manhattan clam chowder. But it actually comes from Chiapas and uses *shuti*, the small river snails that thrive in the creeks that flow into the three rivers running through the town of Chiapa de Corzo and then to the southern part of the state. The recipe, which Ricardo has replicated, is a specialty of the Zoque people who live near the highland source of the rivers.

Here, I have replaced the snails with small clams, and although not quite the same, they are reminiscent of what I have enjoyed in Chiapa de Corzo. If you do get to this riverside town, try to find the *caldo* made with the snails. It is well worth the search.

The *chile chamborote*, which grows in the warm regions of Chiapas, is a small red chile that can be either very hot or quite mild—it's a gambler's choice—but *chile serrano* can be substituted.

If the clams are freshly dug, I always drop them into a large bowl or pot with cold water to cover and 1 tablespoon cornmeal and let them stand for 1 to 2 hours. This helps to expel any sand. Then I rinse and drain them. Otherwise, just scrub them well under cold running water.

Bolillos (crunchy bread rolls) or French bread are perfect for sopping up the tasty broth.

Serves 4

1 pound ripe tomatoes (about 3 medium), roughly chopped, or 1 (14½-ounce) can diced tomatoes, drained

¼ cup roughly chopped white onion

2 chiles chamborotes or 1 chile serrano, roughly chopped

2 pounds hard-shell clams (about 60) such as East Coast littlenecks or cherrystones or any of the small Pacific Coast varieties, well scrubbed

½ teaspoon sea salt

3 tablespoons canola or safflower oil

1 sprig fresh epazote or cilantro

2 limes, preferably Key lime, quartered

Put the tomatoes, onion, and chiles in a blender and process until smooth. Set aside.

Place the clams in a large pot, add 4 cups water and the salt, and bring to a boil over high heat. Lower the heat to medium, cover, and cook until the clams open, 5 to 8 minutes. Remove from the heat. Using a slotted spoon, scoop into a large bowl, discarding any clams that are still closed. Reserve the broth.

While the clams are cooking, heat the oil in a *cazuela* or heavy skillet over medium-high heat until shimmering. Add the tomato mixture, lower the heat, and simmer, stirring frequently, until the sauce thickens and darkens, about 5 minutes. Pour in the reserved broth, add the epazote, and continue cooking for 10 minutes.

Just before serving, add the clams to the broth and reheat. Ladle immediately into warmed deep, shallow bowls and serve right away. Put the limes close by for squeezing in the juice to heighten the flavor of the broth. Have a separate bowl nearby for the discarded shells.

SOPA DE CILANTRO
Cilantro Soup

One of the most memorable meals that I ever shared in Mexico was at the lovely home of María Dolores Torres Yzábal. As we gathered around her colorfully decorated table, she served her version of this classic cilantro soup with its subtle chile personality. It was a perfect taste prelude to the more distinct flavors that followed in her French-influenced *chiles poblanos rellenos de queso y envueltos en pasta hojaldre* (page 194). For dessert, there was a dramatic presentation of *isla flotante* (page 262), another of María Dolores's specialties.

Serves 6

FOR THE SOUP
1½ teaspoons sea salt

4 small zucchini (about 1 pound), cut into chunks

5 cups chicken broth (page 25)

1 cup firmly packed, roughly chopped fresh cilantro, thick stems removed

2 tablespoons unsalted butter

1 tablespoon canola or safflower oil

2 white onions, minced

2 tablespoons cornstarch, dissolved in a small amount of cold water

2 chiles serranos, stemmed and partially slit lengthwise

2 bay leaves

FOR THE SOUP: Pour a small amount of water into a saucepan, add ½ teaspoon of the salt, and bring to a boil over medium-high heat. Add the zucchini, lower the heat, cover, and simmer until crisp tender, about 3 minutes. Do not overcook. Remove from the heat and scoop the zucchini into a blender. Add 2 cups of the broth and the cilantro and process briefly, leaving some texture.

Melt the butter with the oil in a *cazuela* or heavy saucepan over medium heat. Add the onions and sauté just until translucent. Stir in the cilantro mixture, the remaining 3 cups broth, the diluted cornstarch, whole chiles, bay leaves, and

FOR THE TOPPING

¼ cup Mexican crema (page 23), crème fraîche, or thick sour cream thinned with 1 tablespoon whole milk

¾ cup totopos (page 21), in ½-inch squares

½ pound queso panela or fresh mozzarella cheese, cubed

the remaining 1 teaspoon salt and simmer over low heat for 10 minutes.

Remove and discard the chiles and bay leaf and ladle into warmed bowls. Top each serving with a swirl of *crema* and a scattering of the tiny *totopos* and cheese.

SOPA DE HONGOS
Wild Mushroom Soup

During the summer rainy season in central Mexico, an abundance of wild mushrooms in an array of colors and shapes arrives in the local markets. Ricardo enjoyed this voluptuous mushroom soup accented with chiles on a cold, rainy Sunday in a rustic restaurant in the Ajusco Mountains, on the southern outskirts of Mexico City. The tightly packed darkness of this forested area is where many of the residents of the more chaotic Mexico City come for contact with nature and to escape the stress of city life. It is unlikely that you will find the same wild mushrooms where you live, but if you are a forager or frequent a farmers' market with a mushroom vendor, use what you can find, such as morels in spring or chanterelles in early fall. You can also make this with a combination of wild and cultivated mushrooms, such as oyster, cremini, porcini, or shitake. I like to add a dried shitake or chanterelle to the broth for a more intense flavor. The important thing is to have a variety of different mushrooms.

To clean the mushrooms, use a soft-bristled brush to whisk away any debris and a lightly dampened paper towel on stubborn spots of dirt. Do not wash the mushrooms.

This soup pairs nicely with Chiles Poblanos Rellenos de Picadillo Norteño (page 198).

Serves 6 to 8

FOR THE SOUP

4 large chiles guajillos, stems, membranes, and seeds removed

⅓ cup minced white onion

1 tablespoon minced garlic

2 teaspoons sea salt

FOR THE SOUP: Soak the chiles in a bowl in very hot water to cover until soft, about 30 minutes. Remove the chiles, reserving the water, and tear into smaller pieces. Put the chiles, onion, garlic, and salt in a blender and process until a smooth

¼ cup freshly rendered pork lard (page 24) or canola or safflower oil

6 cups chicken broth (page 25) or water

1 dried shitake or chanterelle mushroom (optional)

Olive oil for frying

2 pounds mixed wild and cultivated mushrooms, at least four types, brushed clean, hard stems removed, and sliced

25 fresh epazote leaves, roughly chopped (optional but recommended)

▎ FOR THE GARNISH

1 cup totopos (page 21), in ¼-by-1-inch strips

6 tablespoons Mexican crema (page 23), crème fraîche, or thick sour cream thinned with 1 tablespoon whole milk

2 tablespoons chopped fresh cilantro, thick stem ends removed

sauce forms, adding some of the reserved soaking water if needed to release the blades.

Heat the lard in a large *cazuela* or Dutch oven over medium heat until it is shimmering. Pour the chile mixture in all at once and cook, stirring constantly with a wooden spoon, until the color deepens, about 10 minutes. Lower the heat and gradually stir in the broth and then the dried mushroom (if using). Bring back to a simmer and cook, uncovered, for 20 minutes to blend the flavors. Remove the mushroom (if using), slice it, discarding the tough stem if necessary, and return the slices to the broth.

Meanwhile, heat 2 teaspoons olive oil in a large skillet over high heat. Add one variety of the mushrooms in a single layer and fry, turning often, until golden. Transfer the mushrooms to the soup and repeat with the remaining mushrooms, frying only one type each time, keeping the temperature high, and adding more oil to the pan with each batch. This method ensures that the mushrooms retain their texture and flavor and do not exude so much liquid that they become bland and soggy.

Add the epazote to the soup, then taste and add more salt if needed.

Ladle the soup into warmed bowls, making sure each serving has plenty of mushrooms. Garnish with the *totopos*, a swirl of *crema*, and a scattering of cilantro.

SOPA HUASTECA DE ESPINACA Y CALABACITA

Spinach and Zucchini Soup

While researching the foods of the Huastecs living in northeast Veracruz and the adjacent state of San Luis Potosí, Ricardo noticed that the cooks, not wanting to waste anything, use any tiny bits of leftover pork or chicken to flavor their simple vegetable soups.

To enliven this soup, add a spoonful of Salsa de Cuaresmeños (page 32) or Salsa Verde Cocida con Aguacate (page 31). A bowl of this soup pairs quite happily with Gorditas de Frijoles Negros (page 68).

Serves 6 to 8

1 tablespoon canola or safflower oil

¼ cup finely chopped white onion

1 cup fresh or thawed frozen corn kernels

2 large cloves garlic, minced

4 cups chicken broth (page 25) or vegetable broth

1 cup shredded cooked chicken (page 25) or pork (optional)

3 small zucchini (about ¾ pound), cut into ¼-inch cubes

¼ cup chopped fresh epazote leaves (cilantro or Italian parsley can be reluctantly substituted)

1 teaspoon sea salt

¼ pound spinach leaves (1 cup firmly packed), roughly chopped with some small leaves left whole

Heat the oil in a large *cazuela* or Dutch oven over medium-high heat. Add the onion and fry for a few seconds. Add the corn and garlic and cook, stirring frequently so nothing burns, for about 5 minutes. Add the broth, shredded meat (if using), zucchini, epazote, and salt, lower the heat, and simmer for 5 minutes longer to heat through and blend the flavors. Taste and add more salt if needed.

Add the spinach, allow it to wilt, and then immediately ladle the soup into warmed deep bowls and serve.

SOPA DE FLOR DE CALABAZA Y HONGOS SILVESTRES
Squash Blossom and Wild Mushroom Soup

Some years ago, one of Mexico's truly great cooks, María Dolores Torres Yzábal, was consulting for a large Monterrey company in Nuevo León when the owner's wife asked her to prepare a meal for a visiting celebrity, Luciano Pavarotti. She served this delightfully savory soup of golden squash blossoms and mushrooms imbued with a flavor reminiscent of the forest where they had recently been gathered. Pavarotti liked it so much that when he was next in Mexico City, María Dolores was asked to make another batch for him, which his chauffeur picked up. He even had the recipe translated into Italian.

The colorful appearance and the complex, earthy flavor of this soup make the effort and expense worthwhile for a special occasion. In some parts of the country, the knobby morels can be picked by lucky foragers during several weeks in April and May, or purchased at some specialty produce markets, but the dried ones are available year-round in most grocery stores. As a bonus, their soaking liquid can be added to the soup.

The large, delicate deep gold squash blossoms are also seasonal, appearing on plants of thick-skinned squashes during the summer months. They are often available in farmers' markets or occasionally at Italian grocery stores. If you grow them in your garden, pick only the male flowers, the ones with long, enlarged stamens, but leave some on the plant for pollinating other flowers. It is important to use the blossoms as soon as possible, preferably the same day they are cut as they wilt quickly. If you have to keep them overnight, place them in a pitcher of water, like a bouquet. To prepare the squash blossoms, cut off the stems and remove the green sepals from the calyx, the fleshy base, then rinse lightly and shake off any remaining water. Some cooks also remove both the calyx and the stamen, but they are also removing texture and flavor.

The potato starch can be found in most supermarkets, usually in the section in which Jewish foods are stocked.

This will be a never-to-be-forgotten meal when served at summer's end with the celebratory Chiles en Nogada (page 200) and perhaps Flan de Leche (page 259) for dessert.

1 pound fresh morel mushrooms, stems removed, or 2 ounces dried morels

½ pound oyster mushrooms lightly brushed clean and stems removed

2 pounds large male squash blossoms (about 100 flowers), stems and sepals around the base removed

4 tablespoons unsalted butter

½ teaspoon olive oil

2 cups finely chopped white onions or shallots

2 cups chicken broth (page 25)

1 cup whole milk

2 tablespoons potato starch, dissolved in ¼ cup chicken broth

1 teaspoon sea salt

¼ teaspoon freshly ground black pepper

½ cup Mexican crema (page 23), crème fraîche, or thick sour cream thinned with 1 tablespoon whole milk

1 small sprig fresh epazote or flat-leaf parsley, chopped

If using dried morels, put in a bowl and pour in very hot water to cover. Soak until saturated and plump, about 30 minutes. Line a fine-mesh sieve with cheesecloth (or spread open a coffee filter), place the sieve over a bowl, and pour the mushrooms into the sieve. If using freshly picked mushrooms, first flick away any dirt or other debris with a soft-bristled brush. Slice the morels in half lengthwise and then slice them into ¼-inch-wide strips. Chop the oyster mushrooms and set them aside with the morels.

Cut the squash blossoms crosswise into ¼-inch-wide strips, including the small bulbous calyx. Set aside.

Melt the butter with the oil in a soup kettle or pot over medium-high heat. Add the onions and cook, stirring frequently, until soft and barely beginning to brown, about 4 minutes. Add half of the squash blossoms and all of the mushrooms and cook, stirring occasionally, for 2 to 3 minutes. Pour in the broth, cover partially, and bring to a simmer. Lower the heat to medium-low and cook for 5 minutes.

Add the milk, the diluted potato starch, and the salt and pepper and simmer, stirring frequently, until lightly thickened, about 10 minutes.

Add the *crema* and the remaining squash blossoms and simmer just until the *crema* is warm and the blossoms are relaxed. Taste and add additional salt or pepper if needed.

Ladle into warmed bowls and sprinkle with the epazote. Serve right away.

SOPA DE HABAS CON NOPALES
Fava Bean Soup with Crunchy Cactus

Dried flat fava beans, introduced to Mexico by the early Spanish, are the principal ingredient in this long-simmering rustic soup. Ricardo told me that this is a favorite of cooks in the homes and *fondas* of central Mexico, especially when the contrasting sorrel-sour taste and crunchy texture of nopales are added. In predominately Catholic Mexico, this soup is especially popular during Lent, when meat is abstained from, and it is often paired with freshly made *quesadillas con queso* (page 58) on a Lenten menu. I also like to serve this comforting dish on a cold, dreary day, adding some minced ham along with the nopales. You will need to start the soup at least a day in advance. Crusty bread, a green salad, and Pastel de Elote (page 252) can complete the meal.

Serves 4 . . . .

▪ FOR THE SOUP

10 ounces (about 1⅓ cups) dried yellow fava beans

¼ cup extra virgin olive oil

2 cups 1-by-¼-inch nopal strips (from 3 small or 2 medium cleaned paddles, page 23)

⅓ cup minced white onion

2 tablespoons minced garlic

1⅔ cups ¼-inch-cubed ripe tomatoes (about 2 medium), or 1 (14½-ounce) can diced tomatoes, drained

½ cup chopped fresh cilantro, thick stem ends removed

2 teaspoons sea salt

▪ FOR THE GARNISH

6 tablespoons extra virgin olive oil

6 tablespoons Mexican crema (page 23), crème fraîche, or thick sour cream thinned with 1 tablespoon whole milk

1 tablespoon chopped fresh cilantro, thick stem ends removed

FOR THE SOUP: Rinse and sort the beans, discarding any broken pieces. Soak overnight in a large bowl with water to cover by 2 inches (about 2 quarts).

Put the beans and the soaking water in an olla (page 15) or large pot and bring to a boil over medium-high heat. Lower the heat, cover, and simmer until the beans are tender and begin to split apart, about 2 hours. Test frequently for doneness and top with more water if needed to keep the beans submerged.

While the beans are cooking, heat the oil in a large skillet over medium heat until barely shimmering. Add the nopales, onion, and garlic, cover, and cook, stirring occasionally, until softened, about 6 minutes. Add the tomatoes, cilantro, and salt and cook, uncovered, until the slimy liquid from the nopales has been absorbed, about 6 minutes longer. Remove from the heat and set aside.

When the favas are soft and have split apart, stir in the nopal mixture and simmer over low heat for 15 minutes. Remove from the heat and taste for salt. Fava beans often require more salt to bring out their flavor.

Ladle into warmed large bowls and garnish each serving with a fine stream of oil, a drizzle of *crema,* and a scattering of cilantro.

SOPA DE PLÁTANO MACHO
Plantain Soup

When María Dolores Torres Yzábal was served this simple soup by her friend Celia Chávez de Garcia Terrés, she didn't recognize the transformed subtle flavor of the plantain (page 103). This soup provides a soothing balance for a *picante* main course, such as Albóndigas de Pavo en Salsa de Chipotle (page 132).

Serves 4 to 6

2 tablespoons unsalted butter, or more if needed

1½ tablespoons finely chopped leek, white part only

1 large barely ripe plantain (about ½ pound), peeled and sliced into ¼-inch-thick rounds

4 cups chicken broth (page 25)

½ teaspoon sea salt

½ cup Mexican crema (page 23), crème fraîche, or thick sour cream thinned with 1 tablespoon whole milk

Freshly ground black pepper

Melt 2 tablespoons butter in a *cazuela,* Dutch oven, or large saucepan over medium-low heat. Add the leek and sauté until tender but not brown, 4 to 5 minutes. Using a slotted spoon, scoop out the leek, allowing the excess butter to drip back into the pan, and put it in a blender.

Sauté the plantain slices in the same pan over medium-low heat, turning occasionally and adding more butter if needed to prevent scorching, until softened but not browned, 5 to 10 minutes. Remove from the heat, add to the blender along with 2 cups of broth, and process until smooth.

Return the mixture to the pan, stir in the remaining 2 cups broth, and add the salt. Bring to a bare simmer, then lower the heat and cook very gently for 5 minutes to concentrate the subtle flavors.

Ladle into warmed bowls, top each serving with a swirl of *crema* and a hefty sprinkle of pepper, and serve.

SOPA DE LIMA
Lime-Flavored Chicken Soup

According to Ricardo, this traditional chicken soup, while considered typical of Yucatán, may owe its present popularity to Mayan chef Katún, who first prepared it in a Mérida restaurant in 1946. What makes it so magical is the use of the fragrant juice and rind of an unusual citrus fruit known in Yucatán as *lima agria,* or "bitter lime," which has a nipplelike protuberance on its blossom end when ripe. I have occasionally found it in Mexican markets in the Southwest and I have heard that it is available in Chicago. When I cannot find it, I substitute Key limes, which are more sour than bittersweet but are not as astringent as the more common Persian lime.

Every market in Yucatán has a section devoted to displays of large mounds of various *recados,* or spice mixtures, such as the *recado de toda clase* used for this soup. It is best to make these essential Yucatecan seasonings in advance.

Many of the ingredients used by Yucatecan cooks are not available outside the area, but substitutes that approximate the regional taste can be used. For example, the quite mild *chile dulce* can be replaced by the similarly shaped but larger and more aggressively flavored bell pepper. As mentioned earlier, home gardeners can plant the Red Knight bell pepper, which is a particularly good match for the sweet, fruity flavor of the *chile dulce.* In Mexico, there are many plants called oregano that are used for seasoning, and the oregano from Yucatán with its large leaves is one of the most distinctive. But the Mexican oregano widely available in the United States can be substituted.

This is a flavorful but mild soup, so bowls of either Salsa Xnipec (page 36) or Salsa de Chile Habanero (page 39; sometimes called *salsa tamulada* in Yucatán because it is made in a *tamul,* a Yucatecan *molcajete*), or both, are always nearby so they can be added. This *habanero* salsa is blistering hot, so just a drop or two is needed.

Queso Relleno (page 205), followed by a plate of Dulce de Papaya (page 246) and cheese, would complete this festive Yucatecan meal.

▌ FOR THE RECADO DE TODA CLASE

1 tablespoon black peppercorns, toasted
(page 19)

3 whole cloves, toasted (page 19)

5 whole allspice, toasted (page 19)

¾-inch stick Mexican true cinnamon bark
(page 88), toasted (page 19)

1 teaspoon cumin seeds, toasted (page 19)

3 tablespoons dried oregano, preferably
Yucatecan or Mexican, toasted (page 19)

8 small cloves garlic, roasted (page 18), then
peeled and minced

1 tablespoon freshly squeezed bitter orange
juice (page 26) or diluted unseasoned rice
vinegar (page 50)

▌ FOR THE SOUP

2 quarts chicken broth (page 26)

1 teaspoon recado de toda clase

Sea salt

2 tablespoons canola or safflower oil

3 tablespoons finely chopped white onion

3 tablespoons finely chopped green chile dulce
or green bell pepper

1 cup peeled, seeded, and finely chopped ripe
tomatoes or drained diced canned tomatoes

3 cups totopos (page 21)

2 bitter limes or 3 Key limes, thinly sliced
(12 slices)

About 1 cup shredded cooked chicken
(page 25)

6 to 12 tablespoons freshly squeezed bitter
lime or Key lime juice

FOR THE RECADO: Put the peppercorns, cloves, allspice, cinnamon, cumin, and oregano in a spice grinder or coffee grinder and grind to a powder. Put the ground spices in a small bowl, add the minced garlic and orange juice, and smash with a fork to a thick paste. Set aside 1 teaspoon for the soup. Save any remaining *recado* for rubbing on chicken, pork ribs, or even steaks before cooking. It will keep in a covered container in the refrigerator for several weeks.

FOR THE SOUP: Put the broth in a large pot over medium-high heat and bring to a simmer. Add 1 teaspoon of the *recado* and stir until dissolved. Taste and add salt if needed and continue simmering for another 5 minutes.

Heat the oil in a heavy skillet over medium heat. Add the onion and stir in the chile dulce and tomatoes and continue cooking until the vegetables are soft, about 5 minutes. Remove from the heat and set aside.

When ready to eat, put a small handful of *totopos* in the bottom of each warmed shallow bowl and top with a heaping tablespoon of the tomato mixture, 2 lime slices, and a large pinch of the shredded chicken. Ladle in the hot broth, stir 1 tablespoon lime juice into each bowl, and serve immediately.

Canela

Mexican Cinnamon

There are two major types of cinnamon: Cassia (*Cinnamomum aromaticum*), which is labeled and sold as cinnamon in the United States, is the bark of a tree grown in southern China, Indonesia, and Myanmar. These are those tough sticks that are best used to flavor hot punch. When ground, which is the way cassia is usually found on grocery-store shelves, it is harsher in flavor and less aromatic than so-called true cinnamon (*C. verum*, formerly *zeylanicum*).

True cinnamon, soft and flaky, one- to two-foot-long coils of bark, is an essential ingredient in Mexican cooking. Called *canela*, it is used in traditional sweets and in such savory dishes as stews and moles, where it contributes a sweet balance to the heat and spice of chiles. Native to Sri Lanka and the southwest coast of India, it is now being cultivated in the Mexican states of Puebla, Veracruz, and Tabasco, as well as in the West Indies and on islands off the east coast of Africa.

Both aromatic barks are considered cinnamon, although cassia is never used in Mexico and seldom in England or Europe, where *C. verum* has long been the cinnamon of choice. If you do have to use cassia in Mexican cooking, always use a smaller amount than the recipe calls for to compensate for its more penetrating flavor.

Look for true cinnamon in Mexican markets, spice shops, and well-stocked supermarkets that carry a broad selection of spices, or on the Internet (see Sources). Or better yet, bring back a bundle from your next trip to Mexico.

CREMA DE GARBANZO

Cream of Garbanzo Soup

The garbanzo (ceci bean or chickpea), which originated in the Middle East, was a favorite ingredient of the Spaniards and is now used in savory stews and soups throughout Mexico. In this easily made soup, the flavor is often heightened by the addition of *chiles chipotle en adobo*. During the Lenten season, when no meat is to be eaten, this garbanzo bean soup is often made with vegetable broth rather than chicken broth. For more texture, I occasionally add thick slices of Chorizo (page 145). This soup paired with a simple quesadilla (page 58) makes a very satisfying supper.

Serves 6 to 8

2 (15-ounce) cans garbanzo beans, drained and rinsed (about 3 cups)

¼ white onion, roasted (page 18) and roughly chopped

2 cloves garlic, roasted (page 18), then peeled

2 large plum tomatoes, roasted and peeled (page 18)

4 cups whole milk

1½ teaspoons sea salt

½ teaspoon ground allspice

7 tablespoons unsalted butter

6 cups chicken broth (page 25), water, or a mixture

2 teaspoons sauce from chiles chipotles en adobo (if not enough sauce, blend 1 chile with a little water)

1 cup Mexican crema (page 23), crème fraîche, or thick sour cream thinned with 1 tablespoon whole milk

½ cup minced fresh flat-leaf parsley

Put half each of the garbanzo beans, onion, garlic, tomatoes, milk, salt, and allspice in a blender and process until a very smooth mixture forms. Set aside in a bowl. Repeat with the remaining half of these ingredients and add to the first batch.

Melt the butter in a large saucepan over medium heat. Pour in the pureed garbanzo mixture and bring to a simmer. Stir in the broth and chile sauce, then taste and add more salt if needed to bring out the flavor of the beans. Reduce the heat to medium-low, cover, and simmer until piping hot and the flavors are well blended. The earthy flavor intensifies even more if cooled and refrigerated, then reheated later.

Ladle the creamy soup into warmed bowls or mugs. Top each serving with a large swirl of *crema* and a sprinkle of parsley and serve right away.

CALDILLO DE MACHACA
Shredded Dried Beef Soup

The northern stretches of Mexico are cattle-ranching country and beef is, by far, the most popular meat. The first Spanish ranchers, drawing on the methods their families used back home for preserving meat, cut most of the beef they butchered into thin strips and dried it. *Machaca,* the Spanish word for "pounded," refers to meat that is salted, usually sun-dried, and then tenderized by pulverizing before cooking. Even today, *machaca* and the similar *carne seca* provide the basis for many regional beef dishes.

It is hard to raise cattle in the hottest arid swaths of Coahuila and Nuevo León, in the northeast, but the determined little goat seems able to thrive on the area's meager vegetation, and a variation of *machaca* is made with its meat. In the past, venison was also used.

According to some sources, Mexican revolutionary general Pancho Villa was a great aficionado of this soup, which makes sense since he was born, and later died, in Chihuahua, one of the northern states.

A tart Ensalada Clásica de Nopales (page 235) is a perfect contrast to the hearty flavors of this soup. Serve with lots of hot flour tortillas, another regional mainstay.

Serves 4 to 6 generously . . . .

FOR THE SOUP

½ pound beef jerky

¼ cup freshly rendered pork lard (page 24) or canola or safflower oil

1 cup finely chopped white onion

1 tablespoon minced garlic

6 ripe tomatoes (about 2 pounds), cut into small cubes, or 2 (16-ounce) cans diced tomatoes, drained

4 cups beef broth (page 26)

¾ pound small red or Yukon Gold potatoes (about 3 medium), peeled and cubed

Sea salt

FOR THE SOUP: Preheat the broiler. If the jerky is very salty, rinse it under cold running water and then pat dry. Arrange the jerky in a single layer on a baking sheet and place under the broiler until the fat rises to the surface, which will take several minutes. Remove from the broiler, let cool, and tear into shreds about ½ inch long. Set aside. (This can be done a few hours in advance.)

Heat the lard in a large *cazuela* or heavy skillet over medium-high heat. Add the onion and fry, stirring frequently, until lightly golden, about 10 minutes. Add the garlic and continue to stir for another

½ cup chopped fresh cilantro, thick stem
ends removed

Freshly ground black pepper

30 seconds. Do not allow the garlic to
brown. Stir in the tomatoes and cook until
the flavors mingle, about 5 minutes.

Gradually stir in the broth and 4 cups
water and bring to a boil. Add the potatoes
and jerky, reduce the heat to low, and cook just until the potatoes are tender and the broth
has reduced slightly, 10 to 15 minutes.

Taste and season with salt, then ladle into warmed bowls. Garnish with the cilantro and a
liberal grind of black pepper and serve right away.

YUCA EN CHILPACHOLE
Spicy Yuca Soup

In Veracruz, every meal should be joyous, and according to Ricardo, many Mexicans
of African descent enliven one of their staples, the rather innocuous-tasting yuca
(page 232), by substituting the tuberous root for the shrimp or soft-shell crabs in the
traditional spicy seafood soup known as *chilpachole*. If you like, you can add a handful of
shrimp to create a seafood flavor. Serve with a side of Codzitos (page 66) and a cooling
glass of Agua Fresca de Sandia (page 272).

Serves 6 to 8 as a main dish

FOR THE SOUP

2 pounds yuca

1 teaspoon sea salt

6 medium, very ripe tomatoes (about
2 pounds), roughly chopped, or 2 (16-ounce)
cans diced tomatoes, drained

¼ white onion, roughly chopped

4 cloves garlic

1 to 2 chiles chipotles en adobo, to taste

18 fresh epazote leaves, tough stems removed
(cilantro can be reluctantly substituted)

2 tablespoons canola or safflower oil

FOR THE SOUP: Put 3 quarts water in
a large pot and bring to a boil over high
heat. While the water is heating, using
a sharp, heavy knife, cut the yuca into
3-inch lengths. Slit the tough outer skin
lengthwise and then, using a small knife,
pry off the skin and the pinkish layer
under it. Remove any hard central fiber
and cut into 1½-inch cubes.

Add the yuca and salt to the boiling water.
After the water returns to a boil, reduce
the heat to a gentle simmer and cook until

the yuca starts to soften, about 20 minutes. Test with a toothpick. Yuca, just like the young woman in the English nursery rhyme "Mary, Mary Quite Contrary," may be perverse, with some pieces becoming mushy quite quickly, which should be promptly removed and set aside, while others remain stubbornly hard. Turn off the heat and let the hard pieces stand in the water to finish cooking until soft. Remove the pieces with a slotted spoon, saving the cooking water.

Put the tomatoes, onion, garlic, chiles, and epazote in a blender and process until a smooth sauce forms, adding some of the reserved cooking liquid if needed to release the blades.

Heat the oil in a large *cazuela* or Dutch oven over medium-high heat until shimmering. Quickly pour in the tomato sauce and cook, stirring often, for about 15 minutes. Stir in the cooked yuca, adding more of the reserved cooking liquid if needed to cover. Lower the heat and simmer for another few minutes.

Ladle into warmed bowls and accompany with the lime wedges and chiles. Let everyone squeeze in lime juice to accentuate the flavors and add a scattering of chiles for an even more *picante* taste.

VARIATION: CHILPACHOLE DE YUCA CON CAMARONES (SPICY YUCA SOUP WITH SHRIMP)

To add shrimp to the soup, bring 6 cups water in a saucepan to a rolling boil. Add 1 pound extra-large shrimp in the shell (14 to 16 count per pound) and 1 tablespoon sea salt and cook until the shells begin to blush, no more than 3 minutes. Lift the shrimp out with a slotted spoon and set aside. Reserve the cooking water. Make the soup as directed, substituting the 6 cups shrimp broth for half of the water used for cooking the yuca. In Veracruz, the shrimp would be left in the shell but you can peel them if you like. Add them to the soup just before serving.

CHILEATOLE CON POLLO Y CALABACITAS TIERNAS

Fresh Corn and Chicken Chileatole

This soupy, nourishing dish of prehistoric origin is often eaten with tamales for *cena* (a light supper), the chicken obviously a later addition. The very first time I tried *chileatole* was in a kitchen crowded with the friends of the hostess, Mónica Maestretta, in Cholula, a city adjacent to Puebla, the capital of the state of the same name. After my first sip, I was a convert, ignoring everyone around me as I consumed every drop.

While this version from Yolanda Ramos, in the nearby state of Tlaxcala, uses fresh green chiles, I've often eaten it seasoned with dried *chiles anchos* and *chiles guajillos,* and it is equally satisfying. Unlike most masa-based *atoles,* Yolanda's *chileatole* uses fresh corn kernels and becomes more of a soup than a hot beverage. The corn used in Mexico is similar to field corn and hardly sweet at all, so do not buy supersweet corn for this soup.

Guías, the young, tender stems, tendrils, and small, soft leaves of the squash vine, are almost always an ingredient in *chileatole.* If it is summertime and you grow your own squash or buy from a friendly vendor at a farmers' market, you are in luck, as the *guías* will be in abundance. If not, substitute the feathery leaves and stems from a fennel bulb—a similar texture, though a different flavor—which are available from autumn through spring.

Tamales are the traditional accompaniment, and Tamales de Carne de Cerdo y Calabacitas (page 118) would be welcome.

Serves 6 to 8

FOR THE BROTH

1 pound chicken drumsticks (about 4)

1 pound chicken thighs (about 3 or 4)

½ white onion

2 large cloves garlic

½ teaspoon sea salt

FOR THE BROTH: In a large pot, combine 2 quarts water and the chicken and bring to a boil over medium-high heat, skimming off any grayish foam that rises to the surface. Add the onion and garlic, lower the heat to a simmer, cover partially, and cook until the juices run clear when a piece of chicken is pierced with a fork, about 30 minutes.

6 ears corn, husks and silk removed

8 guías (tender stems, tendrils, and small leaves of squash vine), each about 6 inches long, or 2 tablespoons finely chopped fennel leaves

1 clove garlic

½ white onion, roughly chopped

5 small chiles serranos, roughly chopped (about ⅓ cup)

1 tablespoon freshly rendered pork lard (page 24) or canola or safflower oil

5 small or 1 very large zucchini (about 1¼ pounds), cut into ¼-inch cubes

Leaves from 2 sprigs fresh epazote, chopped, or 2 tablespoons chopped fresh cilantro, thick stem ends removed

Sea salt

Take the pot off of the heat and let the chicken rest in the broth for a few minutes. Remove the chicken pieces from the broth and set aside until cool enough to handle, then remove the skin and bones, cut the meat into ½-inch pieces, and set aside. Strain the broth through a fine-mesh sieve into another container, discarding the onion and garlic. Season with the salt and set aside.

FOR THE ATOLE: Slice the kernels from the corncobs and set aside.

Strip off any thick fibers from the squash stems, cut into small pieces, and put in a blender with some of the tendrils and leaves (or add the fennel to the blender). Add half of the corn kernels and the garlic, onion, and chiles and pulverize until smooth.

Heat the lard in a *cazuela* or Dutch oven over medium-low heat until rippling hot. Add the corn mixture and cook, stirring frequently, until thickened, about 3 minutes. Add the reserved broth and stir in the remaining corn kernels, the zucchini, and the epazote. Taste and add salt if needed. Simmer until the zucchini and corn are just tender, no more than 3 minutes. Do not overcook. Add the chicken and heat through.

Ladle the soup into warmed mugs or deep bowls and serve. Alternatively, to intensify the flavors, let the soup cool to room temperature, cover, and refrigerate for several hours or overnight, then reheat to serve.

PLATOS DE DESAYUNO Y CENA CASERA

Casual Meals for Breakfast and Supper

Mexican food does not fit into categories easily. Soups may be served for breakfast, eggs for a light supper dish, and enchiladas and tacos for either. Tamales are a sustaining and popular way to begin and end the day and they appear in variety of sizes and shapes. The most common are wrapped in dried corn husks or banana leaves, but fresh corn leaves and other larger aromatic leaves are also used. All are surprise packages just waiting to be opened.

Combined with *antojitos* and a smattering of recipes from other chapters in this book, these dishes can become part of a meal that resonates with the true flavors of Mexico. I especially like to include them in a buffet for family and friends.

HUEVOS AHOGADOS
Drowned Eggs

Whenever I am in Veracruz, I find the egg dishes extraordinarily special. I often indulge myself in the morning with dishes like these poached eggs, literally drowned in a feisty tomato sauce and served with hot corn tortillas (page 19). They become a light supper dish if served with a green salad and Frijoles Refritos (page 217) made with black beans.

Serves 2

2 small, ripe tomatoes, roasted and peeled (page 18), then chopped, or ¾ cup drained diced canned tomatoes

½ white onion, roughly chopped

1 clove garlic, roughly chopped

1 chile serrano, roughly chopped

1 cup chicken broth (page 25)

1 tablespoon canola or safflower oil

1 sprig fresh epazote or cilantro

½ teaspoon sea salt

4 eggs, at room temperature and as fresh as possible

Put the tomatoes, onion, garlic, chile, and ¼ cup of the broth in a blender and process until the mixture is pureed with some texture.

Heat the oil in an 8- to 9-inch skillet or *cazuela* over medium-high heat until shimmering. Add the tomato mixture and cook, stirring with a wooden spoon, until it thickens and reduces somewhat, about 6 minutes. Stir in the remaining ¾ cup broth, the epazote, and the salt and continue to cook for another couple of minutes. Lower the heat until the sauce is at a gentle simmer.

One at a time, crack the eggs into a shallow bowl and gently slide each egg into the sauce, spacing them evenly. Cook, basting occasionally with the hot sauce, until the whites are set but the yolks are still soft, 4 to 6 minutes. Be careful that the eggs do not stick to the bottom of the skillet.

With a slotted spatula, carefully remove the eggs and set aside on a warmed plate. Pour the sauce into individual bowls or *cazuelitas,* top with the eggs, and serve.

VARIATION: HUEVOS EN RABO DE MESTIZA
(EGGS POACHED IN A TOMATO SAUCE WITH STRIPS OF CHILES)

There is a similar egg dish that goes by the name of *huevos en rabo de mestiza,* or more descriptively, "the tattered rags of a child of a Spaniard and an indigenous person." The main difference is the addition of strips from a roasted *chile poblano* (page 17) and a roughly equal amount of thinly sliced white onion, which are fried together and then added to the simmering chile-tomato sauce. The rest of the process is the same. Crumbled *queso fresco* is often sprinkled on top before serving.

HUEVOS TIRADOS
Black Bean Omelet

This dish of "throwaway" eggs is filled with memories for me. The first time a plate of these eggs drenched with black beans was set across from me was in a small ramshackle place somewhere in the highlands between Mexico City and Veracruz. I was with Diana Kennedy and she said that this was a dish that I just had to try. I did and the fragrant flavor forever changed my idea of what a morning meal could be. Although its appearance may not be appealing, believe me, once you take that first bite, it is addictive.

The next occasion was in Veracruz with Patricia Quintana, another acclaimed Mexican food authority. She introduced me to Luis Lara Pulido, owner of Restaurante Catedral and a member of the same family that owns the well-known Gran Café de la Parroquia, famed for its uniquely served *café lechero:* one waiter pours you a glass of strong coffee, and when you tap on it with a spoon, another waiter appears and, from on high, pours in steaming hot milk. When Luis left the original spot across from the cathedral and opened his own place in a different part of the city, he identified it by bringing the location name and a similar menu with him.

Through the years I came to know Luis, his wife, and some of their grown children, and because this place is where regulars became part of the family, I was saddened by his death. One of my favorite memories is of the postman delivering the mail daily to one of the patrons who was always seated at the same table by the side door.

This is my version of the *huevos tirados* that I always order at Restaurante Catedral. It is usually served by the same waiter, a man with the chiseled features of an Olmec stone head, but with the addition of a generous smile. Then one morning when Ricardo and I were together, he had me try his mother's version, which is very brothy and served in a bowl. I am content with either of them.

Huevos tirados are traditionally served with strips of *jalapeños en escabeche,* Salsa de Verde Cruda (page 31) or Salsa de Pico de Gallo (page 34), and hot corn tortillas (page 19) for scooping up the eggs.

2 tablespoons freshly rendered pork lard (page 24) or canola or safflower oil

4 tablespoons finely chopped white onion

4 eggs, at room temperature

½ cup drained Frijoles de la Olla (page 214), made with black beans, or drained canned black beans

½ teaspoon sea salt

Heat 1 tablespoon of the lard in a heavy 8-inch skillet or omelet pan over medium heat. Add 2 tablespoons of the onion and cook, stirring frequently, until soft, about 5 minutes. Remove from the heat.

Crack 2 of the eggs into a bowl and beat lightly with ½ teaspoon water. Lightly mash the beans, then gently fold half of the beans into the eggs and mix in

¼ teaspoon of the salt. Return the skillet to medium heat, pour the egg mixture over the onion, and stir until well mixed. Lower the heat and gently shake the pan back and forth until the eggs begin to set but are still creamy. Then, with a spatula, lift up the edge on one side of the omelet and tilt the pan so the uncooked egg runs underneath the omelet. Using the spatula, roll one side of the omelet halfway over, then tilt the pan toward the now-empty space and fold the other third on top, shaping the omelet into an oval. Quickly turn the pan upside down, lowering the omelet onto a warmed plate.

Wipe out the pan, heat the remaining 1 tablespoon lard, and repeat with the remaining ingredients to make a second omelet. Serve right away.

VARIATION: HUEVOS TIRADOS EN CALDO (EGGS AND BLACK BEANS IN HOT BROTH)

Save 1 cup of the broth from the home-cooked beans. If using canned beans, add water or chicken broth (page 25) to the can liquid as needed to equal 1 cup. Make the omelets as directed. Meanwhile, bring the bean broth to a boil. When the omelets are cooked, place each one in a warmed wide, shallow bowl and pour the hot broth over and around them.

HUEVOS AL ALBAÑIL

Bricklayer's Eggs

Masons and bricklayers, who are known as *albañiles*, are held in high esteem throughout Mexico, and special ceremonies featuring this rustic omeletlike dish with a tangy green sauce are held in their honor. This is my version of the *huevos al abañil* that I often enjoy in Oaxaca, although elsewhere the eggs may be scrambled. Serve the eggs with Frijoles Refritos (page 217) and hot corn tortillas (page 19).

1 pound tomatillos (about 9 or 10), husked and well rinsed

3 chiles serranos, stemmed

1 teaspoon plus ¼ teaspoon sea salt

½ white onion, roughly chopped (about ⅔ cup)

1 clove garlic, roughly chopped

2 sprigs fresh epazote, or 4 sprigs fresh cilantro

1 tablespoon canola or safflower oil

1½ cups chicken broth (page 25)

4 eggs, at room temperature

4 teaspoon sea salt

2 tablespoons unsalted butter

½ cup roughly chopped fresh cilantro, thick stem ends removed

1 ripe Hass avocado, halved, pitted, peeled, and cut into small chunks (optional)

1 small, ripe tomato, diced (optional)

Put the tomatillos and chiles in a saucepan, add water to cover and the 1 teaspoon salt, and bring to a simmer over medium-high heat. Cook until tender, about 15 minutes. Drain and put in a blender or food processor. Add the onion, garlic, and epazote and process until quite smooth but still with some texture.

Heat the oil in a heavy skillet over medium-high heat until shimmering. Pour in the sauce and stir with a wooden spoon until it darkens in color and thickens, about 10 minutes. Stir in the broth and when it begins to bubble again, lower the heat and continue to cook until it becomes even thicker, about 10 minutes. Taste and add more salt if needed, then keep hot until serving. The sauce can be made up to 1 day in advance, cooled, covered, and re-frigerated. Reheat before starting the eggs.

Break 2 of the eggs into a bowl and beat lightly with a fork. Add ½ teaspoon water and a pinch of salt and mix well.

Gently warm an 8-inch omelet pan or skillet with sloping sides over very low heat and add half of the butter. As the butter melts, tilt the pan so the bottom and sides are coated. Remove from the heat and quickly pour in the egg mixture, then return the pan to the heat. Shake the pan gently back and forth with one hand and quickly stir the eggs in a wide circular motion with the other hand. When the eggs are nearly cooked but still very moist, lift up the edge on one side of the omelet with a spatula and tilt the pan so the uncooked egg runs underneath. The omelet should still be creamy on top. Using the spatula, fold over one-third of the omelet. Then tilt the pan, flipping the other third over as you flip the omelet onto a warmed plate. Make the second omelet the same way and spoon the hot sauce over both. Serve immediately sprinkled with the cilantro, avocado, and tomato (if using).

CHILAQUILES VERDES CON POLLO
Broken-Up Tortillas with Green-Sauced Chicken

Chilaquiles are not only a satisfying homey dish but also a good way to use up leftover corn tortillas or *totopos*. Occasionally, when I have an urgent craving for *chilaquiles*, I even use store-bought tortilla chips, scouting the shelves for the thickest ones I can find.

Chilaquiles are simple to prepare, making them one of Mexico's favorite dishes for breakfast, a special brunch, or a light supper. In this version, crunchy day-old tortillas are simmered in a pungent chile and tomatillo salsa until slightly chewy and then served with shredded chicken. You can just as easily make them with Salsa Cocida de Jitomate (page 31) and crumbled Chorizo (page 145), with maybe fried eggs on top for a more substantial meal.

Serves 4 to 6 . . . .

FOR THE CHICKEN
2 boneless, skinless chicken breasts (about ¾ pound)

¼ white onion

3 cloves garlic, halved

1 teaspoon sea salt

FOR THE SAUCE
2 pounds tomatillos (about 20), husked and well rinsed

3 chiles serranos, stemmed

2 cloves garlic, coarsely chopped

¼ white onion, roughly chopped, plus 1 small white onion, cut into rings (or use the inner rings of a large onion)

¼ cup roughly chopped fresh cilantro, thick stem ends removed

2 tablespoons canola or safflower oil

1 cup broth reserved from cooking chicken

½ teaspoon sea salt

FOR THE CHICKEN: Put the chicken, onion, garlic, and salt in a saucepan, add water just to cover, and bring to a boil over medium-high heat, skimming off any foam that rises to the surface. Lower the heat to a gentle simmer, cover, and cook until the chicken is just cooked through when tested with a knife, 20 to 30 minutes. Remove the chicken from the pot and let cool until it can be handled, then shred the meat and set aside. Strain the broth through a fine-mesh sieve and set aside for making the sauce. This step can be done up to 2 days in advance. Cover and refrigerate the broth and meat until needed.

FOR THE SAUCE: Put the tomatillos and chiles in a saucepan, add water just to cover, and bring to a boil over high heat. Lower the heat to a gentle simmer and

14 store-bought corn tortillas made into totopos (page 21), or ½ pound lightly salted thick tortilla chips

1 cup Mexican crema (page 23), crème fraîche, or sour cream thinned with 1 tablespoon whole milk

¾ cup crumbled queso fresco

1 firm but ripe Hass avocado, halved, pitted, peeled, and cut into wedges (optional)

1 small, ripe tomato, chopped (optional)

cook until the tomatillos are quite soft but not falling apart, 5 to 10 minutes. Drain the tomatillos and chiles, reserving the water.

Put the tomatillos, chiles, and ⅓ cup of the reserved water in a blender and add the garlic, chopped onion, and cilantro. Process very briefly so some texture remains.

In a large *cazuela* or Dutch oven, heat the oil over medium-high heat until shimmering. Pour in the tomatillo mixture and stir with a wooden spoon until it darkens and thickens, about 5 minutes. Add the reserved broth and cook for another 5 minutes, then season with the salt (you might want to use less salt if you are using packaged tortilla chips). The sauce, without the cilantro, can be made up to several hours in advance; add the cilantro just before reheating.

Carefully stir in the *totopos* and let them soak up the sauce until they are quite moist, about 2 minutes. Just before serving, scatter the shredded chicken and onion slices on top, then drizzle on the *crema*, sprinkle with the cheese, and scoop onto warmed plates. The avocado wedges and chopped tomato make colorful and tasty additions.

MOGO MOGO VERDE
Savory Well-Fried Green Plantains

Ricardo calls this dish, which originated with the descendants of former African slaves in Veracruz and includes garlic and salt, savory or green *mogo mogo*, to distinguish it from sweeter versions. This type of *mogo mogo* is also called *plátanos machucos* (or just *machucos*), or "crushed plantains," and is similar to the *fufu* of West Africa. Although it is traditionally made with starchy, barely ripe plantains, riper ones can be used. In the Veracruz communities where *mogo mogo* is common, it is often served as a one-course meal with a salsa, but you may want to include some Frijoles de la Olla (page 214) made with black beans. It is also a surprisingly tasty side dish alongside grilled pork ribs.

3 barely ripe plantains (page 103), still mostly yellow with some black spots

1 head garlic, cloves separated and roasted (page 18), then peeled and mashed

½ cup freshly rendered pork lard (page 24) or canola or safflower oil

Sea salt

Put the plantains in a wide saucepan, add water to cover, bring to a boil over medium-high heat, and cook until soft, 30 to 45 minutes. The riper the plantains are, the less cooking time they will need. Remove the plantains from the water, let cool, then peel. Mash the plantains and garlic to a pulp with a bean or potato masher.

Heat the lard in a large skillet or *cazuela* over medium-high heat until shimmering. Add the plantain mixture and fry as if making Frijoles Refritos (page 217), then add salt to taste. Serve hot or warm.

▇ VARIATION: MOGO MOGO DULCE DE PLÁTANO MACHO (SWEET PLANTAIN MOGO MOGO)

According to Ricardo, it is the custom in many of the communities surrounding San Andres Tuxtla in southern Veracruz to serve sweet *mogo mogo* for breakfast with *bolillos* (French-style rolls) and black coffee.

To make this sweeter version, cut 3 black-ripe plantains in half crosswise, place in a wide saucepan with water to cover, and bring to a boil over high heat. Lower the heat and simmer until the plantains are quite soft, about 20 minutes. Remove the plantains from the water and let cool, then peel. Using a bean or potato masher, mash the plantains in a bowl until smooth, or puree in a blender or food processor. Add ¼ cup firmly packed light brown sugar and 1 teaspoon sea salt and mix well, then taste and add more sugar and salt if needed.

Heat ½ cup freshly rendered pork lard (page 24) or canola or safflower oil in a large skillet or *cazuela* over medium-high heat until shimmering. Add the puree and fry as if making Frijoles Refritos (page 217), continuing to mash the plantains until smooth. Serve immediately.

Plátanos

Plantains

In Mexico, the large, yellow blackish *plátano macho* cooking banana (*Musa paradisiaca* var.) is considered a starchy vegetable-like fruit and is a familiar sight in the southern part of the country. I was amazed to learn that plantains are not native but instead come from Southeast Asia. Arab traders brought them to central Africa in 1500, and they were soon planted throughout southern Africa, where they are still a staple. From Africa, they traveled to the New World as a food source on the slave-trading ships. Even more astounding to me was that bananas and plantains do not grow on trees. They are actually gigantic herbs topped with spreading leaves followed by the fruits. According to my botanist friends, the trunks are leaves tightly coiled around the stem of an underground rhizome. Once the plantains are picked, a new "trunk" with its bountiful crop of fruits emerges the next year.

Plantains are now available in many U.S. supermarkets and Hispanic grocery stores, but they are often shunned by cooks who do not realize that they must be cooked before they are eaten. The greenish and yellow unripe plantains, the type most often seen in stores, are usually thinly sliced and fried as chips or simmered in well-seasoned stews such as Olla Podrida (page 159). For dishes like Plátanos Rellenos con Frijoles Negros (page 52), Mogo Mogo Verde (page 101), and Arroz con Plátanos (page 224), it is best to use the fairly ripe, but not mushy, mottled yellow and black plantains, which have a rich, creamy texture and profuse banana fragrance.

I often leave plantains to ripen on my counter, where they will keep for many days at room temperature. I have one caution, however: I have occasionally had a contrary plantain that chose to harden instead of soften. If you encounter one, just toss it onto your compost pile. When I have extras that are properly ripened, I peel them, wrap them in plastic wrap, put them in a freezer bag, and freeze them until needed.

SOPA DE FIDEO SECO CON FRIJOL NEGRO

Dry Soup of Pasta with Black Beans

One night, in her spacious home overlooking the city of Guanajuato, Luz Ma Gonzáles served me a traditional Mexican meal in which this "dry" soup followed a "wet" soup before the main course. Nowadays, though, it is more common to serve just one or the other type of soup, or to combine the "dry" soup with a salad as a light meal. The *chicharrón* in this dish adds an excellent texture contrast. Make sure you use real double-fried pork rind from a Mexican market and not the snacks sold in cellophane bags in supermarkets. If you cannot find the real thing, omit the *chicharrón*.

Accompany the soup with a crispy Ensalada de Jícama, Melón y Pepino (page 240) for another contrast in flavor and texture.

Serves 4 . . . .

FOR THE FIDEOS

- 4 tablespoons canola or safflower oil
- 1 (8-ounce) package fideos (coils of thin vermicelli), broken into thirds, or angel hair pasta, broken into 4-inch lengths
- ¼ white onion, finely chopped
- 2 cloves garlic, minced
- 4 medium, ripe tomatoes, peeled, seeded, and coarsely chopped, or 1 (14½-ounce) can diced tomatoes, drained
- 1 chile chipotle en adobo, finely chopped
- 2 cups chicken broth (page 25)
- 2 cups drained Frijoles de la Olla (page 214), made with black beans, or 1 (15-ounce) can black beans, drained
- 1 sprig fresh epazote or cilantro
- ¾ teaspoon sea salt

FOR THE GARNISH

- ½ cup Mexican crema (page 23), crème frâiche, or thick sour cream thinned with 1 tablespoon whole milk

FOR THE FIDEOS: Heat 2 tablespoons of the oil in a *cazuela* or large skillet over medium heat. Add the *fideos* and fry, stirring constantly, until just golden, about 3 minutes. Do not let them become too brown. Scoop the *fideos* into a bowl or onto a plate and set aside.

Add the remaining 2 tablespoons oil to the *cazuela* and heat over medium heat. Add the onion and cook, stirring occasionally, for several minutes. Add the garlic and cook until softened. Stir in the tomatoes and chile and cook, stirring often, until the tomatoes start to break down, about 3 minutes. Remove from the heat and let cool.

Transfer the cooled tomato mixture to a blender, add ½ cup of the broth, and process until smooth.

⅓ cup shredded queso panela or Muenster cheese

⅓ cup crumbled chicharrón (optional)

Return the *fideos* to the *cazuela*, stir in the tomato mixture, and cook over medium heat, stirring occasionally, until the noodles are fairly soft, 8 to 10 minutes.

Add the beans, epazote, salt, and the remaining 1½ cups broth, a little at a time, and simmer, stirring continuously, until the liquid is almost absorbed, about 5 minutes. (Depending on the type of pasta used, the amount of liquid needed may vary. Use whatever amount it takes for the *fideos* to become tender.) Taste and add more salt if needed.

Spoon the *fideos* into a serving dish or serve directly from the *cazuela*. Garnish with the *crema*, cheese, and *chicharrón* (if using).

FRIJOLES PUERCOS CON CHORIZO
Beans with Pork and Chorizo

In times past, pork was much too expensive to waste, and with no refrigeration, all parts of the pig were utilized as soon as the animal was butchered. When Ricardo and his family would return to Tabasco to visit his grandmother, other relatives and friends from widely scattered villages would congregate to welcome them back. The event would always culminate in the sacrifice of a pig to create a multitude of dishes for the large group. The feet were pickled and the meat from the head was made into *queso de puerco* (headcheese). Lard was so precious that the tin cans that held the rendered pork fat were ornately decorated and used over and over again. The small intestine was used to encase spiced, chopped pieces of pork for chorizo, and a pot of black beans was seasoned with any remaining bits of pork.

On the northern Pacific coast of Sinaloa, Sonora, Colima, Michoacán, and Jalisco, a similar dish made with reddish beans is a favorite. It is served as a main dish for *almuerzo* (brunch) or a light supper and is also frequently included as one of many dishes for a celebration.

1 tablespoon freshly rendered pork lard (page 24) or canola or safflower oil

¼ pound lean ground pork

½ pound Chorizo (page 145) or store-bought good-quality Mexican chorizo, casings removed if links and meat crumbled

½ cup finely chopped white onion

1 cup chopped ripe tomatoes (about 1 large)

3 cups partially drained Frijoles de la Olla (page 214), made with pinto or red beans, or partially drained canned pinto or red beans

Sea salt

3 ounces queso fresco, crumbled

6 small pickled chiles jalapeños, sliced lengthwise

Totopos (page 21) or flour tortillas, warmed

Heat the lard in a large, heavy skillet over medium heat. Add the pork and fry, stirring occasionally, just until lightly browned. Add the chorizo and continue cooking until almost crispy, about 5 minutes longer. Stir in the onion and fry for 1 minute, then add the tomato and mix well. Lower the heat to medium and add the beans, smashing and stirring them, until they pull away from the edges of the pan, about 5 minutes. Taste and add salt if needed.

Spoon onto a warmed platter and top with the cheese and chiles. Serve with ample *totopos* for scooping up the tasty mixture, or the beans can be scooped onto a warmed tortilla, rolled up, and eaten by hand.

FRIJOLONES CON COSTILLA DE PUERCO
Beans with Meaty Pork Ribs

In Oaxaca, these large, voluptuous beans are called *frijolones*, but they are better known in other parts of central Mexico as *ayocotes* (see the recipe for *texmole* on page 186). You can identify them by their size more than by their color, as these show-offy beans come in many hues: black, white, purple, brown, burgundy, and even splotchy pinto-pony patterns. They are displayed with pride in the markets and are so highly regarded that they are usually served whole in broth and seldom mashed or fried.

One winter day, I was driving with Emelia Cabrera and one of her daughters, Pilar, near Zaachila, the most southern of the villages encompassing the city of Oaxaca. On one side of the road, two oxen were pulling a cart with a young one trailing behind. On the other side was a field of low plants covered with red flowers. We stopped to look at them, stepping over and around the sprawling squash plants that were sharing the area with what Emelia said were from the blossoms of *frijolones*. I soon realized that similar scarlet runner beans grow up a wooden fence at my own home as an ornamental. As I have begun to eat more and more *frijolones* prepared in many different ways, I have gained a real appreciation of this tasty legume, especially enjoying them in Mole Coloradito con Frijolones (page 182) and with eggs and stews. My favorite way to prepare the dried beans is to cook them simply with pork and then to top them with strips of the local *chiles de agua* and white onions, just as Emelia prepared them one day for me, explaining that the dish is traditionally made with *patitas de puerco* (pig's feet) instead of pork ribs, as they are more economical.

Emelia served these beans with *tacos de berros* (page 62), tortillas filled with watercress and crunchy radishes that we dipped into the bowls of *frijolones* to soak up the rich broth.

Serves 4 to 6

4 cups frijolones (dried runner beans; see Sources)

1 head garlic, outer papery skin removed and pointed top cut off to expose flesh

¼ white onion

2 pounds boneless, meaty country-style pork ribs, trimmed of excess fat and cut in half

1 large sprig fresh epazote or cilantro

2 tablespoons sea salt

▌ FOR THE TOPPING

2 chiles de agua or chiles jalapeños, roasted, peeled, and cut lengthwise into strips (page 17)

¼ white onion, sliced vertically

2 tablespoons dried oregano, preferably Mexican

2 limes, preferably Key lime, quartered

Rinse and sort the beans, discarding any broken pieces. Put the beans in a large olla (page 15) or large, heavy pot and add water to cover by at least several inches (about 3 quarts). Remove and discard any beans that float to the top, then bring the water to a boil over high heat. Depending on the pot used, this will take from 10 to 30 minutes. When it begins to boil, immediately lower the heat to a gentle simmer and add the garlic and onion. Cover and cook, stirring occasionally and adding hot water if needed to keep the beans covered by at least ½ inch, for 2 hours.

Remove the garlic, discard any papery skins, and smash the cloves. Stir the cloves back into the broth. Add the pork, epazote, and salt, raise the heat slightly, and bring to a low boil. Cover and simmer until the beans are completely soft and the meat is almost falling apart. This could take from 2 to 3 hours longer, depending on the age of the beans. These beans should not have al dente centers. Taste and add more salt if needed.

Serve the beans in bowls with lots of broth. Accompany with chile strips, onion slices, oregano, and lime for adding as desired.

FRIJOLES NEGROS CON JAIBAS
Black Beans with Crab

During the time I was cooking and eating with Antonieta Avila Salinas, she was very apologetic that no small soft-shell crabs were available for her to prepare this dish, a favorite of those of African descent living in the lush coastal region of northern Oaxaca. When the crabs are in season, her husband, a fisherman, collects them in the nearby lagoon and brings them, well washed but still with a hint of tidal waters, to the *mercado* in nearby Pinotepa Nacional.

It is traditional to flavor black beans with either pungent epazote or with the leaves of the native avocado tree, which add a whiff of anise to this dish. Leaves from hybrid avocado trees just won't do.

Since we can only get the large Dungeness crab in the Pacific Northwest, I take the meat out of the shell. But if you are using the smaller crabs, break them apart with your fingers before adding them to the pan. Eat this dish with lots of hot corn tortillas (page 19) and Salsa de Chiles Costeños (page 33). Your favorite Mexican beer or a Michelada (page 268) is always a welcome beverage, with cooling Helado de Mango (page 248) for dessert.

Serves 4

¼ cup freshly rendered pork lard (page 24) or canola or safflower oil

¼ cup finely chopped white onion

1½ cups drained Frijoles de la Olla (page 214), made with black beans, or drained canned black beans, plus 2 cups bean broth or liquid from can with water added if needed

8 small blue crabs, cleaned and broken in half, or 1 cup Dungeness crabmeat from a 1½-pound crab

2 dried avocado leaves (optional; see Sources)

½ teaspoon sea salt

¼ cup finely chopped fresh cilantro, thick stem ends removed

Heat the lard in a *cazuela* or heavy skillet over medium-high heat. Add the onion and fry until lightly browned, about 5 minutes, then scoop in the beans and mash with a bean or potato masher until pastelike but still lumpy. Stir in 1½ cups of the bean broth and continue mashing the beans until almost smooth. Gradually stir in the remaining ½ cup broth. When the bean broth begins to simmer, add the small blue crabs, avocado leaves, and salt, lower the heat to a gentle simmer, and continue to cook until the crabs are cooked through, about 15 minutes. If using the Dungeness crabmeat, stir it in right before serving just to heat through.

If the broth becomes too thick, stir in additional broth or hot water.

Spoon the beans and the crabs into warmed wide, deep bowls, sprinkle with the cilantro, and serve right away.

FRIJOLES PUERCOS CON CHILORIO
Beans with Chile-Seasoned Pork

Chilorio, with its brazen flavors of chiles and cumin, is a traditional pork dish for fiestas in Sinaloa on Mexico's west coast. Any leftovers find their way into other dishes, such as Alma Cervantes Cota's version of *frijoles puercos* served with hot flour or corn tortillas, making savory tacos for breakfast or *cena* a special treat. These beans also make a tasty *botana* served with *totopos* (page 21).

Serves 8

2 tablespoons freshly rendered pork lard (page 24) or canola or safflower oil

¼ cup finely chopped white onion

3 cups drained Frijoles de la Olla (page 214), made with any brown or tan beans, or drained canned brown or tan beans, plus 1 cup bean broth or liquid from can with water added if needed

1 teaspoon sea salt

2 cups chilorio (page 70)

FOR THE GARNISH

3 ounces queso fresco, crumbled (optional)

2 tablespoons finely chopped white onion (optional)

3 chiles jalapeños en escabeche, sliced lengthwise (optional)

Heat the lard in a heavy skillet over medium-high heat until shimmering. Add the onion and fry, stirring frequently, until quite brown, about 4 minutes. Add the beans, lower the heat to medium-low, and begin to mash the beans with a bean or potato masher until almost pureed. The mixture will be something like biscuit dough. Add the bean broth and salt and continue to smash and stir for several minutes, allowing the beans to absorb the liquid. Continue cooking until the beans resemble thick, lumpy brown gravy and a spoon scraped across the bottom of the pan leaves an empty space that stays clear for a moment. Gently fold in the *chilorio,* then taste and add more salt if needed.

As soon as the mixture is heated through, spoon onto a warmed platter. If you like, garnish with the cheese, onions, and chiles. Set on the table for everyone to use as filling for tacos.

TAQUITOS PLACEROS CON MOLE COLORADITO

Crispy Marketplace Tacos with Red Mole

The Cabrera family in Oaxaca has played an integral role in my Mexican culinary life, becoming close friends in the process, especially with the mother, Emelia, who has shared many meals with me throughout the years. Neither of us speaks the other's language very well, but once in a while we do have a long conversation on the phone, punctuated by many pauses and laughs. One of Emelia's daughters, Pilar, not only gives cooking classes but also runs the family restaurant, La Olla, with her husband, Luis. This is the recipe for one of their most popular dishes and one I like to serve friends for an informal supper with Frijoles Refritos (page 217), a crisp green salad, and a malty Mexican beer.

Most visitors to Oaxaca rave about the diversity of the moles they have eaten there, forgetting to mention another important specialty, *quesillo de Oaxaca*, flat, tightly wound skeins of ivory-tinted cheese. Both the mole and the cheese are included in this recipe, though an alternative to the Oaxacan cheese is given.

Makes 12 tacos; serves 4 to 6 . . . .

▪ FOR THE MOLE COLORADITO

10 chiles anchos, stems, seeds, and membranes removed, then toasted (page 18)

5 chiles guajillos, stems, seeds, and membranes removed, then toasted (page 18)

¼ cup unhulled sesame seeds

Pinch of sea salt, plus ½ teaspoon

1-inch stick Mexican true cinnamon bark (page 88), broken up

1 tablespoon dried thyme

1 tablespoon dried marjoram

1 tablespoon dried oregano, preferably Mexican

¼ teaspoon freshly ground black pepper

1 medium tomato, roasted and peeled (page 18)

FOR THE MOLE: Soak the chiles in a bowl of very hot water to cover until soft, about 30 minutes. Drain the chiles and tear into smaller pieces.

Put a small dry skillet over medium heat and toast the sesame seeds with the pinch of salt, stirring constantly, until the seeds become very fragrant, about 4 minutes. Scoop out and set aside. (Pilar adds the pinch of salt to help prevent the seeds from popping out of the pan.)

Put the chiles, cinnamon, thyme, marjoram, oregano, and black pepper in a blender and process until a smooth sauce forms, adding ½ to ¾ cup water as needed

¼ medium white onion, roasted (page 18)

3 cloves garlic, roasted (page 18), then peeled

2 tablespoons freshly rendered pork lard
(page 24) or canola or safflower oil

3 cups chicken broth (page 25)

1 (3½-ounce) tablet Mexican chocolate,
roughly chopped (about ½ cup)

1 tablespoon sugar

FOR THE TAQUITOS

Canola or safflower oil for frying

12 white corn tortillas, homemade (page 19) or
store-bought

1 cup shredded cooked chicken (page 25)

FOR THE GARNISH

6 tablespoons finely shredded quesillo de
Oaxaca or Muenster cheese

24 thinly sliced small onion rings (from several
onions)

½ cup shredded romaine lettuce

Leaves from 1 small bunch fresh flat-leaf
parsley, coarsely chopped

to release the blades. Depending on the power of your blender, the pureed chiles may have to be pressed through a medium-mesh sieve to achieve a smooth sauce. Set the puree aside.

Rinse out the blender, then add the tomato, onion, garlic, and sesame seeds and process until smooth. Set aside.

Heat the lard in a *cazuela*, heavy saucepan, or Dutch oven over medium-high heat until shimmering. Pour in the pureed chile mixture and fry, stirring occasionally, until the sauce thickens and darkens, about 5 minutes. Pour in the tomato mixture, lower the heat to medium, and simmer, stirring constantly, for 5 minutes. Pour in the broth, add the chocolate, sugar, and the remaining ½ teaspoon salt, and continue to cook, stirring occasionally, for at least 25 minutes. The mixture should be just thick enough to coat the back of a spoon. Taste and add more salt if needed.

FOR THE TAQUITOS: Pour the oil to a depth of ½ inch into a heavy skillet and heat over medium-low heat. Using tongs, quickly pass 1 tortilla at a time through the hot oil, just long enough for it to become pliable. Drain on absorbent paper, then put several large pinches of the shredded chicken in a line down the center of each hot tortilla and roll up.

Place 2 or 3 *taquitos* on each warmed individual plate and spoon the hot sauce on top. Garnish with the cheese, onion rings, lettuce, and parsley and serve.

ENCHILADAS POTOSÍNAS
Enchiladas San Luis Potosí Style

The mile-high silver city of San Luis Potosí must have more plazas than any other colonial city in Mexico, most with food vendors making almost identical versions of enchiladas with tortillas not rolled but folded, more like a chile-seasoned quesadilla. How to decide among them appears to be based more on the cooks' persuasive personalities than their culinary skills.

Although the *manchego* cheese used to stuff the enchiladas has the same name as the wonderful firm, pale Spanish *manchego* cheese made from sheep's milk in the region of La Mancha, the Mexican version is instead a butter yellow cheese made from cow's milk and quite different in taste and texture. It is available in some Mexican markets but Monterey Jack can be substituted. The filling can be made up to several hours in advance.

These enchiladas are usually served with a scoop of Frijoles Refritos (page 217) and with Guacamole Clásico (page 43) on the side.

Makes 16 enchiladas; serves at least 6 to 8 hungry eaters . . . .

▊ FOR THE FILLING
5 ounces tomatillos (3 or 4), husks removed and rinsed

2 small chiles serranos, stemmed

1 clove garlic

½ teaspoon sea salt

10 ounces Mexican manchego or Monterey Jack cheese, shredded

▊ FOR THE MASA
6 large chiles anchos, stems, membranes, and seeds removed

1 pound freshly made masa for corn tortillas, or 2¼ cups masa harina for tortillas reconstituted with 1 cup plus 2 tablespoons quite warm water (page 19)

½ teaspoon sea salt

Canola or safflower oil for frying

FOR THE FILLING: Put the tomatillos and chiles in a small saucepan with water to cover barely. Bring to a simmer, then lower the heat slightly and cook until soft, about 8 minutes. Drain, then mash and grind them together in a large *molcajete* with the garlic and salt. If you do not have a *molcajete*, use a blender, but be careful not to pulverize the mixture, as it should still have a rough texture. Stir in the cheese and set aside.

FOR THE MASA: Soak the chiles in a bowl of very hot water to cover until soft, about 15 minutes. Drain the chiles and tear into smaller pieces. Put in a blender and puree until smooth, adding just a small amount of water to release the blades.

FOR THE TOPPING

1 cup Mexican crema (page 23), crème
fraîche, or thick sour cream thinned with
1 tablespoon whole milk

Put the fresh masa or the reconstituted masa harina in a large bowl, add the pureed chiles and the salt, and mash together with your hands until thoroughly incorporated. Divide the dough into 16 equal portions and shape each portion into a ball about 1¾ inches in diameter. Cover the balls with a slightly damp towel.

Following the directions on page 19, use a tortilla press to press each masa ball into a tortilla about 5½ inches in diameter, then cook on a *comal*, griddle, or heavy skillet over medium-low heat.

Layer half of each tortilla with a handful of the cheese mixture, leaving a ½-inch border uncovered around the edge. Fold over like a quesadilla, pressing down along the edges to close.

Heat the oven to 200°F. Pour the oil to a depth of ½ inch into a large, heavy skillet and heat over medium-high heat to 375°F on a deep-frying thermometer. Fry 2 or 3 filled tortillas in the hot oil on one side for about 30 seconds. Using a slotted spatula, flip over and briefly fry the other side. Using the spatula, lift each tortilla—now an enchilada—out of the oil, allowing the excess oil to drip off, and drain briefly on absorbent paper, then put on a baking sheet and keep warm in the oven. Working quickly, fry the remaining enchiladas the same way.

Top the enchiladas with the *crema* and serve right away on a warmed platter or individual plates.

ENCHILADAS PLACERAS
Enchiladas of the Plaza

When dusk descends over the Plaza Chica in Pátzcuaro, the sky turns plum purple, signaling that portable food stands will soon appear. Along the sidewalk, oversized metal *comales* with rounded depressions in the middle are set up over charcoal-burning portable stoves. Long-established vendors use the *comales* to prepare enchiladas that they turn into entire meals with the addition of chicken, carrots, and potatoes, all covered with a gutsy chile sauce. Each vendor will have a few colorful oilcloth-covered tables with small stools or benches jammed around them, but since you usually have to wait and jostle for a seat, many people eat standing up with plate in hand.

On a cool night, the masa-thick *atole* is the beverage to drink, with those flavored with the aromatic *guayaba* (guava) or other fruits the usual choice. There is also a stand nearby that sells the very special *atole de anís,* with its faint hint of licorice, and the sour-hot *atole agrio* (page 277). This whole scenario is duplicated in towns throughout Michoacán.

This recipe is a combination of all my favorite *enchiladas placeras* eaten in Michoacán over many years. My notes are sometimes chile-smeared but still bring back wonderful memories. Although the directions may appear complicated, everything except for the final preparation can be done in advance. I have found that it is helpful and fun to have friends or family help assemble the enchiladas for this informal meal. You can easily double the recipe to serve a small crowd.

Serves 6 . . . .

FOR THE CHICKEN

1 teaspoon sea salt

6 chicken thighs, drumsticks, and/or breasts

¼ white onion

FOR THE SAUCE

4 chiles anchos, stems, seeds, and membranes removed, then toasted (page 18)

3 chiles guajillos, stems, seeds, and membranes removed, then toasted (page 18)

2 cloves garlic, roughly chopped

1 teaspoon dried oregano, preferably Mexican

1 teaspoon sea salt

½ teaspoon freshly ground black pepper

FOR THE VEGETABLES

10 ounces carrots (4 or 5), peeled and cut into ½-inch cubes

¼ cup mild white vinegar such as vinagre de piña or diluted unseasoned rice vinegar (page 50)

1½ teaspoons sea salt

10 ounces red or Yukon Gold potatoes (about 4 small), unpeeled, cut into ½-inch cubes

FOR THE CHICKEN: Bring a large saucepan of water to a boil over medium-high heat and add the salt, chicken thighs and/or drumsticks, and onion. When the water returns to a boil, skim off any foam that rises to the surface, reduce the heat to medium, cover partially, and simmer for 20 minutes. If using chicken breasts, add them now and continue cooking for 15 minutes, skimming off any additional foam. Remove the pan from the heat and let the chicken cool in the broth.

Remove the chicken pieces from the broth and set aside. Strain the broth through a fine-mesh sieve, let stand for several minutes, then skim off any fat floating on the surface. Set the broth aside to cool completely, then cover and refrigerate until needed. Lift off and discard any fat on the surface before using. The chicken can be cooked up to 1 day in advance, covered, and refrigerated, then brought to room-temperature before frying.

FOR THE ENCHILADAS

5 tablespoons canola or safflower oil, plus more as needed

18 store-bought thick corn tortillas

1 cup grated queso cotija or Monterey Jack cheese

½ cup finely chopped white onion

FOR THE TOPPING

½ cup finely shredded cabbage or lettuce

1 small white onion, thinly sliced and separated into rings

3 chiles jalapeños en escabeche, seeded and cut lengthwise into narrow strips

2 ripe Hass avocados, halved, pitted, peeled, and sliced

⅔ cup Mexican crema (page 23), crème fraîche, or thick sour cream thinned with 1 tablespoon whole milk

FOR THE SAUCE: Tear the toasted chiles into smaller pieces, put in a small bowl, cover with very hot water, and soak until soft, about 20 minutes. Drain the chiles and put in a blender. Add the garlic, oregano, salt, and pepper and process to a smooth sauce, adding 1 cup or more of the reserved broth as needed to release the blades. Strain the sauce through a medium-mesh sieve into a wide, shallow bowl or pie pan and set aside.

FOR THE VEGETABLES: Pour 2 cups water into a saucepan and bring to a boil over medium-high heat. Add the carrots, vinegar, and salt and cook for 4 minutes. Add the potatoes and continue to cook until the carrots and potatoes are just tender, about 6 minutes. Do not overcook. Drain thoroughly and set aside.

FOR THE ENCHILADAS: Have all of the toppings ready and nearby, as now you will have to work quickly to fry the chicken and vegetables and make the enchiladas. Heat the oven to its lowest setting and warm 6 large plates and 1 smaller one.

Heat 3 tablespoons of the oil in a large, heavy skillet (or even a wok) over medium-high heat until it is sizzling. Pat the potatoes and carrots dry, add to the hot oil, and fry quickly, just until beginning to brown. Using a slotted spoon, lift them out of the oil, allowing the excess oil to drip off, and drain on absorbent paper. Keep warm in the oven.

Add the chicken to the same hot oil, adding more oil if necessary, and fry, turning occasionally, until golden brown on all sides. Using a slotted spatula, remove the chicken, allowing any excess oil to drip off, and drain on absorbent paper, then keep warm in the oven.

Either scrape out any debris from the skillet or use another large skillet, add the remaining 2 tablespoons oil, and heat over medium-high heat. When the oil is rippling, dip and drag the tortillas, one at a time, through the sauce, coating both sides, then fry briefly on each side in the hot oil, using the slotted spatula to turn. Lift the tortilla from the oil, allowing any excess oil to drip off, and put on the warmed small plate. Lightly fill the tortilla with 2 heaping teaspoons cheese and 1 teaspoon onion. Fold one side of the tortilla over the filling and then lap over the other side to make an enchilada and put on one of the heated large plates. Repeat to make 2 more enchiladas, slightly overlapping them, and then add a piece of the chicken to the side of the plate and keep the plate warm in the oven. Continue making the other enchiladas the same way, adding more oil to the skillet as needed.

Pour any remaining sauce over the enchiladas and cover with the fried carrots and potatoes. Top each serving with the cabbage, onion, chiles, avocado, and a dollop of *crema* and serve immediately.

ENCHILADAS SUIZAS
Swiss Enchiladas

Ricardo speaks of these creamy enchiladas as "enchiladas of the two lies," as they are neither very chile flavored nor Swiss. In fact, this is a very Mexico City–style preparation that originated in La Casa de los Azulejos, or the "House of Tiles," a building in the city's old downtown that housed the first Sanborn restaurant, opened around 1919.

According to my longtime friend María Lorens, who lived in Mexico City for her first thirty-six years before moving to British Columbia, the history of the House of Tiles started with a modest home built by the first Count of Orizaba around 1530. Over the years, different heirs made additions to the abode, ending in 1828, with the death of the seventh count, who was responsible for decorating the facade of the now-majestic house with the blue tiles known as Talavera of the Queen.

Some years later, a friend of the family bought the home, where he regularly entertained the most prestigious writers of that time. Eventually it was sold to two American brothers, Walter and Frank Sanborn, with the condition that the building be maintained and the architecture preserved. In 1919, the Sanborn brothers converted the historic home into a popular restaurant, preserving the colonial style of the building but adding a vaulted glass ceiling to cover the courtyard and wall murals by the famous artists Diego Rivera and José Clemente Orozco.

Although today many other Sanborn stores with restaurants are found throughout Mexico, whenever you go to Mexico City, you must visit the beautiful House of Tiles and eat *enchiladas suizas* in their original setting, a Mexico City tradition.

Serve the enchiladas as a light supper, or *cena*, with just Frijoles Refritos (page 217) or perhaps a salad. They also make a hearty breakfast dish and a savory part of a brunch buffet.

FOR THE SAUCE

1½ pounds tomatillos (15 to 18), husked and well rinsed

4 small chiles serranos, stemmed

½ white onion

4 cloves garlic

2 tablespoons canola or safflower oil

1 large sprig fresh cilantro, thick stem ends removed, finely chopped

1 cup chicken broth (page 25)

1½ cups shredded Mexican manchego or Monterey Jack cheese

2 cups heavy cream

1½ teaspoons sea salt

FOR THE ENCHILADAS

3 tablespoons canola or safflower oil, plus more if needed

18 store-bought thick corn tortillas

2⅔ cups shredded cooked chicken breast meat (page 25)

FOR THE TOPPING

½ pound Mexican manchego or Monterey Jack cheese, thinly sliced

1 tablespoon finely chopped fresh cilantro, thick stem ends removed

FOR THE SAUCE: Put the tomatillos in a saucepan with water just to cover and bring to a simmer over medium-low heat. Add the chiles, onion, and garlic and continue to simmer until the tomatillos have softened but still hold their shape, about 20 minutes longer. Remove from the heat and let cool slightly. Pour half of the tomatillo mixture into a blender, process until very smooth, and pour into a bowl. Repeat with the remaining tomatillo mixture and add to the first batch.

Heat 2 tablespoons of the oil in a heavy skillet or *cazuela* over medium heat until shimmering. Carefully stir in the blended tomatillo mixture and cook, stirring constantly as it spews and sputters, for 5 minutes, then add the cilantro and broth.

Put the shredded cheese in a bowl and stir in the cream and salt. Add to the tomatillo sauce, reduce the heat to low, and continue to cook, stirring occasionally, for 10 minutes more to melt the cheese and blend the flavors. Remove from the heat and keep warm.

FOR THE ENCHILADAS: Heat the oven to 350°F. Heat the remaining 3 tablespoons oil in a heavy skillet over medium heat until shimmering. Using a spatula or tongs, quickly dip each tortilla into the hot oil—you may have to turn it over—until hot but still soft. Quickly remove and drain on absorbent paper. Keep warm while you heat the remaining tortillas the same way, adding more oil if necessary.

One at a time, dip each tortilla by hand in the sauce, coating evenly. Spread a little of the shredded chicken down the center of each tortilla and fold or roll. Place the enchiladas in a 14-by-10-by-2½-inch baking pan, arranging them in two rows. Smother them with the creamy sauce. Top with the cheese slices.

Bake just long enough to reheat the enchiladas and melt the cheese, 10 to 15 minutes. Remove from the oven and place 3 enchiladas on each plate. Sprinkle with the cilantro and serve right away.

TAMALES DE CARNE DE CERDO Y CALABACITAS
Tamales with Pork and Zucchini

The culture and food of the Huastec people fascinate me, especially the oversized tamales, the most spectacular being the *zacahuil*, which can be over five feet long and has to be cooked in a special oven. These indigenous people, related to the Maya, still live predominately in San Luis Potosí and northern Veracruz. The culture dates back to 1100 to 900 B.C., but was at its peak between the fall of Teotihuacán and the advent of the Mexica (Aztec) civilization. From all that I have learned, the Huastecs were more than a little sybaritic. They seldom wore clothes other than ceremonial attire, both young boys and young girls partnered with adult men, and they were known for their musical abilities and for their spectacular cloaks made of iridescent bird feathers, later demanded as tribute by Motecuhzoma and other Mexica rulers.

When Ricardo was in Zozocolco de Hidalgo, Veracruz, one of the village women, Guadalupe Gómez Alonso, told him that these remarkable tamales of pork and small chunks of zucchini are made to celebrate their Days of the Dead (November 1 and 2). Do not worry about the amount of salt in the filling. The steam will remove much of it.

Makes 9 large tamales; serves 4 to 6

FOR THE WRAPPINGS
9 (12-inch) squares banana leaf, thawed if frozen and softened (page 22), plus more leaves for lining and covering the steamer rack

FOR THE DOUGH
1¼ cups freshly rendered pork lard (page 24)
2 teaspoons sea salt
1 tablespoon baking powder

FOR THE WRAPPINGS: Prepare the banana leaves.

FOR THE DOUGH: Using an electric mixer, beat together the lard, salt, and baking powder in a large bowl until light and meringuelike, about 5 minutes. With a large spoon or with your hands, gradually mix in the fresh masa or the reconstituted masa harina alternately with 1 cup

2 pounds freshly made masa for corn tortillas, or 2½ cups masa harina for tortillas
reconstituted with 2 cups quite warm water
(page 19)

▋ FOR THE FILLING

¼ cup peanut oil

¼ cup chopped white onion

1 tablespoon minced garlic

2 tablespoons minced chiles serranos
(about 3)

9 ounces zucchini (about 2 medium), cut into
½-inch cubes

2 cups ½-inch-cubed ripe tomatoes (about
4 medium)

1 pound pork loin, preferably the rib end, or
boneless pork shoulder, excess fat trimmed
and cut into 1-inch pieces

1 tablespoon plus ½ teaspoon sea salt

lukewarm water until smooth and free of
lumps. Continue beating with the mixer
until the masa is light and fluffy, about
10 minutes. Pat the masa mixture into an
8-inch square pan with 2-inch sides and
cut the dough into 9 equal portions.

FOR THE FILLING: Heat the oil in a large,
heavy skillet over medium heat until shimmering. Add the onion and garlic and fry
until lightly golden, about 2 minutes. Add
the chiles and zucchini and continue to fry
for several more minutes. Stir in the tomatoes and salt and cook for 10 minutes. Add
the meat and cook until the vegetables
are soft and well incorporated into the
tomatoes and the meat has begun to lose
its raw appearance, about 5 minutes more.
Remove from the heat and taste and add
more salt if needed.

Pour water to a depth of at least 2 inches into a *tamalera* (page 16) or other large pot for
steaming the tamales. Bring the water to a low bowl. Drop in a few coins to rattle in the
bubbling water, their silence signaling the need to add more boiling water to the steamer.

Arrange the prepared banana leaf squares shiny side up on a work surface. Place 1 masa
square in the center of each leaf and spread into a 4-by-2-by-¾-inch rectangle. Spoon
½ cup of the meat and zucchini mixture evenly on top of the masa. Facing the long side of
the masa rectangle, bring up the two sides of the banana leaf parallel to the rectangle and
fold together, tucking one side over the other. Then fold both ends of the leaf toward the
center. You should have a packet about 5½ inches long by 3 inches wide by ¾ inch thick. I
like to pull off narrow strands from an extra banana leaf, knot 2 strands together, and tie
the knotted strand horizontally around the packet. Repeat to make 8 more tamales.

Line the steamer rack with some of the extra banana leaves. Place 3 tamales, with the seam
side up, horizontally on the steamer rack, spacing them evenly. Arrange 3 more tamales,
again with the seam side up, on top, placing them perpendicular to the first layer. Arrange
the final 3 tamales, seam side up, on top, placing them perpendicular to the second
layer. This pattern leaves plenty of empty space around the tamales so that the steam can
surround them. Cover the tamales with more banana leaves and then a clean dish towel.
Place the steamer rack over the bubbling water and cover with a tight-fitting lid.

Steam the tamales over medium-high heat for 1 hour without opening the pot. Remember, if you don't hear the coins jingling, you need to add more boiling water to the pot. After 1 hour, turn off the heat and let the tamales rest for 30 minutes. Remove a tamal from the steamer and let it sit for several minutes. If the leaf lifts off easily, the tamales are done. If not, return the tamal to the pot and steam the tamales for another 5 minutes or so. These tamales are also excellent resteamed for 20 minutes and served the next day.

TAMALES DE PIÑA CON COCO
Pineapple and Coconut Tamales

In Veracruz and Oaxaca, pineapples and coconuts are an abundant source of food and drink. Nothing is more refreshing on a sweltering day than stopping at one of the many roadside stands south of the port of Veracruz and drinking freshly crushed and strained pineapple juice. The local pineapples are also combined with coconut to make sweet tamales that are traditionally served for brunch or a light supper. These same tamales can be served for dessert: put two tamales on each plate and accompany with a scoop of vanilla ice cream topped with toasted almonds and cubes of fresh pineapple.

Serve the tamales on a platter and place a second dish nearby for the discarded husks.

Makes about 26 tamales

FOR THE WRAPPINGS
35 corn husks, soaked and softened (page 22)

FOR THE TAMALES
1¼ cups freshly rendered pork lard (page 24)

½ teaspoon sea salt

1 tablespoon baking powder

2 pounds freshly made masa for corn tortillas, or 2½ cups masa harina for tortillas reconstituted with 2 cups quite warm water (page 19)

2 cups ¼-inch-cubed fresh pineapple

1 cup sugar

¾-inch stick Mexican true cinnamon bark (page 88), ground

FOR THE WRAPPINGS: Prepare the corn husks.

FOR THE TAMALES: Using an electric mixer, beat together the lard, salt, and baking powder in a large bowl until light and meringuelike, about 5 minutes. With a large spoon or with your hands, gradually mix in the fresh masa or the reconstituted masa harina alternately with 1 cup lukewarm water until smooth and free of lumps. Continue beating with the mixer until the mixture is light and fluffy, about 10 minutes. Using your hands, fold in the pineapple, sugar, cinnamon,

1 cup blanched almonds, toasted and finely chopped

1 cup shredded fresh coconut (page 276) or unsweetened dried coconut (if unavailable, sweetened can be substituted)

¼ cup raisins

almonds, coconut, and raisins until thoroughly blended.

Pour water to a depth of at least 2 inches into a *tamalera* (page 16) or other large pot for steaming the tamales. Bring the water to a low boil. Drop in a few coins to rattle in the bubbling water, their silence signaling the need to add more boiling water to the steamer.

Place about ⅓ cup of the masa mixture in the center of a corn husk near the broad end, leaving a wide margin of husk. Fold the long edges over to cover the filling, and then bend the longer empty part of the husk toward the opposite end. Repeat to make the remaining tamales. You should have about 26 tamales. You can pull off 2 narrow strands from a corn husk, knot them together, and tie the knotted strand horizontally around each packet.

Place some of the extra pieces of corn husks on the steamer rack, and put a small metal funnel or empty can with holes in it in the center of the rack. Layer the tamales, propped upright, in concentric circles around the funnel or can. Don't pack them too tightly. Cover with more husks and a small, thick kitchen towel. Place the steamer rack over the bubbling water and cover with a tight-fitting lid.

Steam the tamales for 1 hour without opening the pot. Remember, if you don't hear the coins jingling, you need to add more boiling water to the pot. To test for doneness, remove a tamal from the pot, let sit for a few minutes, and then open it. The dough should easily pull away from the husk and feel spongy. If not, continue cooking for another 15 minutes. Turn off the heat, take off the cover, and let the tamales rest for 1 hour, then serve hot. The tamales can be stored tightly covered in the refrigerator for up to 2 days, and then reheated in the steamer for about 20 minutes.

Sal de Mar

Sea Salt

A pinch of salt, a spoonful of salt, or even a small handful in a large pot of stew adds flavor and provides necessary nutrients. But never in my life had I imagined the quantity of salt I saw in front of me one afternoon on Yucatán's northern coast: vast ranges of snow white mountains of sea salt.

The famous salt flats of Las Coloradas have been exploited for over two thousand years. The Maya gathered the salt by hand and used it as a highly treasured trading commodity, especially the unusual pink crystals from a pond close to the sea. The color of the crystals is a result of tiny marine invertebrates that contain beta carotene. This is a region of hurricanes and strong winds, or *nortes*, and the rough waves that wash over the coastal sand dunes are always creating even more shallow salt ponds. I watched as huge trucks scooped up the salt from the nearby enormous piles and placed it on a long conveyor belt that carried it to cargo ships for transport to the United States and other destinations.

Earlier that day, I had gone out birding in the mangrove-filled estuaries of the nearby Río Lagartos Biosphere Reserve, home to the largest concentration of pink flamingos in Mexico. The birds feed on the same invertebrates found in the nearby salt ponds. It was a truly pink-tinted day.

I have also visited salt flats on the Pacific coast of Mexico, especially in Guerrero Negro in Baja California Sur. Much farther south, on the coast of Oaxaca, an excellent salt is gathered by hand by the village women from near Salina Cruz on the Isthmus of Tehuantepec. And in Chiapas markets, I found a wonderful salt that is mined from an underground deposit of what was once sea salt. I use many of these salts daily in my cooking.

TORTITAS DE CAMARONES ESTILO TEHUANTEPEC

Shrimp Fritters from the Isthmus of Tehuantepec

María Gómez Perea lives in a unique region of Mexico: the sweltering lowlands of the Isthmus of Tehuantepec that girdle the roughly 140 miles that separate the waters of the Gulf Coast from the Pacific Ocean. Her home is in Salina Cruz, named for the nearby *salinas* (salt lagoons) where generations of local residents have made their living harvesting salt. Oaxaca's third-largest city, Salina Cruz is now a huge petrochemical center, and I am always amazed by the juxtaposition of big industry and the fishermen who net fish and shrimp for dishes like these fritters.

María's grandfather emigrated here from Spain and married a local woman, and together they raised a family, all the women becoming skilled at preparing the complex cuisine of the isthmus, combining it with the techniques from their Spanish heritage.

For this dish, María prefers to use the freshly caught small, sweet shrimp that are sun-dried on mats for several days to concentrate their flavor. With their heads and tails on, these *camarones de laguna* are about two inches long, an ideal size. In this part of Oaxaca, these shrimp fritters in tomato sauce are a traditional dish for *desayuno*, the first meal of the Mexican day, or for a light *cena* in the evening.

If you have access to dried shrimp, use them. They are available in most Mexican and Asian markets and are a coveted ingredient in Cantonese and Thai cooking, imparting unami, the "fifth taste," to dishes. Since they will not be freshly dried, reconstitute them by rinsing twice in cold water, removing the heads and legs, and then soaking in cold water for 5 minutes. Surprisingly, you may also need to add extra salt to the shrimp. I have made these fritters both the traditional way with dried shrimp and with fresh shrimp. Pair the *tortitas* with Arroz con Platános (page 223). For a colorful contrast, I serve a salad such as Escabeche de Verduras (page 236).

Serves 4

2 teaspoons sea salt

1 pound medium-large shrimp in the shell, fresh or dried and reconstituted (about 25 shrimp)

Bring a large pot of water and 1 teaspoon of the salt to a boil over high heat. Add the shrimp, cover, and cook until the fresh shrimp just turn pink or the dried ones become plumper, about 3 minutes. Do not

4 large, ripe tomatoes, roasted and peeled (page 18)

1 chile serrano, roasted (page 17), then stemmed

2 small cloves garlic

3 tablespoons canola or safflower oil, plus more as needed

1 large sprig fresh epazote or cilantro

4 eggs, at room temperature, separated

overcook. Remove from the heat, drain, and spread the shrimp on absorbent paper. When cool, peel the shrimp and set aside, then return the shells to the broth. Cover and simmer the broth for 15 minutes. Strain through a fine-mesh sieve.

Put the tomatoes, chile, and garlic in a blender and process until smooth, adding 1 or more cups of the shrimp broth as needed to release the blades.

Heat 1 tablespoon of the oil in a skillet or *cazuela* over medium-high heat until shimmering. Add the tomato mixture, epazote, and the remaining 1 teaspoon salt, lower the heat to medium-low, and simmer, stirring occasionally, until the sauce thickens, 5 to 8 minutes. Remove and discard the epazote. Keep the sauce warm.

Beat the egg whites in a bowl, preferably copper, with a whisk until quite firm peaks form when the whisk is lifted. In a separate bowl, lightly beat the egg yolks with a fork. Gently fold the yolks into the whites until well incorporated. Working on a plastic cutting board or a sheet of waxed paper, snuggle 3 or 4 shrimp tightly together to form a circle about 3 inches in diameter. Repeat with a second batch of shrimp. Spoon enough of the egg mixture over the top of the shrimp to cover completely.

Heat the remaining 2 tablespoons oil in a large, heavy skillet over medium heat. When the oil is quite hot, using a slotted spatula, carefully slide each shrimp circle, or *tortita*, into the oil and fry until golden brown, 2 to 3 minutes. Turn and fry until lightly browned on the other side. Using the spatula, lift the *tortitas* out of the oil, allowing any excess oil to drip off, and carefully slip them into the hot tomato sauce. Assemble and fry the remaining *tortitas* the same way, adding more oil to the pan as needed and slipping the *tortitas* into the sauce. When all of the *tortitas* are in the sauce, transfer to a warmed shallow platter and serve.

TORTITAS DE NOPALES CON SALSA ROJA
Cactus Fritters in Red Chile Sauce

Now, as when she was a young girl, Arminda Flores, a native Purépecha, often searches out the young, tender paddles of nopal cacti in the fields close by Santiago Tzipejo, Michoacán, for making this vegetarian dish that her extended family likes to eat for a light *cena*. The nopales can be found in most Mexican markets and in some supermarkets.

Serves 4

FOR THE SAUCE

6 chiles guajillos, stems, seeds, and membranes removed, then toasted (page 18)

¼ white onion

1 tablespoon olive oil

½ teaspoon sea salt

FOR THE TORTITAS

6 eggs, at room temperature, separated

4 to 6 small, firm nopales, cleaned, cut into narrow 1-inch-long strips, and boiled (page 23)

½ cup peanut or canola oil, or more if needed

2 sprigs fresh cilantro, thick stem ends removed and chopped

FOR THE SAUCE: Soak the chiles in a bowl of very hot water to cover until soft, about 20 minutes. Spoon the chiles into a blender with 1 cup of the soaking water and the onion and process until a smooth sauce forms. If needed, strain the sauce through a medium-mesh sieve, pressing and scraping with a spoon until only bits of the skin remain in the sieve.

Heat the olive oil in a skillet over medium-high heat until very hot but not smoking. Add the chile mixture and salt and cook, stirring frequently, until the sauce thickens, about 10 minutes. Cover and set aside until ready to use.

FOR THE TORTITAS: Beat the egg whites in a bowl with a whisk until quite firm peaks form when the whisk is lifted. Arminda is fortunate always to have a copper bowl to use as they are made in the nearby village of Santa Clara de Cobre. She finds the whisked eggs produce much more volume when she uses a copper bowl instead of a glass one. In a separate bowl, lightly beat the egg yolks with a fork. Fold the yolks into the whites until well incorporated. Pat the drained nopales dry and fold them into the egg mixture.

Heat the oven to 200°F. Heat the peanut oil in a large skillet over medium-high heat until shimmering. Using a tablespoon, scoop up some of the egg mixture and carefully slide it into the hot oil. The *tortita* should be about 2 inches in diameter. Repeat to form more *tortitas,* being careful not to crowd the pan. Reduce the heat to medium and cook until browned on the bottom, about 2 minutes. If necessary, use two spatulas and press the sides of the *tortitas* inward so they do not spread out too much. Do not pat down. Using a slotted spatula, turn the *tortitas* over and cook until golden brown on the other side, 1 to 2 minutes longer. Using the slotted spatula, lift the *tortitas* out of the oil, allowing any excess oil to drip off, and drain on absorbent paper. Transfer to a baking sheet or heatproof platter and keep warm in the oven. Fry any remaining batter the same way, adding more oil if needed.

Reheat the sauce, then slip the hot *tortitas* into the sauce and let sit for several minutes. Lift out the *tortitas* with a slotted spatula and serve on warmed plates or a warmed platter. Spoon any remaining sauce on top and sprinkle with the cilantro.

POZOLE BATIDO
Beaten Pozole, Pork, and Chicken Soup

Throughout Mexico, and especially in the central region of the country, a big, hearty bowl of pozole made with softened, plump white corn kernels, also called pozole and commonly known as hominy in the United States, is the classic street- or market-stand dish to eat at night—or whenever the urge strikes you. There is the herby *pozole verde* served every Thursday in Acapulco and other parts of the state of Guerrero. In Guadalajara, it is the plain cousin, *pozole blanco*, that is featured, but enlivened by a potent dose of *salsa de chiles de árbol* (page 37), and in many parts of Michoacán and other regions, it is the already chile-laden *pozole rojo* that is favored. There is no hard-and-fast rule, but all varieties have an abundance of toppings, such as sliced radishes, chopped onions, shredded cabbage or lettuce, and *chicharrón*, to provide texture and additional taste. Recipes for these pozoles may be found in my other cookbooks.

In Michoacán, I found yet another way of preparing pozole, *pozole batido*, a longtime favorite in Morelia. The pozole in this soothing version is beaten until almost gruel-like before the toppings are added at the table. Whenever I am in Morelia during the chilly winter months, I return to Cenaduría Lupita for a bowl of this comforting dish, maybe with some *tacos de pescado* (page 64) alongside.

No matter the texture or the color of the pozole, all start with the same dried field corn that has been softened in boiling water with powdered lime (calcium hydroxide) so its tough hulls can be removed. This is the same first step in making masa, but instead of being ground, the kernels are cooked again in fresh water until soft. The pozole is then added to various hearty soups, but especially to the soup with the same name. In the United States, prepared pozole can be purchased in Mexican markets freshly made or frozen. Canned white hominy can be used as a substitute but lacks the earthy fragrance.

This is not a soup to throw together at the last minute. Making pozole takes up to eight hours from start to serving time, so it is best to start a day or so in advance and store the broth and meat separately in the refrigerator.

Given enough notice, most butchers in Mexican markets can get you the pig's head and cut it in half for you. I recommend that you try to find one, as it provides a rich consistency to the broth, although pig's feet are a good substitute.

Serves 10 to 12

▪ FOR THE POZOLE

½ small pig's head, about 2 pounds, or 2 pig's feet, halved lengthwise

1 pound fresh or thawed frozen prepared pozole or drained and rinsed canned white hominy

2 heads garlic, outer papery skin removed and halved crosswise

1 large white onion, quartered

1 pound boneless country-style pork ribs

1 tablespoon sea salt

1 small chicken, about 2 pounds, halved, or an equal amount of chicken parts

▪ FOR THE TOPPING

2 white onions, finely chopped

3 cups finely shredded cabbage or lettuce

20 red radishes, thinly sliced or chopped

⅓ cup dried oregano, preferably Mexican

½ cup ground chile de árbol or other picante chile

9 Key limes, quartered

FOR THE POZOLE: Rinse the pig's head or feet in several changes of cold water, then soak in cold water to cover for about 1 hour.

If using the prepared pozole, put it in a large pot, add the garlic, onion, and water to cover, and bring to a boil over high heat. Lower the heat to a simmer and cook for 2 hours, until the pozole is almost tender. Do not stir during this process.

Add the pig's head or feet to the pot and bring to a boil. (If using the canned hominy, which will be added later, put the pig's head or feet in a large pot of water to cover with the garlic and onion and bring to a boil.) Skim off any grey foam that rises to the surface, lower the heat, partially cover, and simmer for about an hour, until the meat can easily be cut off the bone. Remove the meat from the pot, and when cool enough to handle, cut off the skin, cut the meat into pieces, and return the meat

to the broth. Lupe, my Seattle friend who grew up in Uruapan, Michoacán, always says to save the ear. It is a delicacy to be cut up and added to the pot.

Add the pork ribs, salt, and the canned hominy, if using. Bring the broth back to a simmer and cook, uncovered, over low heat until the meat is almost falling apart, about 2 hours. Add the chicken and hot water if necessary to keep everything well submerged and cook until the chicken is very tender, about 30 minutes.

Remove the pork and chicken, onion, and garlic from the broth. Put the garlic and onion in a blender with a little of the broth and process until smooth, then return the mixture to the pot. Beat and mash the pozole and broth together with a potato masher until gruel-like. You can instead use a food processor but do not overprocess, as the coarse texture is important.

Remove and discard the skin and bones from the chicken. Shred both the pork and chicken meat, stir them back into the pot, and reheat until piping hot, about 10 minutes. Taste and add salt if needed, which is usually the case.

Dish up a large bowl of the pozole for each person. Set out bowls of all of the toppings on the table for adding to the soup.

MONDONGO TABASQUEÑO
Tabasco-Style Tripe Soup

Although *tripes à la mode de Caen* is a classic French dish, and gourmets in many countries consider tripe a special treat, it is often treated with disdain by even the most adventurous eaters in the United States, with the exception of Mexican Americans. Mexicans love to eat the tiny bits of tender tripe in a richly seasoned menudo soup, especially on a Sunday morning to diminish a hangover after partying on Saturday night. The late Merle Ellis, a longtime butcher, food columnist, and cookbook author, once told me that some historians credit tripe with having given the starving troops wintering at Valley Forge enough energy to go on and win the Revolution. The dish they ate is now known as Philadelphia pepper pot. Set aside your prejudices and try this savory tripe.

I first savored *mondongo*, the Gulf Coast version of the northern states' menudo, at a small restaurant in Mérida, Yucatán, owned by the very persuasive and quixotic Raul Lixa, one of the many Lebanese with considerable culinary and financial input in this city. In spite of my hesitation, Raul set a large bowl in front of me, sat down across from me, and looked expectantly until I took that first spoonful. What else could I do but eat it, and then I asked him to replenish my bowl.

Beef tripe, the wall from various parts of the first or second stomachs of the animal, has many descriptive Spanish names: *toalla* (towel), *libro* (book), *manzana* (apple). Any one of them can be used in this soup, but I prefer to use the more available honeycomb tripe, which comes from the wall of the second stomach and is quite tender. The honeycomb tripe that I buy at meat markets in the United States is always thoroughly washed, scraped, softened, and sometimes even partially cooked. It does, however, still require long, slow simmering to make it tender, and the dish should be started a day in advance.

When Ricardo consulted people in southern Mexico about *mondongo*, they gave him so many different recipes it was difficult to choose. Ricardo prefers this version of Spanish origin, because it is similar to the one eaten in his home in Tabasco, where it is served with an additional salsa made from the fiery tiny Tabascan *chiles amaxitos*. You can make a meal of this dish by including hot corn tortillas (page 19) and Guacamole Clásico (page 43) and washing it all down with Micheladas (page 268).

Serves 6

FOR THE TRIPE

2 pounds precleaned honeycomb beef tripe

1 tablespoon coarse sea salt

Juice of 1 small lime

6 cloves garlic

2 bay leaves

1 teaspoon dried oregano, preferably Mexican

2 teaspoons fine sea salt

FOR THE MONDONGO

1 large tomato, roughly chopped

1 white onion, roughly chopped

1 tablespoon chopped garlic

1 teaspoon oregano, preferably Mexican

1 tablespoon canola or safflower oil

2 cups drained and rinsed canned garbanzo beans

½ pound waxy white or red potatoes, peeled and cut into ¼-inch cubes

7 ounces carrots (about 3), peeled and cut into ¼-inch cubes

FOR THE TRIPE: Thoroughly rinse the tripe in cold water and put on a tray. Mix together the coarse salt and lime juice and rub on both sides of the tripe. Let sit for 30 minutes. Rinse the mixture completely off the tripe, then cut the tripe into ½-inch squares. Put the pieces into a large pot and add the garlic, bay leaves, oregano, fine salt, and water to cover by at least 2 inches. Bring to a simmer over medium heat, then lower the heat and cook, uncovered, for 1 hour. Cover and continue simmering until the tripe is very tender, 2 to 3 hours longer. Remove from the heat and let cool, then pour into a bowl or other container, cover, and refrigerate for at least 6 hours or up to overnight.

FOR THE MONDONGO: Put the tomato, onion, garlic, and oregano in a saucepan, add water to cover by ½ inch, and bring to a boil over medium-high heat. Lower the

½ cup pitted green olives

¼ cup raisins

3 tablespoons small capers, rinsed

▌FOR THE SALSA DE AMAXITO

2 teaspoons finely chopped chiles amaxitos or
chiles serranos

⅓ cup freshly squeezed lime juice

½ teaspoon sea salt

heat, cover, and simmer, stirring occasionally, until the tomato and onion are soft, about 10 minutes. Remove from the heat, let cool, then pour the tomato mixture into a blender and process until very smooth, adding some of the reserved tripe broth or water if needed to release the blades.

Heat the oil in a large *cazuela* or Dutch oven over medium-high heat until shimmering. Pour in the sauce and stir constantly with a wooden spoon as it sizzles and thickens slightly, about 10 minutes.

Using a slotted spoon, spoon the tripe from the broth into the sauce. Add the garbanzos, potatoes, carrots, olives, raisins, and capers and cook over medium-high heat, stirring occasionally, until the potatoes and carrots are fork-tender, about 10 minutes. Add some tripe broth or water if the dish seems dry.

FOR THE SALSA: Combine the chiles, lime juice, and salt in a *molcajete* and crush thoroughly, leaving some texture.

Serve the *mondongo* steaming hot in warmed deep bowls. Have the salsa nearby for anyone who wants to add some zip to the soup.

PLATOS FUERTES

Main Dishes

I n Mexico, families and friends traditionally gather around tables in the midafternoon, either at home or at their favorite restaurant, to socialize while they eat *comida*, the most substantial meal of the day. Following various lighter courses, the heart of the meal appears, often some type of meat, poultry, or seafood enveloped in a lush savory sauce—the most important element of the dish. The exceptions are dishes that are roasted, grilled, sautéed, or, like *fiambre* (page 155), an arrangement of pickled meats and vegetables. They may be as simple as an ample cluster of *camarones al mojo de ajo* (page 176), or one of the more regional preparations served for festive occasions, such as a dark and fruity *mole de Xico* (page 183), *adobo de puerco huasteco* (page 143), or *chiles poblanos* transformed into the celebratory *chiles en nogada* (page 200). These classic dishes are the center of Mexico's gastronomical traditions.

POULTRY

ALBÓNDIGAS DE PAVO EN SALSA DE CHIPOTLE
Spicy Turkey Meatballs in Chipotle Sauce

Years ago, Aurora Cabrera Dawson, an excellent cook from Oaxaca, gave me this simple and tasty recipe for meatballs using ground turkey or chicken instead of beef or pork. It is a favorite of her family for a light meal, alongside boiled new potatoes matching the size of the *albóndigas*. I like to have a crunchy salad such as Ensalada de Piña con Lechugas (page 234) for a contrasting flavor and texture.

Makes about 30 meatballs; serves 6 to 8

FOR THE SAUCE
- 1 pound tomatillos (about 9 or 10), husks removed and well rinsed
- 1 cup chicken broth (page 25), plus more if needed
- 2 cloves garlic, roughly chopped
- 1 chile chipotle en adobo, with a little sauce, roughly chopped
- ½ teaspoon sea salt
- 1 tablespoon olive, canola, or safflower oil

FOR THE MEATBALLS
- 1½ pounds ground turkey or chicken
- 1 egg, lightly beaten
- 2 tablespoons fresh bread crumbs or raw medium-grain white rice
- 1 tablespoon minced fresh mint (about 3 sprigs)

FOR THE SAUCE: Put the tomatillos in a saucepan with water to cover and bring to a simmer over medium heat. Cook until fork-tender, 10 to 15 minutes. Drain, transfer to a blender, add the broth, garlic, chile, and salt, and blend until smooth. Taste and add more chile or salt if needed.

Heat the oil in a large *cazuela* or Dutch oven over medium-high heat until sizzling hot. Pour in the tomatillo mixture and cook, stirring occasionally as it bubbles and spews, for 5 minutes. Lower the heat and simmer until the sauce begins to thicken and change color, about 5 minutes longer. Remove from the heat and set aside. (The sauce can be made up to 4 days in advance. Let cool, cover, and refrigerate, then reheat just before needed.)

½ chile chipotle en adobo, finely chopped

1 teaspoon sea salt

½ teaspoon freshly ground black pepper

FOR THE MEATBALLS: Put the turkey in a bowl and mix in the egg, bread crumbs, mint, chile, salt, and pepper. You can start with a fork but hands are always the best tools to use.

Return the sauce to the stove top over medium heat and bring to a slow boil. Scoop up a nugget of the turkey mixture, roll between your palms into a 1½-inch ball, and carefully place in the hot sauce. Repeat until all of the turkey mixture has been shaped into balls and the balls are submerged in the sauce. You may need to add more broth or water to submerge the balls. Cover the pot, reduce the heat to low, and simmer the meatballs, stirring often to ensure they cook evenly, until cooked through, about 20 minutes.

Serve the meatballs in warmed deep plates with plenty of sauce.

ALMENDRADO HUASTECO
Chicken in Silky Almond Sauce

Not the usual inconsequential chicken dish at all, but one so prized that in the small Huastec village of Zozocolco de Hidalgo in Veracruz, it is reserved for baptisms or other special occasions. The sauce is so important that it is scooped up with hot corn tortillas and eaten after the meat is finished. Local cook Guadalupe Gómez Alonso makes this dish from meat of native deer when it is available, and Ricardo especially likes to prepare it with venison loin.

Ceviche de Dzilam de Bravo (page 53) would be a welcome starter, with Arroz Blanco (page 223) and hot corn tortillas (page 19) served alongside the chicken and perhaps Budín de Frutas (page 256) for dessert.

Serves 4 to 6

FOR THE CHICKEN

6 large chicken thighs, 2½ to 3 pounds

½ white onion

2 large cloves garlic, halved

2 teaspoons sea salt

FOR THE CHICKEN: Put the chicken in a pot and add the onion, garlic, sea salt, and water to cover. Bring to a boil over medium-high heat, skimming off any foam that rises to the surface. Lower the heat to a gentle simmer and cook until

FOR THE SAUCE

6 large chiles guajillos (about 1½ ounces), stems, seeds, and membranes removed, then toasted (page 18)

4 large chiles anchos (about 1½ ounces), stems, seeds, and membranes removed, then toasted (page 18)

4 chiles pasillas (about 1½ ounces), stems, seeds, and membranes removed, then toasted (page 18)

½ white onion, roasted (page 18)

3 large cloves garlic, roasted (page 18), then peeled

5 black peppercorns, toasted (page 19) and ground

5 whole allspice, toasted (page 19) and ground

¼ cup freshly rendered pork lard (page 24) or canola or safflower oil

¾ cup blanched almonds, toasted and chopped

Sea salt

FOR THE GARNISH

6 blanched almonds, toasted and slivered

Small sprigs fresh flat-leaf parsley

no pinkish flesh is found near the bone when a thigh is cut into with a sharp knife, about 30 minutes. Remove from the heat. Remove the chicken pieces from the broth and set aside. Strain the broth through a fine-mesh sieve and reserve.

FOR THE SAUCE: Tear the chiles into smaller pieces and place in a bowl. Add 5 cups hot water and let soak until soft, about 30 minutes. Drain the chiles, reserving the water. Put the chiles, onion, garlic, peppercorns, and allspice in a blender and process until a smooth sauce forms, adding some of the reserved water as needed to release the blades.

Heat the lard in a large *cazuela* or Dutch oven over medium-high heat until sizzling hot. Add the chile mixture and fry, stirring constantly with a wooden spoon, until the color darkens, about 2 minutes. Lower the heat and continue to cook, stirring often, until thickened, about 10 minutes longer.

Meanwhile, put the chopped almonds and 3 cups of the reserved broth in the blender and process until a very smooth sauce forms. When the chile mixture is ready, slowly stir in the almond sauce, then taste and add salt if needed. Add the chicken pieces and simmer until everything is pleasantly hot.

Transfer the chicken pieces to a warmed platter and cloak with an abundance of the sauce. Garnish with the almond slivers and parsley sprigs.

Every day throughout the Yucatán Peninsula, Mayan women bring their *nixtamal* to the local *molino* to be ground into masa for tortillas, tamales, or various *antojitos*. The *nixtamal* is made by soaking dried corn kernels in boiling water with powdered lime (calcium hydroxide) until soft and then rubbing off the remaining skins.

Seafood is a major source of nutrition for the Costeños, African Mexicans living in isolated settlements near the northern Oaxacan coast. Casting nets is the traditional way of catching the abundant fish in the nearby lagoons.

Antonieta Avila Salinas often prepares this *barbacoa de pescado* (page 167) with the small red snappers caught by the men in her family. Freshly made tortillas are kept warm in a *jícara,* a container made from a dried bottle gourd.

Spain's traditional churros (page 263) are paired with Mexico's chocolate (page 280) for the perfect light evening snack. The disks of ground cacao, sugar, cinnamon, and sometimes almonds are dissolved in simmering water or milk, and then a carved wooden *molinillo* is vigorously whirled to create a layer of foam.

A group of young people gather in Mexico City for a fun-filled evening of *antojitos*, guacamole, and *cervezas*.

Abigail Mendoza, a Zapotec woman in Teotitlán del Valle, Oaxaca, grinds *nixtamal* in the traditional manner on her volcanic-stone *metate*, using a heavy, cylindrical *mano*. She is making the masa for her family's daily *tlayudas*, the enormous regional tortillas.

Arroz a la tumbada (page 164) combines well-seasoned rice with a medley of the plentiful seafood found in the waters off the coast of Veracruz. This popular dish reflects the influence of both the Spaniards and their African slaves.

Small glass barrels of *aguas frescas* are a common sight throughout Mexico. This vendor has a variety of the thirst-quenching drinks, including the coffee brown *agua fresca de tamarindo* (page 273), the milky white *horchata* (page 275), and the crimson *agua fresca de jamaica* (page 272), made from the sepals of a variety of hibiscus.

Drinking the "water" directly from the coconut is a refreshing treat for this young woman, who lives on the hot and humid coast of northern Oaxaca.

The dish shown above, *chiles en nogada* (page 200), adorned with the red, white, and green of the Mexican flag, was first made by the Augustine nuns of Puebla for a visit by Mexico's then emperor Don Augustín de Iturbide, who, following the War of Independence, remained in power for less than a year. It is usually served around Independence Day, September 16, when pomegranates and fresh walnuts can be found in the markets.

Cemita (page 73) is the name for both these sesame seed–topped rolls and these famous *tortas* of Puebla, which are found only in the local markets. The *tortas* are offered with a choice of fillings, the most popular of which is beef *milanesa* smothered with *quesillo de Oaxaca*, onions, avocados, *chiles chipotles*, and *pápalo,* a pungent herb that is definitely an acquired taste.

The earthy *frijoles de la olla* (page 214), can be revolutionized into *frijoles charros* (page 220), the cowboy beans of Jalisco. The added flavors and colors of chiles, bacon, tomato, and cilantro make *frijoles charros* as brash and brazen as the elaborately costumed horsemen who perform every Sunday at a local rodeo, or *charreada*.

In a market *fonda*, a cook deftly lays tortillas on a clay *comal* before flipping them over to finish cooking.

A local *palenquero* (small *mezcal* producer) in Matátlan, Oaxaca, checks the fermenting roasted agave mash before distilling it in his copper still.

Throughout central Mexico, nopales (cactus paddles) and their fruit, which may be the tart *xoconoxtle* or the sweeter *tuna*, depending on the species of the cactus, are common ingredients in many dishes.

In Tabasco, the freshwater *pejelagarto*, a type of gar, is an important part of the regional cuisine. It is sold in local markets with a wooden stick running through it to make transporting and grilling it easier.

ASADO DE POLLO EN ESCABECHE
Braised Marinated Chicken with Sherry

Mónica Maestretta, who is from a family with a long history in the large colonial city of Puebla, came on one of my first culinary trips and we quickly became good friends, spending many hours together in each other's homes and kitchens.

Mónica's family arrived in Mexico from countries in Europe other than Spain. Recounting her family history may seem superfluous, but I think it gives a better understanding of the culture and cuisine that is now Mexican. Carlos, Mónica's grandfather and an engineer, came from Milan to Querétaro to supervise the building of bridges and dams. After he married, Carlos moved to Puebla and Mónica's father, Marco, was the first of his seven children. When Marco was seventeen, he also went to Milan, but because of unrest there, returned to Mexico and later married Mónica's mother, Sara Cobel, whose family was from Budapest.

Sara's grandfather, Segismund Kobelishek (changed by custom officials to Edmundo Cobel), came to Mexico in 1854 and served in the army under Maximilian. After Maximilian was executed, Segismund remained in Mexico and settled in Puebla, married, and had five children. One of his boys married María Zamora, who so loved to cook that she handwrote many of her recipes into a book. The youngest of her four daughters, Sara (Mónica's mother), was sixteen when María died, and since she was also passionate about cooking, the other sisters gave this cookbook to Mónica's mother. Now, Italy comes back into the scenario, as Sara married a handsome man with blue eyes "like a prince," who arrived from Italy. Even with six children, she always cooked elegant meals for him, especially when they had guests. To spoil her husband, she often made dishes of the family's heritage, but also Spanish and French food, which was the custom at the time. From a young age, Mónica helped her mother cook, and the following recipe for braised marinated chicken comes from grandmother María's recipe book.

Serve with Arroz Blanco (page 223) or boiled small potatoes. Ensalada de Habas Verdes Descalzas (page 238) is a pleasant accompaniment.

Serves 4 . . . .

- ¼ cup olive oil

- 5 or 6 large chicken thighs, about 2½ pounds

- ½ cup Spanish dry (fino) sherry

- ¼ cup mild white vinegar such as vinagre de piña or diluted unseasoned rice vinegar (page 50)

- 6 cloves garlic, quartered

- ½ white onion, halved and cut into ½-inch-thick slices

- 4 carrots, peeled, quartered lengthwise, and cut crosswise into 1½-inch-long strips

- 4 black peppercorns

- 2 chiles de árbol

- ½ teaspoon dried oregano, preferably Mexican

- ½ teaspoon dried thyme

- ½ teaspoon sea salt

- 1 cup pitted small green olives

Heat the oil in a large *cazuela* or Dutch oven with a tight-fitting lid over medium heat until shimmering. Add the chicken and cook, turning as needed, until golden brown on all sides, 5 to 10 minutes. Pour off any excess oil from the pot. Add ½ cup warm water, sherry, vinegar, garlic, onion, carrots, peppercorns, chiles, oregano, thyme, and salt, cover tightly, lower the heat until the liquid barely simmers, and cook, shaking the pot occasionally so the chicken does not stick to the bottom, until the chicken is tender, about 45 minutes. Just before the chicken is ready, stir in the olives.

Scoop out the chicken and vegetables onto a warmed platter and serve.

PATO A LA BASURA
"Garbage-Style" Duck

Gloria Mejía Coronado, who shared this recipe with me, was one of three girls in a family of five children who early on helped with the large parties held for distinguished guests at the family home on Lake Pátzcuaro, in Michoacán. At the time, there were no roads on their side of the lake, so canoes and horses were the only means of transportation. They grew all their own produce and raised poultry, pigs, and cows. Some of the beef was salted to make *cecina*, cut into strips, and dried in their large pantry. Gloria's mother, Marina, created this dish with its preposterously concocted name using the wintering migrating ducks from Canada and the United States. It was always a favorite and has won several regional cooking awards in recent times.

Today, the nearby hillsides are still pincushioned with various species of opuntia cactus, just as they were when Gloria was growing up. One species produces sour, egg-shaped edible fruits known as *xoconoxtles*, which are used in this dish. They add an appealing acidic flavor that contrasts nicely with the duck. Unfortunately, there is no adequate substitute.

Since household ovens were not available in Mexico until relatively recently, chicken and other fowl were usually simmered in large *cazuelas,* as this duck is here. Gloria's father was of Spanish descent, so olive oil was the choice for frying most ingredients.

Use two to three wild ducks; the number depends on whether they are a larger type, such as a mallard or wigeon, or smaller, such as a teal. If using a farm-raised bird, use one Long Island or Muscovy duck. Remove the skin from the ducks, whether wild or domestic, and cut into serving-size pieces with poultry shears, reserving the back and neck for enriching the broth. Long experience has taught me that it is best to presoak wild ducks for at least 2 hours in very salty water to cover with a little baking soda added to take out that very gamy taste of older birds. Drain, rinse repeatedly, and pat dry. If using a domestic bird, you may have to special order it from your butcher.

Sopa de Hongos (page 79) would be a tasty introduction to this dish. Round out the menu with Arroz a la Mexicana (page 224), a good bottle of a Spanish light red wine, and Flan con Licor de Café y Ron (page 259).

Serves 4 . . . .

▌ FOR THE DUCK

2 tablespoons olive oil

4 to 5 pounds duck pieces (legs, breasts), skinned

½ white onion

1 clove garlic

1 teaspoon sea salt

▌ FOR THE BASURA SAUCE

1 tablespoon olive oil

2 spring onions or 6 large green onions, white part only, sliced

2 xoconoxtles (page 211), peeled, seeded, and sliced

1 cup dry white wine such as a Spanish Rioja

1 cup chicken broth (page 25)

2 sprigs fresh thyme, or 1 teaspoon dried thyme

2 sprigs fresh marjoram, or ½ teaspoon dried marjoram

FOR THE DUCK: Heat the oil in a *cazuela* or Dutch oven over medium-high heat until shimmering. Add the duck pieces and cook, turning as needed, until browned on all sides. (If you have the backs and necks of the birds, brown them as well, then discard them when you strain the broth.) Add the white onion and garlic, sprinkle with the salt, and add water to cover by 1 inch. Bring to a boil, lower the heat, cover, and simmer for 15 minutes. Remove the breast pieces and set aside. Continue to cook the legs and thighs for another 15 minutes, then add them to the breast pieces. Pour the broth through a fine-mesh sieve into a bowl, skim off any fat, and set aside.

FOR THE SAUCE: Wipe out the *cazuela,* return it to the stove top over medium-high heat, and add the oil. When the oil

2 bay leaves

½ teaspoon ground allspice, preferably freshly ground

½ teaspoon sea salt

Freshly ground black pepper

▮ FOR THE GARNISH

½ cup green olives

4 whole chiles güeros en escabeche or any pickled light-skinned chiles

is hot, add the spring onions and sauté until softened, about 3 minutes. Add the *xoconoxtles* and cook briefly.

Return the duck to the *cazuela* and pour in the wine, chicken broth, and defatted duck broth. Add the thyme, marjoram, bay leaves, allspice, salt, and several grinds of pepper and stir well. Bring back to a boil, lower the heat to medium-low, and simmer until the liquid is reduced and the duck is tender, about 20 minutes. The domestic duck may take longer. Using a slotted spoon, transfer the duck and *xoconoxtles* to a warmed platter and keep warm.

Skim off as much fat as possible from the broth and strain through a medium-mesh sieve. Return the broth to the *cazuela,* raise the heat to high, and boil until the sauce reduces by one-third. Taste and adjust the seasoning with salt if needed.

Spoon the sauce over the duck and *xoconoxtles,* garnish with the olives and chiles, and serve.

MEAT

. . . .

CONEJO EN ADOBO
Rabbit in Savory Red Chile Sauce

Ricardo learned to make this robust rabbit dish more than twenty-five years ago from a cook in Hidalgo, and together we have enjoyed similar rabbit dishes at numerous roadside eateries in central Mexico.

Order fresh rabbit from any good butcher, or look for frozen rabbit in a well-stocked grocery store. The front legs have little meat on them but should be included in the broth and then discarded before serving. If the rabbit is fresh, the giblets are usually included and can be cooked separately just as you would chicken livers or heart. My husband likes me to fry them with onions and add them to scrambled eggs, with a salsa of course.

I often serve a first course of Ensalada Clásica de Nopales (page 235), then I accompany the rabbit with Arroz Blanco (page 223) and end the meal with Capirotada de Leche (page 254).

Serves 4 . . . .

FOR THE RABBIT

- 1 rabbit, about 3 pounds, cut into 8 pieces
- 1 head garlic, halved crosswise and outer papery skin removed
- 1 small white onion, quartered
- 4 bay leaves
- 1 teaspoon dried oregano, preferably Mexican
- 2 teaspoons sea salt
- ⅓ cup canola or safflower oil

FOR THE RABBIT: Put the rabbit into a large pot, add 2 quarts water, and bring to a boil over medium-high heat, skimming off any foam that rises to the surface. Add the garlic, onion, bay leaves, oregano, and salt, lower the heat to medium, and cook at a very slow boil until the rabbit is tender and cooked through, 20 to 30 minutes. Using a slotted spoon, transfer the rabbit pieces to a platter and pat dry with absorbent paper. Strain the broth through a fine-mesh sieve and reserve.

FOR THE ADOBO

6 chiles moritas, stems, seeds, and membranes removed, then toasted (page 18),
or 2 chiles chipotles en adobo

6 chiles anchos, stems, seeds, and membranes
removed, then toasted (page 18)

6 chiles guajillos, stems, seeds, and membranes removed, then toasted (page 18)

2 pounds ripe tomatoes (about 6 medium),
roasted and peeled (page 18), or
1 (28-ounce) can diced fire-roasted
tomatoes, drained

½ teaspoon cumin seeds, lightly toasted
(page 19), and ground

2 teaspoons sea salt

1 teaspoon black peppercorns, lightly toasted
(page 19) and ground

FOR THE GARNISH

2 slices white onion, smaller center rings only

1 ripe Hass avocado, halved, pitted, peeled,
and diced

Heat the oil in a *cazuela* or heavy skillet over medium-high heat until shimmering. Add the rabbit pieces and fry, turning once, until lightly browned on both sides, 3 to 5 minutes on each side. Using tongs, transfer to absorbent paper to drain. Leave the oil in the *cazuela* and set aside.

FOR THE ADOBO: Tear the chiles into smaller pieces, put in a bowl, add 4 cups of the hot broth, and let soak until soft, about 30 minutes. Drain the chiles, reserving the broth. Put the chiles, tomatoes, cumin, salt, and pepper in a blender and process until a smooth sauce forms, adding the reserved broth as needed (about ¼ cup) to release the blades.

Reheat the oil in the *cazuela* over medium heat until shimmering. Carefully pour the adobo into the oil (it may splatter) and fry, stirring frequently, until it begins to thicken, about 5 minutes. Put the rabbit pieces back in the pan to reheat, adding more broth if needed to cover the meat. The sauce should be quite thick and have a silky texture. Lower the heat and simmer, stirring occasionally, for 10 minutes. (This dish can be made up to 4 days in advance, covered, and refrigerated, then reheated over low heat before serving.)

Spoon the rabbit and sauce into a warmed deep platter or individual plates. Garnish with the onion slices and avocado.

PIERNA DE CERDO AL HORNO
Roasted Pork Leg

When I am with my friend Mónica Maestretta, who now lives in Cholula adjacent to the city of Puebla, our conversations invariably turn to food: What was the best or worse meal we have had recently? How do we prepare a specific dish? Where and what do we want to eat? What recipes do we traditionally make for special occasions? One of Mónica's answers to the last question is this recipe for roasted pork leg from her *abuelita* María's hand-written cookbook.

Fresh ham or pork leg may be difficult to find, but it is well worth the search, as this roasted leg is a great meal to serve a large gathering. Estimate one pound per person. Special order half of a small fresh ham from your butcher.

Arroz a la Mexicana (page 224) and Calabaza con Elote (page 229) are both good companions to the pork, along with a light red Spanish wine. Ante de Coco Marquesote (page 258) would provide a fitting end to the meal.

Serves 6 to 8 . . . .

2 chiles anchos, seeded

⅔ cup chopped white onion

10 cloves garlic, sliced

1 tablespoon freshly ground black pepper

1 teaspoon dried oregano, preferably Mexican

1 cup dry white wine

3 tablespoons freshly rendered pork lard (page 24) or canola or safflower oil

1 tablespoon sea salt

½ bone-in, skin-on pork leg (fresh picnic ham), about 6 pounds

Soak the chiles in a bowl in very hot water to cover until soft, about 30 minutes. Remove the chiles from the water, reserving the water, and tear into smaller pieces. Put the chiles, onion, garlic, pepper, oregano, and wine in a blender and process until a smooth paste forms, adding some of the reserved soaking water if needed to release the blades.

Heat the lard in a *cazuela*, Dutch oven, or skillet over medium-high heat until shimmering. Pour in the chile mixture and stir constantly with a wooden spoon until it darkens in color, gives off an enticing aroma, and becomes quite thick, about 5 minutes. Remove from the heat and let cool.

Using a sharp knife, score the skin of the pork in a diamond pattern (the diamonds should be about 1 inch across), cutting through the underlying layer of fat. With your fingers, rub the chile paste over all sides of the pork, making sure that it penetrates into the incisions. Put the pork in a large container and cover tightly, or in a large resealable plastic bag and seal closed. Marinate in the refrigerator for at least 8 hours or up to 10 hours. If too large for your refrigerator, put it in an ice chest.

To roast the meat, heat the oven to 400°F. Lightly salt the pork, and place it on a rack in a rather deep roasting pan. Insert a meat thermometer, if you have one, in the thickest part of the leg, making certain that it does not touch bone. (If you have only an instant-read thermometer, you will need to remove the leg from the oven to test for doneness.) Add ½ cup warm water to the pan, encase the leg snugly with aluminum foil, and put in the oven. After 30 minutes, reduce the heat to 325°F and continue to roast, basting every 20 to 30 minutes, until the skin is a crusty, deep ruddy brown and the temperature registers 180°F, 2½ to 3 hours. If the drippings start to burn during roasting, add a little more water to the pan.

Remove the pork from the oven and let rest for at least 30 minutes (it will continue cooking while it is resting). Cut off the crusty rind and break it into small pieces or cut into squares for snacking. Starting at the small end, with the knife perpendicular to the bone, thinly slice the meat, then make one long slice to separate the meat from the length of the bone. Arrange the slices on a platter, along with the crunchy skin, and serve.

PUERCO ENCACAHUATADO ESTILO XALAPA
Pork in a Xalapa-Style Peanut Sauce

Ricardo can still remember the first time he tasted this dish. It was at a friend's fifteenth birthday party in Xalapa, Veracruz, and he was immediately won over by the decadently rich peanut sauce lavishly cloaking chunks of tender pork. Both the pork and the sauce can be prepared in advance and refrigerated.

Accompany with scoops of Arroz Blanco (page 223) and hot corn tortillas (page 19) for mopping up the sauce. Traditionally, small individuals bowls of Frijoles de la Olla (page 214) made with black beans would be on the table.

Serves 6 to 8 · · · · · · · · · · · · · · · · ·

FOR THE MEAT
2 teaspoons sea salt

½ white onion, halved

4 cloves garlic, halved

3 pounds boneless pork shoulder, trimmed of fat and cut into 1½-inch pieces

FOR THE SAUCE
1 large chile guajillo, stem, seeds, and membranes removed, then toasted (page 18)

1 chile chipotle en adobo

FOR THE MEAT: Pour 2 quarts water into a large saucepan, add the salt, onion, and garlic, and bring to a boil. Add the pork, bring back to a boil, and skim off any foam that rises to the surface. Lower the heat to a gentle simmer, cover partially, and cook until the meat is fork-tender, about 1 hour. Drain the meat, reserving the meat and broth separately.

FOR THE SAUCE: Tear the chile guajillo into smaller pieces, put in a small bowl,

2 medium, ripe tomatoes, roasted and peeled (page 18), then roughly chopped, or 1 (14½-ounce) can fire-roasted tomatoes, drained and roughly chopped

¼ cup roughly chopped white onion

3 large cloves garlic, halved

1½ cups skinned raw peanuts, toasted

1¼-inch stick Mexican true cinnamon bark (page 19), toasted

10 black peppercorns, toasted (page 19)

4 whole allspice, toasted (page 19)

2 whole cloves, toasted (page 19)

¼ cup canola or safflower oil

½ teaspoon sea salt

▌FOR THE GARNISH

2 tablespoons skinned raw peanuts, toasted and chopped

add 1 cup very hot water, and let soak until soft, about 15 minutes. Transfer the chile and soaking water to a blender, add the chile chipotle, and process until a smooth sauce forms. Pour into a small bowl and set aside.

Add the tomatoes, onion, garlic, peanuts, cinnamon, peppercorns, allspice, cloves, and 3 cups of the reserved broth to the blender and process until a smooth sauce forms. If you do not have a heavy-duty blender, you will need to grind the nuts and spices in a spice grinder or coffee grinder before you add them to the blender.

Heat the oil in a large *cazuela*, heavy skillet, or Dutch oven over medium-high heat until barely shimmering. Pour in the chile mixture and fry, stirring frequently, until it darkens in color and thickens, about 5 minutes. Stir in the tomato mixture and salt, reduce the heat to low, and simmer, stirring occasionally, for 10 minutes to blend the flavors. Taste and add more salt if needed. Stir in the pork and allow to heat through, about 5 minutes.

Spoon the meat with plenty of sauce onto a warmed platter, always remembering that the sauce is the most important element of the dish. Sprinkle on the chopped peanuts and serve.

ADOBO DE PUERCO HUASTECO
Pork Loin in a Savory Red Chile Sauce

The recipe for this special pork dish comes from Guadalupe Gómez Alonso. It is a traditional wedding dish in her small village in the undulating foothills of the Sierra Madre Oriental, halfway between the bustling port of Veracruz and the oil-rich city of Poza Rica, and it involves all of the senses: the sounds, sights, and smells of the preparation and then the wonderful taste at the table. This celebratory dish is always accompanied with

Arroz Blanco (page 223) and hot corn tortillas (page 19). Although not typical, Escabeche de Verduras (page 236) and fresh fruit are two complementary additions to the menu, and I like to pour a California Syrah.

All of the spices can be toasted at the same time; just be careful that they do not scorch. You need a powerful blender to blend everything well. If your blender isn't strong enough, prepare the *adobo* in two batches.

Serves 4 to 6

FOR THE MEAT
3 pounds boneless blade end of pork loin or country-style pork ribs, excess fat trimmed and cut into 1½- to 2-inch pieces

½ white onion

2 cloves garlic, halved

2 teaspoons sea salt

FOR THE ADOBO
12 large chiles guajillos, stems, seeds, and membranes removed, then toasted (page 19)

3 large chiles anchos, stems, seeds, and membranes removed, then toasted (page 19)

¾ pound plum tomatoes (3 large or 6 medium), roasted and peeled (page 18), then roughly chopped

½ white onion, roasted (page 18) and roughly chopped

6 large cloves garlic, roasted (page 18), then peeled

1 bolillo (French bread roll), sliced, lightly fried, and broken into small pieces (about 1 cup)

2-inch stick Mexican true cinnamon bark (page 19), toasted

8 whole allspice, toasted (page 19)

6 whole cloves, toasted (page 19)

1 teaspoon cumin seeds, toasted (page 19)

FOR THE MEAT: Pour 2 quarts water into a large pot, Dutch oven, or *cazuela,* add the pork, onion, garlic, and salt, and bring to a boil over medium-high heat, skimming off any foam that rises to the surface. Reduce the heat to a simmer, cover partially, and cook until the meat is tender, 30 to 45 minutes. Drain the meat, reserving the meat and broth separately.

FOR THE ADOBO: Tear the chiles into smaller pieces, put in a bowl, add 3 cups of the hot reserved broth, and let soak until soft, about 20 minutes.

Transfer the chiles and broth to a blender and add 1 more cup broth, the tomatoes, onion, garlic, bread, cinnamon, allspice, cloves, cumin, peppercorns, oregano, and sugar and blend into a smooth, thick sauce.

Heat the lard in a *cazuela* or deep skillet over medium-high heat until it ripples. Pour in the sauce, lower the heat, and cook, stirring often, for 15 minutes. It will become quite thick and rich looking and it may bubble and spew.

Lower the heat to the lowest setting and add the reserved pork and the salt. Rinse

6 black peppercorns, toasted (page 19)

1 teaspoon dried oregano, preferably Mexican

1 tablespoon sugar

½ cup freshly rendered pork lard (page 24) or canola or safflower oil

1 teaspoon sea salt

the blender jar with 2 cups of the reserved broth to capture any clinging chile sauce and add to the *cazuela*. Simmer for 30 minutes to blend the flavors. Taste and add more salt if needed.

For this joyous occasion, Guadalupe would serve everyone an abundance of both meat and sauce.

CHORIZO
Mexican Red Sausage

The craving for chorizo is just as evident in its adopted home of Mexico as it is in its original home of Spain, and in both countries the cuisine would be unimaginable without the sausage. The main difference between the two is the use of the more potent chile in the Mexican chorizo and the milder dried pimiento in the Spanish sausage.

Over the years, I have spent time in and around Toluca, the capital of the state of Mexico, where a conclave of Spanish settlers introduced pigs into this high valley. The Spanish historian Carlo Cereya suggests that "although the horse was of real significance in the conquest, the hog was of greater importance and contributed to a degree that defies exaggeration." Here, the Spaniards began making their beloved sausage, soon adapting it to local culture by adding chile. One of the main features of the huge, rambling Friday Mercado Juárez (now moved from its longtime site) is stalls cascading with ropes of both red and herb green chorizos, the latter a more recent version. Some of the *chorizos verdes* glisten with an almost-brilliant green artificial coloring and are to be shunned.

This recipe for traditional red chorizo is an adaptation of a recipe used by one of the leading sausage makers in Toluca, second-generation Jorge Figueroa, who makes it in voluminous quantities to sell to the throngs of waiting customers at his family shop, Carnicería La Figueroa. Ricardo and I use chorizo in a wide variety of dishes, from Frijoles Puercos con Chorizo (page 105) to Tinga de Cerdo (page 147).

Athough chorizo is usually stuffed into pork casings, it is a lot less work to make it in bulk and freeze what is not needed right away. I have provided directions for both links and bulk here. If you opt for links, you will probably need to special order the casings (salted, well-cleaned small pig intestines) from a butcher. Do not be deterred and use synthetic casings, as they are not satisfactory.

FOR THE CHORIZO

¼ pound chiles guajillos (about 14), stems, seeds, and membranes removed

¾ cup mild vinegar such as vinagre de piña or diluted unseasoned rice vinegar (page 50), or more if needed

2 pounds coarsely ground pork shoulder

½ pound medium-ground pork fat

4 large cloves garlic, minced

1 tablespoon dried oregano, preferably Mexican

2 teaspoons sea salt

½ teaspoon freshly ground black pepper

¼ teaspoon dried thyme

⅛ teaspoon ground allspice

⅛ teaspoon ground cloves

Large splash of tequila blanco (optional)

FOR THE LINKS

4 to 5 feet small hog casings

¼ cup mild vinegar such as vinagre de piña or diluted unseasoned rice vinegar (page 50)

FOR THE CHORIZO: Soak the chiles in a bowl in very hot water to cover until soft, about 15 minutes. Drain the chiles, tear into smaller pieces, and return to the bowl. Add the vinegar and marinate for 45 minutes, stirring from time to time. Transfer the chiles and vinegar to a blender and process until smooth, adding a bit more vinegar only if needed to release the blades.

Put the pork, pork fat, and garlic in a large bowl and toss until crumbled and well mixed. Add the pureed chiles, oregano, salt, pepper, thyme, allspice, cloves, and perhaps the tequila. Thoroughly squish together all of the ingredients with your hands. Fry a spoonful in a small skillet until thoroughly cooked, taste, and add more salt if needed. Cover the bowl tightly and cure in the refrigerator for at least 1 day and preferably for 3 days, occasionally turning the mixture so the flavors are well blended. At this point, the chorizo can be divided into smaller batches, some to be used immediately in various dishes and others that can be frozen for up to 3 months. If you want, this is also the time to stuff some or all of the meat mixture into casings.

FOR THE LINKS: If you are making links with only some of the chorizo, you will not need all of the casings. Rinse the casings in cool water to remove the salt, then soak them in water to cover mixed with the vinegar for 30 minutes. As you remove the casings from the water, cut in half. Squeeze closed one end of a length and fill the opposite end with water to make sure there are no leaks. If there is a puncture, cut the casing on both sides of the puncture, tie a double knot at one end of each length, and press any water out the other end.

Here now is the real challenge, and the fun: stuffing the filling into the casings. It can be done with just a funnel and any round, flat-ended piece of wood that fits into the opening. But, as always, fingers are the best.

Carefully smooth the open end of the casing over the funnel, pushing it as far up as it will easily go. Before adding the meat mixture, hold the funnel upright and press the casing to remove any excess air. Now, stuff some of the chorizo into the funnel, pushing as much of it as you can down into the casing and adding enough to make a firm package but leaving a little empty space at the end to make another double knot. Twist and tie every 3½ to 4 inches with burlap-type string or narrow strips of dried corn husk. Diana Kennedy, from whom I have learned so much, always waits until she has filled the whole casing and then ties it off to make sure that all of the space is filled.

Hang the links to dry at room temperature for 3 days, then cover and refrigerate and continue to dry for several more days. The links will keep for several weeks in the refrigerator or they can be frozen for a few months.

TINGA DE CERDO
Chipotle-Seasoned Shredded Pork

Puebla is home to some of Mexico's most classic dishes, including *mole poblano, chiles en nogada,* and this simpler but singularly tasty *tinga,* with its complex layers of savory flavors. Ana Elena Martínez, a pastry chef and caterer, as well as my assistant in Mexico, uses it as a main course with *arroz blanco* (page 223) or as a filling or topping for the countless *antojitos* that she makes for her clients. This recipe can be easily doubled or tripled and can be made up to 1 day in advance. Any leftovers can be reheated and used as a topping for tostadas (page 21) or a filling for quesadillas (page 58). Serve with hot corn tortillas (page 19), preferably freshly made, for making tacos, or spoon over Arroz Blanco (page 223).

Serves 4 to 6 with leftovers

⫶ FOR THE PORK

½ teaspoon sea salt

1 pound boneless pork shoulder, trimmed of excess fat and cut into 1-inch pieces

½ white onion, thickly sliced

2 cloves garlic

1 bay leaf

FOR THE PORK: Pour 5 cups water into a saucepan, add the salt, and bring to a boil over high heat. Add the pork, onion, and garlic and return the water to a boil, skimming off any foam that rises to the surface. If the meat is not fully submerged, add more water as needed. Lower the heat to medium-low, add the bay leaf,

FOR THE TINGA

1 tablespoon canola or safflower oil

½ cup chopped white onion

¼ pound chorizo, homemade (page 145) or store-bought, removed from its casing and cut into ¼-inch cubes or crumbled

1 clove garlic, minced

1 pound ripe tomatoes (about 3 mdium), roasted and peeled (page 18), or 1 (14½-ounce) can diced fire-roasted tomatoes, drained

2 chiles chipotles en adobo, chopped, with 2 tablespoons sauce

1 bay leaf

¼ teaspoon dried thyme

¼ teaspoon dried oregano, preferably Mexican

1½ teaspoons sea salt

¼ teaspoon freshly ground black pepper

1 tablespoon tomato paste, if needed

½ teaspoon light or dark brown sugar

¼ teaspoon granulated sugar

FOR THE GARNISH

1 firm but ripe Hass avocado, halved, pitted, peeled, and sliced

and simmer, uncovered, until the pork is tender, about 1 hour.

Remove from the heat, let cool slightly, then scoop the pork into a bowl and set aside. Strain the broth through a fine-mesh sieve and set aside. If cooking the pork in advance, pour 2 cups of the broth over the meat so that it does not dry out, then cover and refrigerate until needed.

FOR THE TINGA: Heat the oil in a *cazuela* or large skillet over medium heat. Add the onion and fry, stirring occasionally, until translucent, about 5 minutes. Add the chorizo and continue to fry, stirring frequently, until well browned, about 10 minutes. Spoon or drain off any excess fat, stir in the garlic, and continue to cook, stirring frequently, for another few minutes. Add the tomatoes, *chiles chipotles* and sauce, bay leaf, thyme, oregano, salt, and pepper. If the tomatoes are not very red and juicy, add the tomato paste and a little of the broth and stir well. Cover partially and cook, stirring frequently, for 30 minutes. Add some of the broth toward the end of cooking if needed to prevent the mixture from drying out.

While the sauce is simmering, shred the pork using your fingers or two forks. When the sauce is ready, stir in both sugars and the shredded pork and simmer for about 15 minutes so the meat will absorb the sweet and spicy flavor.

Scoop this stewlike pork into a warmed serving dish and garnish with the avocado slices.

Achiote

When I first saw the native annatto tree (*Bixa orellana*) in full bloom in Tixkokob, a small village outside of Mérida, the green leaves were polka-dotted with large pink blossoms. It was only when I later returned to Yucatán that I realized that this flowering tree was a source of achiote, the seeds of the flower now encased in prickly red pods. When the seeds are ground, they impart a light flowery flavor, but more important, they imbue a dish with a deep orange tint. Mayan warriors painted their bodies with this coloring, and more recently, it was used to color oleomargarine during World War II. The latter may have looked like butter after my mother stirred in the tiny packets of achiote dye, but believe me, it did not taste like the real butter I spread on my toast today.

If you walk through the large Mercado Municipal Lucas de Gálvez in Mérida, you will see stalls heaped with small mounds of *recados*, or seasoning pastes. Made of different ground herbs and spices, the pastes come in a variety of colors, including olive green, black, and reddish orange. Achiote is the primary ingredient in the reddish orange paste, or *recado rojo*, which is used in many regional dishes, especially *cochinita pibil* (below).

In the markets of Tabasco, I have seen pure ground achiote paste for sale. It is typically mounded on plates that are held waist high by women lining the stairs and entrances.

COCHINITA PIBIL DE YAXUNAH
Steam-Roasted Pork from Yaxunah

Even though the Mayan community of Yaxunah in Yucatán is only twenty miles from the famous archaeological site of Chichén Itzá, it remains a small, isolated village. Here, Silvio Chumul Mex, along with his neighbors and compadres, owns a cooperative raising *pecarís* (peccaries, the native wild pigs), for their own use and occasionally for selling to friends. The cooperative, knowing that consumption of the animal is restricted, follows all government regulations regarding its slaughter. The prized *pecarí* is used in place of the more common pig for *cochinita pibil* only when a great fiesta is planned or an outsider makes a special request, as when Ricardo arranged a meal of this succulent animal to honor a small group of us.

To prepare the *cochinita* required the entire community's involvement. The men in the cooperative dug the pit and lined it with stones. Before the fiesta, they built a fire to heat the stones, slaughtered the *pecarí*, and slathered the *achiote recado rojo* (achiote seasoning paste) made by the village women on the pig. The animal was then wrapped in banana leaves and buried in the pit, where it cooked for four to five hours.

Local families greeted our party as we entered the village. Soon after our arrival, the pit was uncovered and we gathered and watched the men shoveling out the dirt. Then, the pan of succulent *cochinita pibil* was lifted up and the meat was put on large platters that were carried to our table. A seemingly never-diminishing pile of freshly made small yellow corn tortillas sat alongside the meat. Each of us quickly piled a small heap of the pork on a tortilla and topped it with a few drops of an unmercifully hot but addictive *salsa de chile habanero* (page 39). Next came a layer of *ensalada de col* (page 46), followed by a layer of crunchy *salsa de rábanos* (page 44). The result was one of the most succulent tacos I have ever eaten. Our hosts poured two famous local beers, Montejo and the darker León, though you may want to uncork a bottle of Chianti Classico for your table.

The villagers did not share their exact method for preparing the *cochinita pibil*, so this is Ricardo's version of what we ate, simplified for oven baking and for a smaller gathering. The *recado rojo* seasoning paste can usually be found packaged in a Mexican market, or you can make your own using the achiote seeds that are readily available in Mexican markets.

Serves 6 to 8 . . . .

▦ FOR THE RECADO ROJO SEASONING PASTE

¼ cup achiote seeds (page 151)

1 teaspoon black peppercorns

1 teaspoon cumin seeds

12 whole allspice

1 teaspoon dried oregano, preferably Mexican

▦ FOR THE MEAT

5 to 6 pounds boneless pork shoulder, trimmed of excess fat and cut into 2-inch cube

FOR THE RECADO: Combine the achiote seeds, peppercorns, cumin seeds, and allspice in a *molcajete* and pulverize until finely ground. (Alternatively, use a spice grinder or coffee grinder.) Add the oregano and continue grinding to a fine powder. Transfer to a bowl and mix in 2 to 3 tablespoons water to form a thick paste. Measure out ½ cup for seasoning the meat. If not using right away, transfer to an airtight container and refrigerate. It will keep for a few months in the refrigerator or it can be frozen.

⅓ cup recado rojo

2 cups freshly squeezed orange juice

½ cup freshly squeezed lime juice, preferably Key lime

4 cloves garlic, mashed

⅓ cup melted freshly rendered pork lard (page 24) or canola or safflower oil

1 teaspoon sea salt

2 to 3 banana leaves, softened (page 22)

FOR THE MEAT: Place the pork in a large bowl or other large vessel. Put the *recado rojo* in a bowl and add the orange juice, lime juice, garlic, lard, and salt and mix well. Add the achiote mixture to the meat and mix well. Cover and refrigerate, turning the meat occasionally, for at least 4 hours or up to overnight.

Heat the oven to 350°F. Line a deep baking pan with the banana leaves, arranging them shiny side up and crisscrossing them. The leaves should extend 5 to 6 inches over the sides of the pan.

Add the pork and its marinade to the pan, then fold the overhanging leaves over the pork to enclose completely. Do not worry if some of the citrus juice leaks out of the leaf lining into the pan, which often happens. Cover the pan completely with aluminum foil to make a tight seal and put in the oven. Bake until the meat is very tender, 2½ to 3 hours.

Remove the pan from the oven, then remove and discard the foil and fold back the banana leaves. Using two forks or your fingers, roughly shred the meat, pile it on a platter, and serve.

NOTE

You can find premade achiote or *recado rojo* seasoning paste, labeled *condimento de achiote,* on the shelves of Mexican markets, but it will have often been sitting there for a while and will need a flavor boost. Ricardo has devised a simple way to enliven a store-bought achiote paste. Combine ½ teaspoon black peppercorns, 3 whole allspice, 3 whole cloves, and ½-inch stick Mexican true cinnamon bark (page 88) in a *molcajete* and pulverize until finely ground. (Alternatively, use a spice grinder or coffee grinder.) In a bowl, using a fork, mash together 6 cloves garlic, roughly chopped, and 1 (3½-ounce) container *condimento de achiote* until a paste forms. Add the ground spices and mix well. Transfer to an airtight container and refrigerate, then dilute with 1 teaspoon water before using.

AJIACO DE PUERCO DE YUCATÁN
Yucatecan Pork Stew with Garlic

The *ajiaco* of Mexico, undoubtedly a derivative of one of Cuba's popular dishes, is one of the oldest recorded dishes in the Americas, showing up in a surprising number of tasty variations.

Cuban anthropologist Fernando Ortiz equates the diversity of his country's ingredients to the global makeup of Cuba's population, all being melded together in new ways. Root crops—some indigenous, others from Africa—were mixed with other vegetables and whatever meat was most readily available. More often than not, it would have been viscera for the enslaved blacks and the more desirable parts of the animal for the Spanish ruling class.

This same diversity of ingredients is found in Mexico's *ajiaco*, redolent of garlic. The *ajiaco* of Tabasco, similar to the early Cuban stew, is made with beef tripe sautéed with lots of garlic, tomato, achiote, allspice, oregano, and garbanzos. It also sometimes includes plantains, pumpkin, squash, yuca, yams, and the very nutritious dark green *chaya*, a leafy plant native to tropical Mexico and long cultivated by the Maya.

In Guerrero, some families serve an *ajiaco* of chicken or turkey made with plenty of garlic and *longaniza* (sausage) fried in lard and with tomatoes, olives, pickled chiles, raisins, herbs, and allspice. I enjoyed such a dish while staying in the village of Teloloapan, high in the Sierra Madre, with the family of Geno Behena, a former chef in Rick Bayless's restaurants in Chicago.

All of these various ways of making *ajiaco* reflect the lives of the people where it is made, but the garlic is constant. To make this Yucatecan pork *ajiaco*, it helps to have the *recado* seasoning paste prepared in advance. The pork also can be simmered ahead of time and reheated and then the vegetables and saffron added.

In Mexico, there are more than fifteen varieties of the herb the Spanish called *orégano*, many even of different species and none the same as the one they used in Spain. But the one found in the Yucatán is the most unusual, with a larger, rather fleshy leaf.

Served with hot corn tortillas (page 19), this dish is a meal in itself. If you like, you can add some small, crispy Codzitos (page 66), rolled and fried little tacos, and Guacamole Clásico (page 43).

▌ **FOR THE RECADO BLANCO**

12 black peppercorns

3 whole cloves

1-inch stick Mexican true cinnamon bark (page 88)

1 teaspoon coriander seeds

½ teaspoon cumin seeds

10 cloves garlic, roasted (page 18), then peeled

8 dried Yucatecan orégano leaves, or 1 teaspoon dried oregano, preferably Mexican

1 teaspoon sea salt

1 tablespoon mild white vinegar such as vinagre de piña or diluted unseasoned rice vinegar (page 50)

▌ **FOR THE AJIACO**

2 pounds pork loin, trimmed of excess fat and cut into ¾-inch cubes

1 teaspoon sea salt

¼ cup mild white vinegar such as vinagre de piña or diluted unseasoned rice vinegar (page 50)

1 pound red or Yukon Gold potatoes (about 4 medium), peeled and cut into ¼-inch cubes

7 ounces carrots (about 2 medium), peeled and cut into ¼-inch cubes

1 chayote (about ¾ pound), peeled and cut into ¾-inch-thick slices

1 pound zucchini or round calabacitas (summer squashes found in some Mexican markets), cut into ¼-inch cubes

Pinch of saffron threads

4 cups Arroz Blanco (page 223)

½ cup freshly squeezed bitter orange juice (page 26)

FOR THE RECADO: Combine the peppercorns, cloves, cinnamon, coriander, and cumin in a dry skillet and toast over medium-low heat just until you can smell the heady aroma, then pour onto a plate to cool. Smash the garlic in a *molcajete* or garlic press. Grind together the cooled spices and the *orégano* in a spice grinder or coffee grinder and transfer to a small bowl. Add the garlic and mix well. Add the salt and stir in the vinegar to make a paste. Set aside.

FOR THE AJIACO: Pour 2 quarts water into a large pot, *cazuela*, or Dutch oven, bring to a boil over high heat, and add the pork and salt. Return the water to a boil, skimming off any foam that rises to the surface, then lower the heat to a simmer and cook for 5 minutes. Add the vinegar and simmer for another 15 minutes.

Stir in the *recado*, add the potatoes, carrots, and chayote, and cook until the vegetables are nearly tender, about 10 minutes. Add the zucchini and saffron and cook for 10 minutes longer. At this point, the vegetables and meat should be tender. Stir in the rice, return to a simmer, and cook until the rice is heated through. This is a thick, rather than a brothy, stew, so add hot water only if needed to achieve the correct consistency.

As soon as everything is piping hot, ladle into warmed shallow soup bowls or deep plates and add some of the bitter orange juice to each serving. Serve right away.

CARNE DE VENADO ASADO ESTILO DE PAMES

Venison Cooked in the Pame Style

The close to six thousand indigenous Pame, descendants of the earlier nomadic Chichimec who now live on the rough terrain of the mile-high plateaus of the state of San Luis Potosí, are excellent hunters, and according to Ricardo, the once-abundant deer played an important role in their diet. Since venison is now quite scarce, the more easily available pork is used by the Pame women in dishes like this simple one. If you have access to venison, this is an interesting way to prepare it. A chef from Montana who helped me with testing recipes simply went out in his backyard, shot a mule deer, and cleaned it on the spot, then later trimmed away the silver skin and sliced the meat. Although venison can be special ordered from many meat markets, I use pork, which also contrasts nicely with the brick red sauce. The term *asado* in the name of this recipe may be confusing as it usually refers to cooking directly on a very hot surface or a grill, but it can also mean roasting or even, as in this dish, cooked in liquid.

Chiles chiltepín are tiny fireballs that grow wild on the canyon steps of San Luis Potosí, but the cultivated closely related *piquín* will add a similar kick of penetrating heat. Look for these small chiles in Mexican groceries and in many supermarkets.

Lots of hot corn tortillas (page 19) are a necessity, and Frijoles Chinos (page 216) and Arroz Blanco (page 223) usually accompany this dish.

Serves 4 with leftovers

FOR THE MEAT

2 pounds venison or pork loin, trimmed of excess fat and cut into 1-inch-thick slices

1 small white onion, quartered

3 cloves garlic, halved

1 tablespoon sea salt

1 teaspoon dried thyme

1 teaspoon dried marjoram

1 bay leaf

FOR THE MEAT: If using the pork, put it in a large pot along with the onion, garlic, salt, thyme, marjoram, bay leaf, and water to cover and bring to a boil over medium-high heat, skimming off any foam that rises to the surface. Lower the heat to a gentle simmer, cover, and cook until the pork is tender, about 45 minutes. Remove from the heat and drain. Set the pork aside and discard the remaining contents of the sieve. If using the venison, omit

FOR THE SAUCE

- ½ pound ripe tomatoes (about 2 medium), coarsely chopped, or 1 cup diced canned tomatoes, drained
- 2 cloves garlic, coarsely chopped
- 6 chiles piquíns, crumbled
- 1 teaspoon sea salt
- 2 tablespoons freshly rendered pork lard (page 24) or canola or safflower oil

FOR THE GARNISH

- 1 tablespoon finely chopped fresh cilantro, thick stem ends removed
- 2 teaspoons finely chopped green onion

this precooking step. In a small bowl, mix together half of the salt, thyme, and marjoram and rub the mixture into the venison pieces.

FOR THE SAUCE: Put the tomatoes, garlic, chiles, and salt in a blender or food processor and process until smooth. Coat the meat with the tomato mixture.

Heat the lard in a heavy skillet or *cazuela* over medium-high heat until shimmering. Add the meat and fry, turning as needed, until lightly browned on both sides, about 2 minutes on each side for the pork or closer to 5 minutes on each side for the uncooked venison.

Spoon the meat onto a warmed platter, garnish with the cilantro and green onion, and serve. Any leftover meat can be shredded and used in tacos.

FIAMBRE POTOSINO
San Luis Potosí–Style Cold Meats and Vegetables

This favorite warm-weather, flamboyantly colorful Spanish dish of pickled meats, including tongue and pig's feet, and vegetables was replicated by the colonists in Guanajuato and neighboring states. Every cook developed his or her own variation, some including apples, oranges, bananas, or even jícama. On several occasions in homes in Guanajuato, this dish was proudly offered to me, and although I almost moaned with delight when devouring the tongue, the knack of eating the savory pig's feet without making a mess escaped me. In the end, I just picked up a piece and gnawed on it, sucking the bones clean.

Fresh (not smoked) beef tongue may be a challenge to find, so you may need to special order it from your butcher. Also ask your butcher to split the pig's feet in half lengthwise. It is surprising what your butcher will do for you if you ask. I know that mine misses the days when he actually butchered animals and didn't just wrap packages of precut meat.

This dish is time-consuming to prepare but definitely worth the trouble. Begin preparing it at least a day in advance. I suggest serving a dry Sopa de Fideo Seco con Frijol Negro (page 104) as a substantial and tasty way to start the meal, and the traditional Ante de Coco Marquesote (page 258) with a Café de Olla (page 280) for relaxing at the end.

Serves 8 . . . .

▪ FOR THE MEATS

1 small fresh beef tongue, about 1½ pounds, trimmed of excess fat and rinsed in cold water

4 pig's feet, halved lengthwise, rinsed in cold water, and each pair wrapped in cheesecloth and tied securely to keep their shape, or 2 (9-ounce) jars pickled pig's feet

¼ cup mild white vinegar such as vinagre de piña or diluted unseasoned rice vinegar (page 50)

2 teaspoons sea salt

10 black peppercorns

10 fresh thyme sprigs, or 1 teaspoon dried thyme

1 bay leaf

4 boneless chicken thighs

▪ FOR THE VEGETABLES AND GARNISH

2 beets

Sea salt

1 cup trimmed green beans

4 carrots, peeled and cut into ¼-inch-thick slices

1 pound small red or Yukon Gold potatoes (4 or 5), peeled and cut into ¼-inch-thick slices

3 medium, ripe large tomatoes, sliced

1 white onion, thinly sliced

2 ripe Hass avocados, halved, pitted, peeled, and sliced

1 English cucumber, peeled and cut into ¼-inch-thick slices

8 to 10 interior romaine lettuce leaves (optional)

FOR THE MEATS: Put the tongue and fresh pig's feet in a large pot with cold water to cover and bring to a boil over high heat. Lower the heat to medium and simmer for 5 minutes, skimming off any foam that rises to the surface. Add the vinegar, salt, peppercorns, thyme, and bay leaf, cover partially, and continue to cook until the tongue and feet are tender, 2 to 3 hours. The feet may take less time than the tongue; when they are easily pierced with a knife tip, remove them, let cool, then cover and refrigerate. When the tongue is ready—a two-pronged fork should easily pierce the root end—remove it from the broth and plunge it into cold water. Reserve the broth in the pot. Trim off the ragged root edge and any remaining gristle or bone, then peel off the skin with a knife. Put the meat in a bowl, add some of the reserved broth to keep it moist, cover, and refrigerate. If using pickled pig's feet, skip this step; drain them, rinse them lightly with water, and cover and refrigerate until serving.

Meanwhile, return the broth to a simmer, add the chicken, and cook for 20 minutes. Remove from the heat, transfer the chicken to a bowl, and let cool. Splash the chicken with some of the broth to moisten, cover, and refrigerate. Strain the remaining broth and reserve for another purpose.

FOR THE VINAIGRETTE

¼ cup white wine vinegar

1 tablespoon Dijon mustard

1 tablespoon finely chopped fresh flat-leaf parsley (leaves only)

¾ cup olive oil

½ teaspoon sea salt

Freshly ground black pepper

FOR THE VEGETABLES AND GARNISH: The next day, trim off the stems from the beets, leaving 2 inches intact. Rinse the beets well, put in a saucepan, fill the pan with salted water, place over high heat, and bring to a boil. Lower the heat to medium, cover, and cook until tender, 20 to 30 minutes. Remove from the heat, drain, and rinse under cold water until cool. Slip off the skins, cut the beets into ¼-inch-thick slices, and set aside.

Bring a small saucepan filled with salted water to a furious boil over medium-high heat. Add the beans and cook, uncovered, until barely tender, about 10 minutes. They should still be crispy. Drain, rinse under cold running water, and set aside.

Pour water to a depth of 2 inches into the same saucepan, add a pinch of salt, and bring to a boil over medium-high heat. Add the carrots and potatoes, cover, lower the heat to a gentle simmer, and cook until tender, about 10 minutes. Drain and rinse under cold running water until cool. Set aside. Ready the tomatoes, onion, avocados, cucumber, and lettuce.

FOR THE VINAIGRETTE: Pour the vinegar into a small bowl and whisk in the mustard and parsley. Pour in the oil a little at a time, whisking constantly to emulsify. Whisk in the salt and a liberal grinding of pepper and set aside.

Remove the meats from the refrigerator. Starting at the tip, slice the tongue crosswise on the diagonal into ¼-inch-thick slices.

Arrange the tongue, feet, beans, carrots, and potatoes together on a platter with the lettuce leaves. Intersperse the beet, tomato, onion, avocado, and cucumber slices in and around the meats and other vegetables. Drizzle with the vinaigrette and serve cool or at room temperature.

CHÚRIPO

Fiesta Beef Stew

Cayetana Kambo was, at sixty-five, one of the most vital women I had ever met—doing many things and all of them with verve. Active in politics, she is the undisputed leader of the women in her village of Erongarícuaro on Lake Pátzcuaro in Michoacán. Cayetana sells flour tortillas, owns an Internet café, and raises cattle and pigs behind her home. Plus, a grant made it possible for her to travel to South America, where she learned how to convert the excrement of her home-raised livestock into fuel, which she now burns in her stove and sells to neighbors.

Cayetana is also an accomplished cook who allowed me to spend part of a day with her as she made a typical fiesta meal of *chúripo* and *corundas*, the region's six-sided triangular tamales, before racing off to yet another meeting. The beef can be cooked in advance and then reheated and the chile mixture and vegetables added to finish the cooking.

Arroz a la Mexicana (page 224) can take the place of the *corundas*. As a good contrast to this rustic dish, I often pour an Oregon Pinot Noir during the meal.

Serves 6 . . . .

▌ FOR THE BEEF

1½ pounds bone-in beef shanks, trimmed of excess fat

½ white onion, quartered

1 large or 2 small cloves garlic

1 teaspoon sea salt

1 sprig fresh mint

1 sprig fresh thyme

1 sprig fresh marjoram

▌ FOR THE SAUCE

6 chiles guajillos, stems, seeds, and membranes removed, then toasted (page 18)

½ white onion, quartered and roasted (page 18)

1 clove garlic, roasted (page 18), then peeled

FOR THE BEEF: Put the beef, onion, garlic, salt, and water to cover in a *cazuela,* deep pot, or Dutch oven and bring to a boil over medium heat, skimming off any foam that rises to the surface. Add the mint, thyme, and marjoram, reduce the heat to low, cover partially, and simmer until the meat is tender, 1½ to 2 hours. Remove from the heat and transfer the beef to a plate. Strain the broth through a medium-mesh sieve and return it to the pot.

When the meat is cool enough to handle, cut the meat off the bone, shred it, removing any remaining fat and gristle, and set aside. Return the broth to a simmer.

  3 carrots, peeled and cut into ½-inch dice

  2 small chayotes, peeled, seeded, and cut into
    ½-inch dice

  ½ medium cabbage, sliced into quarters

  2 limes, quartered

FOR THE SAUCE: Soak the chiles in a bowl in very hot water to cover until soft, about 20 minutes. Drain the chiles and transfer to a blender. Add the onion and garlic and process until smooth, adding some of the hot broth as needed to release the blades. Strain through a medium-mesh sieve and stir into the simmering broth.

FOR THE VEGETABLES: Add the carrots and chayote to the simmering broth and cook for 20 minutes. Add the cabbage and continue to cook until all of the vegetables are tender, about 8 minutes longer.

Return the shredded meat to the broth and reheat. Serve the stew in warmed wide, shallow bowls and squeeze on lime juice to accent the favors.

OLLA PODRIDA
Meats, Fruits, and Vegetables Simmered in a Pot

The obscure name of this dish of Spanish origin literally means "rotten clay pot," but in reality it is quite the opposite, being wonderfully aromatic of fruits and chiles. This typical fiesta dish from the village of Ario de Rosales, close to Pátzcuaro, Michoacán, is similar to *manchamanteles* (literally, "tablecloth stain"), a much beloved mole. Even though it takes some time to prepare the fruits and vegetables, it is a favorite celebratory dish of Salvador Corona Delgado, better known as Chavo. It is best made in autumn when the aromatic quinces are readily available, although other fruits, such as pears, can be substituted. It is a perfect dish for a party buffet, as much of it can be prepared ahead and the precooked fruits and vegetables added a little before serving.

Corn tortillas (page 19) are needed to sop up the tasty sauce, and Arroz Blanco (page 223) is always welcome. Since this is a fiesta dish, offer tequila, beer, Micheladas (page 268), or an *agua fresca* such as Agua Fresca de Jamaica (page 272).

8 large chiles anchos, stems, seeds, and membranes removed, then toasted (page 18)

8 large chiles guajillos, stems, seeds, and membranes removed, then toasted (page 18)

Canola or safflower oil for frying

1 white onion, roughly chopped

6 large cloves garlic, sliced in half

1 pound boneless lean lamb, cut into 2-inch chunks

1 pound boneless lean pork, cut into 2-inch chunks

1 pound boneless lean beef, cut into 2-inch chunks

1 pound chicken thighs, boned and cut into large chunks

½ teaspoon dried marjoram

½ teaspoon dried thyme

½ teaspoon dried oregano, preferably Mexican

2 bay leaves

1 quart Mexican beer, plus up to 4 cups more beer, chicken broth (page 25), or water

2 small chayotes

2 cups trimmed and halved green beans

2 carrots, peeled and cut into ¼-inch-thick slices (about ¾ cup)

½ cup fresh or frozen corn kernels

4 tablespoons unsalted butter, plus more if needed

½ teaspoon canola or safflower oil

2 medium quinces (about ½ pound), quartered, peeled, cored, and cut into ⅛-inch-thick slices

2 small apples, halved, peeled, cored, and cubed (about ¾ cup)

¾ cup cubed, peeled fresh or frozen peaches (about 2 peaches)

Soak the chiles in a bowl in very hot water to cover until soft, about 30 minutes. While chiles are soaking, heat ½ tablespoon oil in a large, heavy skillet, *cazuela,* or Dutch oven over medium heat. Add the onion and fry until it starts to turn yellow, about 5 minutes. Add the garlic and continue frying until the onion starts to brown, 4 to 5 minutes longer. Using a slotted spoon, lift out the onion and garlic, allowing any excess oil to drip back into the pan, and put them in a blender. Set the pan with the oil aside.

When the chiles are soft, drain them, tear into smaller pieces, and add them to the blender. Add 1½ cups water and process until a smooth puree forms. If the puree is not completely smooth, pass it through a medium-mesh sieve, pushing the residue through with a wooden spoon. Set aside.

Return the pan to medium-high heat, add the lamb in a single layer, and brown on all sides, turning frequently and adding more oil if needed to prevent sticking. Using a slotted spoon, transfer the lamb to a bowl. Brown the pork and beef separately the same way and add them to the bowl. Lightly brown the chicken on all sides the same way and transfer to a separate bowl.

Add more oil if needed to the skillet and reheat over medium-high heat until the oil starts to shimmer. Pour in the pureed chile mixture and fry, stirring constantly with a flat-bottom wooden spatula and scraping up any meat particles from the bottom of

2 partially black plantains (page 103), halved
lengthwise, peeled, and cubed

Sea salt

the pan, for 5 minutes, being careful that the mixture does not splatter. Stir in the marjoram, thyme, oregano, bay leaves, and beer and heat, stirring occasionally, until the mixture begins to bubble again. Add the lamb, pork, and beef, lower the heat, cover, and cook, stirring occasionally, until the meat is tender, about 1 hour longer, adding more beer if needed to keep the meats covered. (At this point, the meat and sauce can be cooled, covered, and refrigerated overnight, then reheated before continuing.)

Combine the chayotes and salted water to cover in a saucepan, bring to a boil over medium-high heat, and cook until almost tender but still firm, 15 to 25 minutes, depending on size. Scoop out the chayotes and let cool, then peel, halve lengthwise, remove the large seed, and cut the flesh into ½-inch dice. (The edible nutlike seed in each chayote is the cook's reward.) Set the diced chayote aside. Return the water to a boil, add the green beans and carrots, and cook until almost tender, no more than 5 minutes. Add the corn and cook for another 2 minutes. Drain well and set aside, covered. About 15 minutes before serving, stir the vegetables into the simmering chile and meat mixture to finish cooking and heat through.

Meanwhile, melt the butter with ½ teaspoon oil in a large skillet over medium heat. Add the quince slices and sauté until just beginning to change color, about 8 minutes. Using a slotted spoon, transfer the slices to the simmering chile and meat mixture, then add the browned chicken.

Return the skillet to medium heat, add the apples, peaches, and plantains, and sauté until browned, about 5 minutes, adding more butter if needed to prevent sticking. Spoon the fruits into the chile and meat mixture and continue to cook until the chicken is tender when pierced with a fork, about 10 minutes longer. Taste the sauce and add salt if needed. If the sauce is too thick, thin with broth or water.

Ladle into large, shallow soup bowls or deep dinner plates and serve.

MIXIOTE DE CARNERO ADOBADO
Chile and Spice Marinated Lamb Barbacoa

arbacoa in Mexico should never be confused with the grilled or barbecued meats cooked in backyards throughout the United States. Every region of Mexico has its own version of *barbacoa,* but all are steam-roasted in a sealed underground pit, or now more frequently in an oven or even in a pot on the stove top.

Throughout central Mexico, the huge maguey plant with its swordlike *pencas,* or "leaves," dominates the landscape. Besides being made into pulque, *mezcal,* and tequila (pages 270–271), in Tlaxcala and some neighboring states, the tough, transparent skin of the *penca* is stripped and wrapped around pieces of lamb that have been marinated in a rich chile sauce known as *adobado.* The packets are then cooked in a pit, creating a *barbacoa* called *mixiote.* Stripping off this skin from the stalks is now restricted, as it kills the plants, so parchment paper is usually substituted, as it is in this version of *mixiote* created by Yolanda Ramos Galicia.

Lamb can be time-consuming to bone, so ask your butcher to bone it and cut it into kebabs or stewlike chunks. Yolanda always leaves the bone in half of the lamb chunks. The bones make the meat more difficult to eat but they do add flavor. If using the toasted avocado leaves, make sure they are from the small *criollo* tree, the native avocado. Their strong aniselike flavor complements the lamb.

To start this fiesta meal, Yolanda always pours small glasses of local *mezcal* for everyone. For a first course, serve bowls of Sopa de Hongos (page 79) and accompany the lamb with Arroz a la Mexicana (page 224), Salsa Verde Cocida (page 31), and lots of hot corn tortillas (page 19). Offer Pastel de Elote (page 252) and Café de Olla (page 280) to prolong the meal.

Serves 4 to 6 ·

3 pounds boneless lamb shoulder, trimmed of excess fat and cut into ½-inch chunks

2 ounces chiles guajillos (about 6), stems, seeds, and membranes removed

3 ounces chiles anchos (about 4 large), stems, seeds, and membranes removed, then toasted (page 18)

Put the lamb in a large bowl. In a saucepan, bring 3 cups water to a boil, add the *chiles guajillos,* and remove from the heat. Let sit for about 5 minutes. Add the *chiles anchos* and let soak until all the chiles are soft, another 5 minutes. Drain the chiles, tear into smaller pieces, and

4 cloves garlic, roasted (page 18), then peeled and chopped

2 teaspoons sea salt

1 teaspoon ground cumin

1 teaspoon dried oregano, preferably Mexican

½-inch stick Mexican true cinnamon bark (page 88)

¼ teaspoon dried thyme

¼ teaspoon freshly ground black pepper

⅛ teaspoon ground cloves

3 tablespoons cider vinegar

3 bay leaves

8 avocado leaves (see Sources) (optional)

8 to 10 corn husks, plus husk strips for tying (optional)

transfer to a blender. Add the garlic, salt, cumin, oregano, cinnamon, thyme, pepper, cloves, and vinegar to the blender and process until very smooth, adding a bit of water if needed for the mixture to have the consistency of tomato sauce. Scrape the sauce through a medium-mesh sieve onto the lamb. Mix well and stir in the bay leaves. Cover and refrigerate, turning the meat occasionally, for at least 8 hours or up to overnight.

Have eight 9-inch squares of parchment paper in a single layer on your work surface. Remove the bay leaves from the meat mixture and discard. If you are using the avocado leaves, they must be lightly toasted first. Heat a *comal* or heavy skillet over medium-low heat. Toast the leaves, a few at a time, turning them over often, until they are very aromatic and lightly browned, about 1 minute. Place a leaf in the center of each square. Divide the lamb chunks evenly among the parchment squares, adding 1 to 2 tablespoons of the sauce to each mound. Gather the edges of each parchment square to the center and tie with kitchen string or a strip of dried corn husk, securing the packet well so that meat juices do not leak out.

Pour water to a depth of 2 to 3 inches into a steamer and put the steamer rack in place. Make sure the water does not touch the rack. Arrange the packets in a single layer on the rack, cover them with the corn husks, and then cover the steamer with the lid. Place the steamer over medium-high heat and bring the water to a boil. Lower the heat to medium and steam the packets for 2 hours, checking the water level from time to time and adding more water if it threatens to boil away. (You can drop a few coins into the pot to rattle in the bubbling water; if they are quiet, you know you need to add water.) To test if the *mixiote* is ready, remove a packet from the steamer and open it; the meat should be tender but not falling apart. If it is not, retie the packet, return it to the steamer, and steam for at least 10 minutes longer. The *mixiote* can be steamed several days in advance, cooled in the packets, and refrigerated, then resteamed just before serving until hot.

Heap the packets onto a large platter and let your guests help themselves.

SEAFOOD

ARROZ A LA TUMBADA
Rice with Seafood

A *la tumbada* means "thrown together" and this rather soupy mixture of rice infused with the very essence of the sea is indeed traditionally made from whatever seafood has just been caught. It is also probably the first dish that I really fell in love with in Mexico. The place was Pardiño's, the largest of the many seafood restaurants along the riverfront in Boca del Rio, then just a small, friendly Veracruz town on the wide mouth of the lazy Jamapa River. Folks on the side streets sat outside their homes on rocking chairs and smiled as we visitors were on our way to enjoy the dishes that they cooked on a daily basis.

This is my version of Pardiño's colorful medley of seafood and rice with additional adjustments based on many years of straying to eateries in other nearby fishing villages. I use a combination of whatever seafood is fresh, but shrimp are always included and often squid and crab. Because I live in the Pacific Northwest, a few tiny clams or mussels are sometimes added to my mix.

This substantial dish needed only *guacamole clásico* (page 43) and *totopos* (page 21) to nibble on while we listened to the white-clad musicians play their unusual guitars and harps, singing their just-made-up ribald lyrics. It helps if you know Spanish. Serve with a salad and a dry white Spanish wine like an Albariño from Galicia.

Serves 6

6 tablespoons olive oil

1 pound medium shrimp in the shell

1 large white onion, roughly chopped

4 cloves garlic, roughly chopped

3 medium tomatoes or 4 large plum tomatoes, coarsely chopped, or 1 (14½-ounce) can diced tomatoes, drained

Heat 4 tablespoons of the oil in a large *cazuela*, Dutch oven, or similar deep pot over medium heat until shimmering. Add the shrimp and cook briefly on both sides until the shells turn pinkish. Using a slotted spoon, transfer the shrimp to a plate and set aside to cool.

4 cups fish, shrimp, or clam broth, or more if needed

1½ cups medium-grain Spanish rice such as Valencia or other medium-grain rice

2 or 3 chiles jalapeños en escabeche, stemmed and partially sliced through on two sides

4 fresh epazote leaves, finely chopped, or 2 sprigs fresh cilantro

2 teaspoons finely chopped fresh chives

1 teaspoon dried oregano, preferably Mexican

½ teaspoon sea salt

2 firm-fleshed white fish fillets such as red snapper or sea bass (about 2 pounds), ¾ to 1 inch thick, cut into wide strips or 1-inch pieces

½ pound cleaned squid, cut into ¼-inch-wide rings (optional)

12 small clams, well scrubbed (optional)

12 small mussels, well scrubbed and debearded (optional)

½ pound freshly cooked crabmeat (optional)

½ pound shucked small oysters (optional)

½ cup finely chopped fresh flat-leaf parsley (leaves only)

Add the onion and garlic to the pot and cook, stirring occasionally, until the onion is translucent, about 5 minutes. Stir in the tomatoes and continue cooking, stirring occasionally, until the tomatoes have softened, about 5 minutes. Remove from the heat, let cool slightly, pour into a blender or food processor, and process until smooth, adding up to ⅓ cup of the broth if needed to achieve a good sauce consistency. If necessary, strain through a medium-mesh sieve to eliminate lumps.

In a small pan, heat the 4 cups broth. Meanwhile, wipe out the *cazuela* and heat the remaining 2 tablespoons oil over medium heat. When the oil is quite hot, add the rice and fry, stirring often, until just golden. Stir in the tomato mixture, chiles, epazote, chives, oregano, and salt and continue to cook, stirring often, for about 3 minutes to blend the flavors. Stir in 3 cups of the heated broth, cover, and cook over low heat for 15 minutes.

While the rice is cooking, peel the shrimp, leaving the tail segments intact.

When the rice is partially cooked and much of the liquid has been absorbed, add the shrimp and fish, and the squid, clams, and mussels, if using. Stir in the remaining 1 cup broth and bring back to a simmer. Cover and continue cooking until the rice is tender, the clams and mussels have opened, and the seafood is just cooked, 5 to 10 minutes. Stir in the crabmeat and oysters, if using, and bring to a simmer again. Remove from the heat and let sit for a few minutes; the rice should be moist and surrounded by some liquid. Remove and discard the chiles and discard any clams and mussels that failed to open.

Spoon the rice into warmed, shallow soup bowls or deep plates, sprinkle with the parsley, and serve.

AJIACO DE CAMARONES
Soupy Rice with Shrimp

This colorful medley of shrimp, rice, and vegetables is just another example of how the people from a specific region combine ingredients available to them to make a tasty bowl of goodness. My friends in Colombia tell me it is their national dish and it is thick with chunks of potatoes, chicken, and corn. In Cuba, *ajiaco* means "containing many ingredients," and it may have both beef and pork along with yuca, sweet potatoes, and plantains. The inclusion of achiote, sweet pepper, and the explosive *chile habanero* makes this version uniquely Yucatecan, which is where Ricardo first savored this soupy rice dish. Since one can never get enough seafood when on the Gulf Coast, begin this informal meal with Ceviche de Dzilam de Bravo (page 53) and serve with meager drops of hot salsa and a squeeze of lime.

Serves 6

▌FOR THE RICE
3 tablespoons canola or safflower oil

1 cup medium- or long-grain white rice

1 teaspoon sea salt

▌FOR THE TOMATO SAUCE
1 cup roughly chopped ripe tomato

½ cup olive oil

½ cup ½-inch-cubed, peeled black-ripe plantain (page 103)

½ cup finely chopped white onion

1 tablespoon minced garlic (about 3 cloves)

4 bay leaves

½ teaspoon dried oregano, preferably Mexican

¼ teaspoon ground cumin

¼ teaspoon freshly ground black pepper

2 tablespoons achiote condiment (see note, page 149), diluted with 1 cup water

FOR THE RICE: Heat the canola oil in a heavy skillet or *cazuela* over medium heat. Add the rice and salt and fry lightly, stirring continually, until almost chalky white and starting to turn pale gold, about 4 minutes. Remove from the heat and reserve.

FOR THE SAUCE: Put the tomato in a blender and process until very smooth. If necessary, strain the pureed tomato through a medium-mesh sieve to eliminate any lumps. Set aside.

Heat the olive oil in a large heavy pot or *cazuela* over medium heat until sizzling hot. Drop in the plantain cubes and fry, turning as needed, until deep gold on all sides, about 6 minutes. Lift out with a slotted spoon, allowing any excess oil to drip back into the pan, then drain on absorbent paper.

FOR THE VEGETABLES AND SHRIMP

1 cup diced zucchini

1 cup chopped ripe tomato

1 cup diced, peeled red or Yukon Gold potatoes

½ cup diced, peeled carrot

⅓ cup finely chopped green chile dulce or green bell pepper

18 large shrimp, peeled

1 teaspoon sea salt

½ cup chopped fresh cilantro, thick stem ends removed

FOR SERVING

2 limes, quartered

Salsa de Chile Habanero (page 39)

To the same pot, add the onion and garlic and fry lightly. Add the pureed tomato and the fried plantains, stir in the bay leaves, oregano, cumin, pepper, the diluted achiote condiment, and 6 cups water, and bring to a low boil.

FOR THE VEGETABLES AND SHRIMP: Stir the zucchini, chopped tomato, potatoes, carrot, green pepper, and rice into the tomato sauce, cover, lower the heat to a gentle simmer, and cook until the rice is cooked and the dish is brothy thick, about 10 minutes, adding more water only if needed.

Add the shrimp and salt and cook until the shrimp are opaque and tender, 5 to 6 minutes. Sprinkle in the cilantro, then ladle into warmed bowls and serve. Pass the limes and salsa at the table.

BARBACOA DE PESCADO
Chile-Marinated Steamed Fish

Antonieta Avila Salinas, who is of African descent, lives in El Ciruelo on Oaxaca's northern Costa Chica. She prepares this traditional dish on top of her small stove, though her father always cooked the freshly caught fish over coals. Antonieta often uses a local variety of red snapper caught by her husband, but striped sea bass or another firm-fleshed white fish also works well, if small enough. I sometimes substitute freshwater trout, which are widely available. Antonieta always keeps the head on her fish, but you may find that the fish will fit in your pan more easily if the head is removed. This dish can also be made with thick pieces of halibut.

Serve with Arroz Blanco (page 223) and with hot corn tortillas (page 19) to help scoop up the fish and sop up the tasty broth. I like to add a crispy Ensalada de Jícama, Melón y Pepino (page 240) and offer a slightly sweet German Riesling to drink.

2 chiles puyas, stems, seeds, and membranes removed

3 chiles guajillos, stems, seeds, and membranes removed

1 white onion, roughly chopped

2 cloves garlic

½ teaspoon dried oregano, preferably Mexican

Large pinch of ground cloves

½ teaspoon freshly ground black pepper

½ teaspoon sea salt

2 tablespoons canola or safflower oil

4 small whole fish, each 10 ounces to 1 pound and 10 inches long, cleaned, fins removed, and patted dry

▌FOR THE TOPPING

2 ripe tomatoes, sliced

½ white onion, sliced

1 or 2 bay leaves

Soak the chiles in a bowl in 2 cups very hot water until quite soft, about 30 minutes. Transfer the chiles and soaking water to a blender and add the onion, garlic, oregano, cloves, pepper, and salt and process until smooth. Taste and add more salt and oregano if needed. Set aside.

Select a large, heavy skillet or other pan wide enough to hold the fish and heat the oil over medium-high heat until shimmering. Add the fish and fry, turning once, until crispy brown on both sides, no more than 2 minutes on each side. If necessary, fry the fish in two batches.

If the fish was fried in batches, return all it to the pan. Cover with the chile sauce and top with tomato and onion slices. Add the bay leaf, cover tightly, and cook over medium-low heat until the flesh flakes when nudged with a knife tip, 5 to 8 minutes.

Place the fish in a wide, shallow platter or bowl and ladle the sauce over the top. Serve right away.

TRUCHAS CON SALSA DE MACADAMIA
Trout with Macadamia Nut Sauce

When first visiting Michoacán in the early 1980s, my husband and I became close friends with Enrique Bautista. Since then, we have often visited his family's extensive avocado ranch outside the subtropical town of Uruapan. The area's economy has diversified since our first visit, with macadamia nuts and trout now important local products. It was interesting to me that the Bautistas obtained their original fish stock from my home state of Washington. These days, Michoacán and the neighboring state of Mexico are big trout producers, with the roads and highways in both states lined with small, rustic eateries serving the fish grilled or fried. Trout dishes like this unusual one, which features Ricardo's creamy sherry sauce with macadamia nuts, are found in more formal restaurants or in homes.

The macadamia nut tree, which is native to Australia, was introduced to Hawaii in 1832, where it thrived and the nuts became an important crop. The trees were brought to Mexico in the late 1960s and are now widely grown in the hot lands of Michoacán and other states.

Freshly caught or store-bought farm-raised trout can be used in this recipe. Care must be taken to remove the spinal column and the bones. Most fishmongers will do this for you, but some smaller bones may still need to be tweezed out.

The fish is enhanced when paired with a crispy lettuce and fruit salad such as Ensalada de Piña con Lechugas (page 234), and Arroz Verde (page 235) makes a colorful contrast. For dessert, Enrique likes to serve *helado de aguacate* (page 247) made with the avocados from his ranch.

Serves 6 . . . .

FOR THE SAUCE
- ½ cup roughly chopped unsalted macadamia nuts
- ¼ cup slivered blanched almonds
- 1 cup heavy cream
- 3 ounces cream cheese
- 1½ tablespoons sugar
- 2 tablespoons Spanish dry (fino) sherry

FOR THE FISH
- 1 cup all-purpose flour
- ¾ teaspoon sea salt
- ½ teaspoon or more freshly ground black pepper
- 6 medium-size trout, head removed and filleted with skin intact, with each 6- to 8-inch-long fillet weighing 5 to 6 ounces
- 4 tablespoons unsalted butter, plus more if needed
- 1 teaspoon canola or safflower oil

FOR THE SAUCE: Put the macadamia nuts, almonds, heavy cream, cream cheese, sugar, and sherry in a blender and process until smooth. The sauce will be quite heavy as you blend and you may have to stop several times and stir with a spoon before continuing. There should be 2 cups thick sauce when finished.

FOR THE FISH: Put the flour into a shallow container and season with the salt and generously with the pepper. Dredge the fish in the flour, coating thoroughly and shaking off any excess.

Melt the butter in a wide, heavy skillet over medium heat. Add the oil and heat until shimmering. Slide 2 or 3 fish fillets, skin side up, into the bubbling butter and sauté until the flesh is golden brown on the first side, about 4 minutes. Turn and continue cooking until the fish is just opaque throughout, about 3 minutes. Transfer to a warmed platter. Repeat with the remaining fillets, adding more butter if needed to prevent sticking. Add them to the warmed platter.

While the trout is frying, gently warm the macadamia sauce.

Serve the fillets, skin side down, on warmed plates. Spoon the macadamia sauce over and around the fish and garnish with the chives.

CHICHARRÓN DE PESCADO
Crispy Fish

No, this is not the *chicharrón* of crispy pork skin that most think of, but instead one of crispy fish. The crunchy texture of the outer casing keeps the fish moist, and when fried at the correct temperature, the fish absorbs hardly any oil.

Alma Cervantes Cota, who shared this recipe with me, is from the flat, tropical coast of Sinaloa. The people there have a rather simple diet that relies on a plethora of seafood and an abundance of crops, including wheat, which was introduced by the Jesuits in the late sixteenth century. That means that corn tortillas are used, but flour tortillas are just as common. An unexpected condiment, soy sauce is almost a staple in Sinaloa because the port was on the trade route from Asia to the Philippines and on to Mexico. Worcestershire sauce, ketchup, and mustard are more recent additions from the United States.

Gather a group of friends and family around a table with a platter of this fish in the center. Surround it with a basket of hot flour tortillas, bowls of Guacamole Clásico (page 43), Salsa Verde Cruda (page 31), and the even more potent Salsa de Chiles de Árbol (page 37). Always have Frijoles Refritos (page 217) on the table, and for a typical *comida* in Sinaloa, include the regional pork specialty *chilorio* (page 70), which is also scooped up with the tortillas. A pitcher of Agua Fresca de Sandia (page 272) and cold bottles of Pacífico, the local pilsner-style beer, are always welcome.

Serves 6 . . . .

FOR THE FISH

2 pounds sea bass, red snapper, mahimahi, or other firm-fleshed white fish fillets, cut into 3-inch pieces

2 teaspoons sea salt

¼ cup whole milk

¼ cup Worcestershire sauce

¼ cup soy sauce

1 clove garlic, minced or crushed

FOR THE DIP

1 tablespoon olive oil

3 to 4 chiles de árbol, depending on tolerance

1 clove garlic, finely chopped

¼ cup tomato ketchup

1 tablespoon Dijon mustard

3 tablespoons good-quality mayonnaise

FOR SERVING

Peanut or sunflower oil for deep-frying

1 cup all-purpose flour

½ teaspoon sea salt

½ teaspoon freshly ground black pepper

FOR THE FISH: Pat the fish dry with absorbent paper and sprinkle 2 teaspoons salt on both sides.

Mix together the milk, Worcestershire sauce, soy sauce, and garlic in a flat bowl or pan. Add the fish pieces, drenching them completely in the sauce, cover, and marinate in the refrigerator, turning occasionally, for 2 hours. Remove from the marinade and pat dry.

FOR THE DIP: Heat the olive oil in a large skillet over medium heat. Add the chiles and fry briefly, just until the aroma becomes pronounced and their color deepens. Using a slotted spatula, lift out the chiles, allowing any excess oil to drip back into the pan, and drain on absorbent paper. Set the oil in the pan aside to cool.

Crush the chiles into smaller pieces and transfer to a blender. I always use the seeds, but you may want to remove some of them for a milder-tasting mixture. Add the garlic, ketchup, and cooled oil to the blender and process until smooth. Transfer to a bowl and stir in the mustard and mayonnaise.

FOR SERVING: When ready to serve, pour the peanut oil to a depth of 2 inches into a deep, heavy 9- to 10-inch skillet and heat until the oil is shimmering or registers 350°F on a deep-frying thermometer. Stir together the flour, salt, and pepper on a large, flat plate. Working in batches, add the fish pieces, turn to coat lightly on all sides, and shake off the excess. When the oil is ready, fry several pieces of fish at a time, turning them often, until golden and crispy, about 4 minutes. Make sure not to overcook. Using the slotted spatula, transfer to absorbent paper to drain.

When all of the fish pieces are cooked, put them on a platter with a bowl of the chile-flavored dip and serve right away.

Hierba Santa

Holy Herb

Hierba santa, also widely known as *hoja santa*, has long been an essential flavoring in many of southern Mexico's regional dishes. Its large leaves, which impart a subtle aromatic aniselike taste, are usually used as wrappings for fish, meats, or tamales, but occasionally they are torn and used in stews, sauces, *pipianes*, or moles, such as Oaxaca's ubiquitous *mole amarillo de res* (page 180). If you are in Chiapas, *hierba santa* (*Piper auritum*) goes by *momo;* in Oaxaca, it is known as *yerba santa;* and in Tabasco and Veracruz, it may be called *acúyo*— same plant, different names.

In Texas, these large plants grow wild along riverbanks, and even with snow and frost, they come back year after year. When I was a small child, our family lived for a while outside of Corpus Christi. I can remember walking with my dad along the nearby river and the excitement I felt when he had me rub the big, heart-shaped leaves and my fingers smelled like my favorite licorice stick. It started with that first touch, then the scent, and now the taste—all are special to me.

I often try to grow *hierba santa* in large whiskey barrels, but it definitely needs more sun than the Pacific Northwest can provide. I'm lucky if I end up with even ten leaves to use (see Sources for where to buy seeds).

MONE DE ROBALO

Sea Bass Wrapped in Aromatic Leaves

Mone is an ancient way of preparing fish. It calls for wrapping it in banana and other aromatic leaves such as *hierba santa* to add flavor before placing it on smoldering coals to cook slowly. In Tabasco and Chiapas, carrots, squash, plantains, and tomatoes are traditionally included in the packet, and nowadays the whole dish is often oven-steamed.

Ricardo uses moist sea bass in his *mone* because he believes it's the tastiest choice, but red snapper or a similar fish can be substituted. In Tabasco, the small green sweet pepper known as *chile dulce* is used, but the similar green bell pepper can be substituted. Nestle a mound of Arroz Verde (page 225) alongside and finish with the regional white custard delicacy Manjar Blanco (page 244).

Serves 6

2 tablespoons canola or safflower oil, plus more if needed

3 almost black-ripe plantains (page 103), peeled and cut into ⅜-inch-thick slices (36 slices total)

1 small green chile dulce or green bell pepper, halved, seeds and membranes removed, and cut lengthwise into ¼-inch-wide strips

½ cup thinly sliced white onion

6 (12-inch) squares banana leaf, softened (page 22)

6 large hierba santa leaves (optional but recommended; page 172)

Sea salt

18 ripe tomato slices, each ⅜ inch thick (from about 4 tomatoes)

6 sea bass or other similar fish fillets, 5 to 6 ounces each

1 tablespoon minced garlic (about 3 cloves)

½ teaspoon freshly ground black pepper

6 sprigs fresh flat-leaf parsley

6 tablespoons freshly rendered pork lard (page 24) or unsalted butter, melted

Heat the oil in a heavy skillet over medium-high heat. Add the plantain slices and brown, turning once, about 2 minutes on each side. Using a slotted spoon, transfer to absorbent paper to drain. Add the *chile dulce* and onion to the same pan and sauté until softened, about 3 minutes or so, adding another dribble of oil if needed to prevent scorching. Set aside.

Have six 12-inch squares of aluminum foil, shiny side up, in a single layer on a work surface. Place a banana-leaf square, shiny side up, on each foil square. Then put a *hierba santa* leaf, if available, on top of each banana leaf. Place 6 fried plantain slices in the center of each leaf, salt them lightly, and add 3 tomato slices. Top with a fish fillet, spread with a little garlic, and sprinkle with salt and a hefty amount of pepper. Divide the *chile dulce* and onion mixture into 6 equal portions and place a portion on each fish fillet. Top each fish fillet with a parsley sprig, 1 tablespoon lard, and a pinch of salt. To form each packet, fold in the opposite sides and then fold in the ends, as if making a tamal. Wrap the leaf packet in the aluminum foil, making sure the foil is well sealed.

Pour water to a depth of 1 to 2 inches into a steamer and put the steamer rack in place. Make sure the water does not touch the rack. Bring the water to a boil over high heat. Add the packets of fish to the rack, lower the heat just until a steady amount of steam envelops the fish, cover tightly, and steam for 20 minutes.

Remove a packet from the pot and let it sit for a few minutes. Open the packet and check to see if the fish will flake easily. If it doesn't, rewrap the packet, return it to the rack, and steam the packets for another 5 to 10 minutes. When the packets are ready, remove them from the steamer and remove and discard the foil. Place the banana-leaf packets on individual plates and serve. Let guests open their packets to reveal the multiple colors and aromas inside.

PESCADO TIKIN XIK
Achiote-Rubbed Grilled Fish

When meandering along the northern shoreline of the thumblike Yucatán Peninsula, which juts out between the moody waters of the Gulf of Mexico and the Caribbean, you will find many small places, even homes, with signs offering *tikin xik*, a grilled fish rubbed with achiote paste. According to the present-day Maya, *tikin* means "dry" and *xik* is the word for "armpit," so in the case of this particular dish the name likely refers to the fin of the fish, which becomes especially crispy when grilled.

I first had *tikin xik* in a small restaurant west of the port of Chuburna, where the owner and his wife used a fire of wood and coconut husks they built in a shallow indentation in the sand. The large fish was butterflied, rubbed with an achiote paste diluted with bitter orange juice, placed on coconut palm leaves, and grilled on a grate over smoldering coals.

Ricardo encountered his favorite preparation of *tikin xik* farther along the coast in Dzilam de Bravo, where his friend Edwin Raul Nadal Aldecua shared with us how he grills the freshly caught *lisa* (gray mullet), which he prefers for its delicious buttery-tasting flesh. *Huachinango* (red snapper), *mero* (grouper), or sea bass can also be used.

The whole fish is cut in half, from the head to the tail, the cook often pounding on the knife with a hammer to chop through the head. The spine and rib bones are left on one side to provide additional flavor. I sometimes compromise and cut off the head.

Two things are especially important when cooking this fish: the coals must deliver white-hot heat and the fish must be in a hinged device so that it can be easily flipped on the grill. You can use a purchased grilling basket or make one out of chicken wire. Although not traditional, you can also cook *tikin xik* in a 400°F oven for 8 to 10 minutes per pound.

Serve with freshly made corn tortillas (page 19), Frijoles Negros Colados a la Yucateca (page 218), and the lip-blistering Salsa Xnipec (page 36) and invite guests to make their own fish tacos. At Edwin's small seafood restaurant, he served *ensalada de col* (page 46), *cebolla morada curada* (page 45), and a heaping bowl of *ensalada de papas glaceadas con queso* (page 54) as accompaniments. A pitcher of Horchata con Coco (page 275) is always welcome, as is a sprightly Michelada (page 268) or lemonade made with mineral water.

Serves 6 . . . .

▌FOR THE ACHIOTE SAUCE

¼ cup canola or safflower oil

1 cup thinly sliced white onion

2 pounds very ripe tomatoes (about 4 large or 6 medium), chopped, or 3 (16-ounce) cans diced tomatoes, drained

1 xcatic, Anaheim, banana, or similar blond chile, stem, seeds, and membranes removed, then thinly sliced

¼ cup achiote condiment (see note, page 151), diluted with 1 cup water

½ teaspoon sea salt

▌FOR THE FISH

1 (4- to 5-pound) sea bass, red snapper, or other firm-fleshed white fish (or 2 smaller fish), head and tail removed if desired and butterflied with backbone and other bones removed

Canola or safflower oil for grill

1 teaspoon sea salt

FOR THE SAUCE: Heat the oil in a large skillet or *cazuela* over medium-high heat. Add the onion and when it just starts to change color, add the tomatoes and chile, lower the heat to a gentle simmer, and cook, stirring occasionally, for 5 minutes.

Stir the diluted achiote condiment into the tomato mixture and continue to simmer, stirring from time to time to prevent scorching, until the mixture thickens and is pastelike, about 10 minutes. Stir in the salt, then taste and add more salt if needed. Remove from the heat and set aside.

FOR THE FISH: Prepare a hot fire in a charcoal grill. Rinse the fish with cold water and pat dry. Lightly oil your grill basket. Sprinkle the salt on the cut side of the fish and lay the fish in the grill basket.

When the coals are covered with gray ash, put the fish, skin side down, over the coals no more than 5 to 8 inches from the heat. Cook for 6 to 8 minutes. Turn the fish and cook until it almost breaks into firm flakes when pressed with your finger but is still moist, 6 to 8 minutes longer. Open the grill basket and rub the achiote sauce on the flesh, which will flavor the fish during the final cooking. Flip the fish over again to char the achiote paste lightly, being careful that it does not burn. Immediately transfer to a warmed platter and serve.

CAMARONES AL MOJO DE AJO

Shrimp Drenched in Garlic

A plate of saucy shrimp and garlic is one of my favorite dishes to eat at Mexico's coastal restaurants and especially this one from Veracruz. Do use fresh or frozen ocean-caught shrimp, not farm-raised.

Serve around a mound of Arroz con Plátanos (page 223). For beer drinkers, have a tangy Michelada (page 268) to drink, and for others, Horchata con Coco (page 275), a refreshing beverage of rice and coconut water.

Serves 4

1 pound medium-large shrimp (about 20), peeled with last joint and tail segments intact

½ teaspoon sea salt

½ teaspoon freshly ground black pepper

Juice of 2 limes

12 large cloves garlic, 6 minced and 6 thinly sliced

3 tablespoons olive oil

½ white onion, finely chopped

1 chile jalapeño, stem, seeds, and membranes removed, then finely chopped (about 1 tablespoon)

¼ cup lightly packed minced fresh cilantro, thick stem ends removed, plus 2 tablespoons chopped for garnish

½ cup dry white wine

Sprinkle the shrimp with the salt and pepper, put in a bowl, and stir in the lime juice and minced garlic. Let the shrimp sit for 3 to 4 minutes, then drain off any liquid.

Heat the oil in a large, heavy skillet over medium heat. Add the onion and chile and cook, stirring, until the onion begins to turn yellow. Stir in the sliced garlic, lower the heat, and continue cooking, stirring occasionally, for about 20 minutes. Stir in the minced cilantro and cook briefly until the flavors are blended. Add the wine and simmer for another minute or two. Add the shrimp and cook until just opaque, about 2 minutes. Do not overcook.

Transfer the shrimp to a warmed platter and scoop the garlic and onion on and around the shrimp. Garnish with the chopped cilantro and serve immediately.

BACALAO A LA MEXICANA
Salt Cod, Mexican Style

Many generations ago, members of Ana María Lopez Landa's family lived in the Basque region of northern Spain, near one of the world's most abundant fishing grounds. Today, freshly caught local fish remain important ingredients in the Basque kitchen, but salt cod, or *bacalao*, rivals them in popularity. The fish has been preserved in this manner for centuries, since Basque whalers sailed from the Bay of Biscay to distant northern waters to satisfy the European demand for whale meat. To provide food for themselves on these long voyages, the whalers would catch, salt, and dry cod on board. The most popular salt cod dish that Basque cooks prepare is *bacalao a la vizcaína* (in the style of the Bay of Biscay).

Now in Mexico, one of Sra. Landa's granddaughters, Ana Elena Martínez, makes an almost identical dish, which she serves on Christmas Eve. Ana Elena's father likes it so much that she always cooks extra for him. He uses the leftover *bacalao* to make *tortas,* stuffing it into *bolillos* (French-style rolls) for eating on Christmas Day.

One of the main differences between the cod dishes of the two countries is that Spanish cooks consider ham and bacon essential ingredients, and Ana Elena and other Mexican cooks insist on olives and capers. Ricardo's family, in Veracruz, also adds slivered almonds and raisins and, like Ana Elena, serves the dish on Christmas Eve.

The families of Ana Elena and Ricardo are large, so a stuffed turkey, soups, salads, and desserts are also on the buffet table. Because Ricardo's family is even larger than Ana Elena's, a roasted leg of pork is served, too. For one of the special desserts, Ricardo's family sets out *ensalada de manzana* (page 250).

Although hard as a slab of wood, salt cod, when properly soaked and cooked, becomes a wonderfully flavored delicacy. Always look for thick, ivory white fillets; Newfoundland and Norway typically produce the best quality. Unfortunately, unlike salt cod sold in Mexico, the fish from both of those sources is usually packed in wooden boxes, which makes it difficult to know exactly what you are buying.

Serves 6 . . . .

2 pounds skinned salt cod fillets

Olive oil for frying

4 cloves garlic, lightly smashed with the side of a knife

2 white onions, roughly chopped

3 small, ripe tomatoes (about ¾ pound), peeled, seeded, and roughly chopped, or 1 (14½-ounce) can diced tomatoes, drained

3 large pimientos, 1 roughly chopped and 2 cut lengthwise into narrow strips

4 cups canned tomato sauce

½ cup sliced pimiento-stuffed green olives

2 tablespoons capers, rinsed

Leaves from 10 sprigs fresh flat-leaf parsley, finely chopped

¾ pound small round potatoes (about 8), cooked and peeled

½ cup dry white wine

1 teaspoon sweet paprika

1 teaspoon hot paprika, or ½ teaspoon cayenne pepper

Sea salt

Place the salt cod in a large bowl and add cold water to cover generously. Cover the bowl and refrigerate for about 36 hours, changing the water 3 or 4 times daily.

The day of serving, pour the oil to a depth of ¼ inch into a large *cazuela* or Dutch oven and place over medium heat. When the oil is hot, add the garlic and fry until barely browned but not burnt, about 2 to 3 minutes. Remove the garlic and discard. Add the onions, lower the heat and cook, stirring occasionally, until translucent but not browned, about 20 minutes. Remove from the heat.

Using a slotted spoon, scoop out the onions, allowing any excess oil to drip back into the *cazuela,* and transfer them to a blender or food processor. Set the pan with the oil aside. Add the tomatoes and the chopped pimiento to the blender and process until smooth.

Reheat the oil in the *cazuela* over medium heat. When it shimmers, add the tomato mixture all at once and let it sizzle, stirring frequently, until it darkens, about 5 minutes. Stir in the tomato sauce, lower the heat and simmer uncovered, stirring occasionally, until the mixture is rich and thick, about 2 hours.

Meanwhile, remove the cod from the soaking water, discarding the water, and put it in a large saucepan or pot. Add water to cover and bring to a boil over high heat. Lower the heat to medium-low and simmer until the fish flakes easily when a knife or fork is inserted into the thickest part. This can take from 10 to 30 minutes, depending on the thickness of the cod. Remove from the heat. Lift out the fish with a slotted spatula and set aside to cool. Reserve the cooking liquid.

When the cod is cool enough to handle, coarsely shred the flesh or cut into small chunks, removing and discarding any errant skin or bones.

Add the cod, olives, capers, and parsley to the tomato mixture, then stir in the potatoes, pimiento strips, and white wine. If the mixture seems too dry, pour in a bit of the reserved cod cooking liquid. Season with the sweet paprika and hot paprika, then taste and add salt if needed. Heat over medium heat to serving temperature, making sure the potatoes are hot throughout. Spoon into a serving dish and serve at once.

The flavor of the dish improves if it is made a day in advance, covered, and refrigerated and then gently reheated just before serving. It can also be frozen. If you are freezing leftovers, remove the potatoes and add new ones when reheating. If you are making the dish ahead and freezing it for a future supper, do not add the potatoes until reheating to serve.

MOLES AND PIPIANES

MOLE AMARILLO DE RES
Oaxacan Yellow Mole with Beef

This is my adaptation of Abigail Mendoza's yellow mole, one of the so-called seven moles of Oaxaca. I say so-called because there are actually many more than just seven types of mole in this southern state, each with its different versions, depending on the village traditions and then the traditions of each family. Most yellow moles are made with chicken or pork, or both, and just occasionally with beef, which in Zapotec villages is butchered only on Wednesdays or for very special occasions. In the time before the Spaniards introduced livestock, deer from the surrounding forested mountains would have been used for this festive dish and still is, when available. When the mole is made with beef, it is traditionally flavored with the aromatic herb *pitiona;* with chicken, cilantro is used; and with pork, anise-flavored *hierba santa*. Because *pitiona* is so regional and there is no substitute flavor, fresh mint is my reluctant compromise.

Although this mole by name is yellow, the actual color is usually more reddish, depending on the dried chiles used for flavoring. In Oaxaca, there are certain yellow-tinted chiles unique to the region: the squat *chilhuacle amarillo*, the slimmer *costeño amarillo*, and the longer *chilcostle*, which is more red than yellow. All are ideal for this mole, although now, even in Oaxaca, they are expensive due to their scarcity and red *chiles guajillos* are often used as a substitute, resulting in a different flavor and color. I have used mild *chiles poblanos* for the *rajas* (chile strips), but the regional feisty *chile de agua* is used in Oaxaca.

Mole amarillo is not just a festive main dish. It is also enjoyed in tamales, and I always make a stop at a restaurant across from the immense two-thousand-year-old cypress tree in El Tule for empanadas filled with shredded chicken enfolded in this mole.

Accompany the mole with Arroz Blanco (page 223) and plenty of corn tortillas (page 19). Abigail always brings out a bottle of smoky *mezcal* with limes and a salt flavored with ground chile and the ground toasted maguey "worms," which really are the larvae of a moth that buries its eggs in the flesh of the spikes of the maguey. They have a special flavor that enhances the *mezcal*.

FOR THE MEAT

2 pounds boneless beef rump or stew meat, trimmed of excess fat and cut into 2-inch chunks

2 pounds beef ribs, trimmed of excess fat and cut into individual pieces

1 white onion, quartered

2 cloves garlic

1 teaspoon sea salt

FOR THE POBLANO CHILE STRIPS

1 chile poblano, roasted and peeled (page 17)

2 tablespoons freshly squeezed lime juice

½ teaspoon sea salt

FOR THE VEGETABLES

¾ pound chayotes (about 2 small), peeled, halved, seeded, and cut into lengthwise strips about ½ inch wide

½ pound small red or Yukon Gold potatoes (about 5), quartered

½ pound green beans, cut on the diagonal into 2-inch pieces

FOR THE MOLE

6 chiles guajillos, stems, seeds, and membranes removed, then toasted (page 18)

3 chiles anchos, stems, seeds, and membranes removed, then toasted (page 18)

4 cloves garlic, roughly chopped

1 teaspoon dried oregano, preferably Mexican

3 black peppercorns, lightly toasted (page 18)

3 whole allspice, lightly toasted (page 18)

3 whole cloves, lightly toasted (page 18)

Pinch of ground cumin

FOR THE MEAT: Put all of the beef in a large, heavy stockpot or *cazuela* and add the onion, garlic, and 3 quarts water. Bring to a boil over high heat, skimming off any foam that rises to the surface. Reduce the heat to low, add the salt, and simmer until all the meat is tender and rib meat is falling off the bones, 1½ to 2 hours. Using a slotted spoon, remove the beef from the broth, place in a bowl, cover, and set aside. Reserve the broth in the pot.

FOR THE CHILE STRIPS: Slit the chile lengthwise, remove the seeds and membranes, and cut lengthwise into narrow strips. Put the strips into a bowl, add the lime juice and salt, and toss to coat evenly. Cover until ready to use. The *rajas* can be made while the meat is cooking.

FOR THE VEGETABLES: Return the broth to a simmer, add the chayotes and potatoes, and cook until tender, about 6 minutes. Using a slotted spoon, transfer to a bowl. Add the green beans to the simmering broth and cook until crisp tender, about 5 minutes. Using the slotted spoon, add the beans to the chayotes and potatoes. Reserve the broth.

FOR THE MOLE: Soak the chiles in a bowl in very hot water to cover until soft, about 20 minutes. Drain the chiles, tear them into smaller pieces, and put in a blender. Add the garlic, oregano, peppercorns, allspice, cloves, and cumin to the blender and process until a smooth sauce forms, adding just enough of the reserved

½ cup masa harina for tortillas

1 tablespoon freshly rendered pork lard
(page 24) or canola or safflower oil

2 small sprigs fresh pitiona or mint

1 teaspoon sea salt

FOR SERVING
4 limes, quartered

broth to release the blades. If you do not have a heavy-duty blender, you will need to grind the spices in a spice grinder or coffee grinder before you add them to the blender. The sauce should be quite thick.

Put the masa harina in a bowl. Mix in up to ⅓ cup of the warm broth until the flour is damp and crumbly.

Heat the lard in a large *cazuela* or Dutch oven over medium heat until shimmering. Pour in the chile sauce, lower the heat to a gentle simmer, and fry, stirring constantly with a wooden spoon, until the color deepens, about 10 minutes. Gradually stir in 2 cups of the reserved broth and bring back to a simmer.

Gradually stir the masa mixture and *pitiona* into the simmering mixture, mixing well. Stir in the salt, then taste and add more salt if needed. Continue to simmer, uncovered, for 10 minutes. The masa will thicken the broth, so stir occasionally. The mole should be thick enough to coat the back of a spoon. If it is too thick, add a little broth to thin as needed.

Add the meat and vegetables to the mole and heat through. Spoon into wide, shallow soup bowls and garnish with the chile strips. Pass the limes at the table for everyone to squirt in juice to taste.

MOLE COLORADITO CON FRIJOLONES
Oaxacan Red Mole with Beans

This simple brick red mole of Oaxacan cook Emelia Arroyo Cabrera is transformed into a very different dish by adding pork and voluptuous local beans to the mole with a platter of Tacos de Berros (page 62) alongside. It helps to make the beans in advance.

Small *buñuelos* were often served after this mole as a special family treat. The wheat-flour dough was stretched paper-thin over Emelia's grandmother's knee, then quickly fried and served with sugar syrup flavored with anise and cinnamon and sprinkled with red-tinted sugar. For a method that requires a less dexterous technique, try my recipe for *buñuelos* (page 265).

3 chiles anchos, stems, seeds, and membranes removed, then broken into large pieces

5 chiles chilcostles or chiles guajillos, stems, seeds, and membranes removed, then broken into large pieces

1 white onion, quartered and roasted (page 18)

1 clove garlic, roasted (page 18), then peeled

1 tablespoon unhulled sesame seeds, lightly toasted (page 19)

½ teaspoon dried oregano, preferably Mexican

¼ teaspoon freshly ground black pepper

Pinch of ground cloves

Pinch of dried thyme

Pinch of dried marjoram

1 to 1½ cups chicken broth (page 25) or water

2 tablespoons freshly rendered pork lard (page 24) or canola or safflower oil

1 teaspoon sea salt

6 cups Frijolones con Costilla de Puerco (page 106)

Soak the chiles in a bowl in very hot water to cover until soft, about 20 minutes. Drain the chiles, tear into smaller pieces, and put in a blender. Add the onion, garlic, sesame seeds, oregano, pepper, cloves, thyme, marjoram, and 1 cup of the broth and process until a smooth sauce forms.

Heat the lard in a large *cazuela* over medium heat until it ripples. Pour in the chile mixture, add the salt, reduce the heat to medium-low, and cook, stirring often, until reduced and thickened, about 10 minutes.

Add the beans and cook until heated through, adding the remaining ½ cup broth if the mixture seems too thick. Spoon the mole into a warmed deep platter or a shallow soup bowl.

MOLE DE XICO
Dark and Fruity Turkey Mole

There are many dark moles, especially the celebratory mole of Puebla and the Oaxacan black mole, both renowned and each with its own regional flavors. But it is the rich prune-dark mole from the small village of Xico in highland Veracruz that I usually prepare for a gathering of appreciative friends. This mole is so famous that there are now several restaurants in Xico that serve it to visitors from all over Mexico.

Like all moles, this one is rather complicated to make. However, it can be prepared in steps and put together on the day of serving, and is actually tastier if made ahead. Because it is time-consuming to prepare, you may want to double the recipe for the mole and freeze the extra, so that all you need to do is add turkey when it is reheated.

In Xico, meals usually begin with a local fruit-flavored liquor, then plates of *gorditas de frijoles negros* (page 68) with *salsa negra con chipotles* (page 41) and a black bean soup made with *xonequi*, a popular regional herb, are served. You can substitute the earthy Sopa de Hongos (page 79) for the black bean soup and accompany the mole with scoops of Arroz Blanco (page 223). To end the meal, offer refreshing Helado de Mango (page 248) followed by Café de Olla (page 280). I like to serve a Chilean Cabernet throughout the meal.

Serves 10

FOR THE MOLE

14 chiles mulatos, stems, membranes, and seeds removed, then toasted (page 18)

6 chiles pasillas, stems, membranes, and seeds removed, then toasted (page 18)

3 quarts chicken broth (page 25)

5 tablespoons canola or safflower oil

½ cup roughly chopped white onion (about 1 small)

5 small cloves garlic

1½ teaspoons sea salt, plus more if needed

2 (½-inch-thick) baguette slices, dried out

1 store-bought small corn tortilla, dried out

½ small black-ripe plantain (page 103), peeled and cut into ½-inch-thick slices

¾ cup pitted prunes, coarsely chopped

½ cup slivered blanched almonds

¼ cup hazelnuts

¼ cup pecans

¼ cup pine nuts

⅓ cup unhulled sesame seeds

½ teaspoon aniseeds, toasted (page 18)

1-inch stick Mexican true cinnamon bark (page 88)

3 black peppercorns, toasted (page 18)

2 whole cloves, toasted (page 18)

2 plum tomatoes, roasted (page 18)

FOR THE MOLE: Soak the chiles in a heatproof bowl in boiling water to cover until soft, about 30 minutes. Drain the chiles and tear into smaller pieces. Transfer half of the chiles to a blender, add ½ cup of the broth, and process until smooth but still with some texture. Add the remaining chiles and continue to process until smooth, adding just enough additional broth (up to 1 cup) to release the blades.

Heat 1 tablespoon of the oil in a large *cazuela*, Dutch oven, or large, heavy skillet over medium heat. Add the onion and garlic and fry, stirring often, until lightly golden, about 2 minutes. Using a slotted spoon, scoop out the onion and garlic, allowing any excess oil to drip back into the *cazuela*, then transfer to the blender with the pureed chiles. Add the salt and process until smooth.

Return the pan to medium heat and add 2 tablespoons of the oil. When the oil is quite hot, pour in the chile mixture and fry gently, stirring often so it doesn't burn, for about 8 minutes. The wondrous chile aroma will be intense. Set the pan aside off the heat.

½ Mexican chocolate tablet (about 1½ ounces), finely chopped

1 tablespoon grated piloncillo (page 42), azúcar morena or other unrefined brown cane sugar, or dark brown sugar

■ **FOR THE TURKEY**

1 skin-on, boneless whole turkey breast, about 3½ pounds, halved

2 tablespoons sea salt

¼ cup canola or safflower oil

In a smaller, heavy skillet, add the remaining 2 tablespoons oil over medium heat. When the oil is hot, add the bread and fry lightly on each side until a dark golden brown. Remove with tongs or a slotted spatula, allowing any excess oil to drip back into the pan, and drain on absorbent paper. Repeat with the tortilla.

Add the plantain slices to the oil remaining in the pan and fry over medium heat until soft, about 4 minutes. Toss in the prunes and continue to cook for another minute or two until hot. Using the slotted spatula, transfer to absorbent paper to drain.

Add the almonds, hazelnuts, pecans, and pine nuts to the oil remaining in the pan and fry until you can smell their nutty fragrance, about 2 minutes. Remove the nuts from the pan and reserve. Wipe out all of the oil in the skillet, add the sesame seeds, and toast, stirring frequently, until they just begin to darken, about 4 minutes. Remove and set aside.

Break up the bread and tortilla, put them in the blender, add 1 cup of the broth, and begin processing. Little by little, add the nuts, all but 1 tablespoon of the sesame seeds, and another 1 cup of the broth and process until smooth. Stir into the chile mixture.

Put the aniseeds, cinnamon, peppercorns, and cloves in a spice grinder or coffee grinder and grind until pulverized. Put the plantain, prunes, and tomatoes in the blender or in a food processor, add the spices, and process until smooth. (This may have to be done in two batches.) Stir into the pot with the chile mixture, place over medium heat, and heat until hot. Add the chocolate and sugar, reduce the heat to medium-low, and simmer, stirring often, for 20 to 30 minutes longer, adding some of the remaining broth if the sauce begins to stick to the bottom of the pot.

Add the remaining broth and continue cooking until the mole is thick and well flavored, about 30 minutes. Taste and add more salt if needed, which I find is usually the case. (At this point, the mole can be removed from the heat, cooled, covered, and refrigerated, then reheated until bubbling before continuing.)

FOR THE TURKEY: While the mole is cooking, sprinkle the turkey with the salt. Heat the oil in a large, heavy skillet over medium-high heat. When hot, place the turkey pieces, skin side down, in the oil. (This may have to be done one piece at a time, depending on the size of your pan.) After about 10 minutes, when the turkey is well browned on the first side, carefully turn the pieces over and brown the other side. Using a slotted spatula, lift the turkey, allowing any excess oil to drip back into the pan, and add it to the mole. Lower the heat, cover, and continue cooking the mole over low heat, basting the turkey and turning it once so that it cooks evenly, until the turkey is cooked through, about 40 minutes. Taste and adjust the seasoning with salt if needed.

Remove the pan from the heat, uncover, and set aside for 20 minutes. Using tongs and a spatula, lift the turkey out of the sauce, scraping off as much sauce as possible, and put on a cutting board. Cut the meat into thick slices. Put 1 or 2 slices on each warmed plate, or arrange the slices on a warmed platter. Spoon the mole over and around the turkey slices. Remember, the sauce is what this dish is all about. Sprinkle with the reserved 1 tablespoon sesame seeds and enjoy.

TEXMOLE CON NOPALITOS
Bean and Cactus Paddle Mole

When I am in central Mexico, I often eat this spicy home-style stew with the descriptive name *texmole*, from the Nahuatl words for masa and mole. Although usually made with young goat, this version, which has been shared by Yolanda Ramos of the east-central state of Tlaxcala, replaces the meat with tender cactus paddles and large, deep purple *ayocotes*, dried runner beans that come in a multitude of shades. Kidney beans or large black beans can be substituted but will provide quite a different flavor to the dish.

To start, a tostada topped with Tinga de Cerdo (page 147) will please those who crave meat with their meals, or make Tacos de Rajas de Chiles Poblanos con Elote (page 62) for a vegetarian meal. Serve hot corn tortillas (page 19) with the *texmole* to sop up all the flavorful sauce and end with Pastel de Elote (page 252).

Serves 8 to 10 . . . .

FOR THE BEANS
  1 pound ayocotes (dried runner beans),
    preferably black or purple

  2 cloves garlic, smashed

  1 slice white onion

FOR THE BEANS: Rinse and sort the beans, discarding any broken pieces. Put the beans in a large olla (page 15) or large, heavy pot and add the garlic, onion, and 2 quarts water. Remove and discard any beans that float to the top, then bring

4 chiles puyas or chiles guajillos, stemmed but not seeded

1 tablespoon canola or safflower oil

½ small white onion, finely diced

1 clove garlic, minced

1 pound nopales, cleaned and cut into 1-by-¼-inch strips as directed on page 25 (about 3½ cups)

½ pound freshly made masa for corn tortillas (page 19), or 1 cup plus 2 tablespoons masa harina for tortillas reconstituted with ½ cup plus 1 tablespoon quite warm water

2 tablespoons freshly rendered pork lard (page 24) or canola or safflower oil

1 good-size sprig fresh epazote (optional but highly recommended)

½ teaspoon sea salt

the water to a boil over medium-high heat. Reduce the heat to medium-low, cover partially, and simmer until the beans are tender, adding more hot water if needed to keep the beans submerged. It should take 2½ to 3 hours, though the timing will vary depending on the type of bean used and how old the beans are. Drain the beans, reserving the broth, and set aside until ready to use. (If cooked in advance, cover and refrigerate until needed.)

FOR THE TEXMOLE: Soak the chiles in a bowl in very hot water to cover until soft, about 30 minutes. Drain the chiles, tear into smaller pieces, and transfer to a blender. Add ⅓ cup of the bean broth to the blender and process until smooth, add more broth if needed to release the blades. Set aside.

Heat the oil in a skillet over medium heat. Add the onion and garlic and fry, stirring occasionally, just until translucent, about 5 minutes. Add the nopales, cover, and cook, stirring occasionally. After 5 minutes, a slimy juice may start to appear and the nopales will change color slightly. Remove the lid and continue cooking until the juice has disappeared and the nopales are still quite crisp. Set aside.

Put the fresh masa or the reconstituted masa harina in a bowl. Stir up to 1 cup water into the masa to make a gruel-like mixture. Add the pureed chiles and stir well.

Heat the lard in a *cazuela* or Dutch oven over medium heat. Add the drained beans and heat for several minutes. Pour in 2 cups hot water and add the masa mixture, nopales mixture, epazote, and salt. Cook, stirring and scraping constantly with a flat-bottom wooden spatula or spoon to keep the mixture from sticking, for about 20 minutes. It will start to thicken immediately and will need to be watched closely so that it does not scorch while the masa cooks. Add up to 1 cup of the remaining bean broth and additional water if it begins to thicken too much. After 20 minutes, lower the heat and cook for a few more minutes, then taste and add more salt if needed.

Spoon into large, shallow bowls and serve. This mole tastes even better when reheated the next day and it freezes well.

PIPIÁN VERDE

Pork in a Green Pumpkin Seed Sauce

Many people think of moles as the ultimate dish of Mexican cuisine, but for me *pipianes* made with pumpkin seeds for both flavor and texture are just as special and simpler to make. Ricardo's rich and creamy green *pipián* from Papantla, the vanilla-growing center of Veracruz, is made with pork but is as delicious when prepared with chicken.

I often accompany this *pipián* with Arroz a la Mexicana (page 224) and serve a light dessert of Gelatina de Rompope (page 242). Throughout the meal, I like to pour one of my favorite red wines, a lush Spanish Tempranillo.

Serves 6

FOR THE PORK

½ white onion, halved

5 cloves garlic

1½ tablespoons sea salt

2 pounds boneless pork loin, cut into 1½-inch pieces

FOR THE PIPIÁN

1 pound tomatillos, husked, well rinsed, and roughly chopped

1½ cups tightly packed fresh cilantro leaves

½ small white onion, roasted (page 18)

5 cloves garlic, roasted (page 18), then peeled

¼ cup canola or safflower oil

3 cups hulled raw pumpkin seeds, toasted (page 19)

3 chiles serranos, stemmed and roasted (page 17)

3 whole allspice

2 whole cloves

1 tablespoon sea salt

FOR THE PORK: Put the onion, garlic, salt, and 2 quarts water in a pot and bring to a rolling boil over medium-high heat. Add the pork, lower the heat to a gentle simmer, and cook until the meat is tender, about 40 minutes. Drain, reserving the broth, and set the pork and broth aside separately. (You should have at least 6 cups broth.) Discard the onion and garlic.

FOR THE PIPIÁN: Put the tomatillos, cilantro, onion, and garlic in a blender and process until a smooth sauce forms. Do not add water.

Heat the oil in a *cazuela* or large, heavy skillet over medium heat until it ripples. Pour in the tomatillo sauce, lower the heat to medium-low, and cook, stirring often, for 10 minutes.

Place half of the pumpkin seeds in a blender and add the chiles, allspice, cloves, salt, and 3 cups of the reserved broth and process until very smooth. Stir the puree into the tomatillo sauce. Repeat this step with all of the remaining pumpkin seeds and 2 cups of the remaining broth, then add the puree to the tomatillo sauce.

Bring the tomatillo sauce to a boil, lower the heat to a gentle simmer, and cook for 5 minutes. Mix in the pork and a final 1 cup broth, then taste and add more salt if needed. Bring back to a simmer and simmer until the meat is heated through, then remove from the heat. The sauce will be thick and care must be taken during cooking to keep the heat low so that no lumps form.

As with most *pipianes*, this dish is best served in deep plates with plenty of sauce.

PIPIÁN VERDE DE XOCONOXTLES
Chicken in a Green Pumpkin Sauce

This elegant dish features *xoconoxtles* (page 211), those rather sour fruits of the nopal cactus, in a *pipián* with chickens or rabbits, which are plentiful in the region of Guanajuato, where Ofelia Rizo de Galindo lives at the Chichimec mission of San Luis de la Paz. Ofelia told Ricardo that *xoconoxtles* are sold in abundance in the village market during much of the year but in the winter are quite scarce. Her solution is to buy *xoconoxtles* in season, then bury them slightly underground to use later.

Tortitas de Nopales con Salsa Roja (page 125) are a tasty starter and yet another way to use the same cactus—this time the paddles. I suggest serving the *pipián* with Arroz Blanco (page 223) and ending the meal with Gorditas de Garbanzo Dulce (page 253) and Café de Olla (page 280).

Serves 6 to 8

FOR THE CHICKEN
6 large chicken thighs, 2½ to 3 pounds

¼ white onion

1 tablespoon sea salt

FOR THE SAUCE
About 4 tablespoons canola or safflower oil

6 to 10 xoconoxtles, depending on size, peeled, halved vertically, seeded, and cut crosswise into ¼-inch-thick slices (about 1 cup)

FOR THE CHICKEN: Put the chicken in a pot and add the onion, salt, and cold water to cover. Bring to a boil over medium-high heat, skimming off any foam that rises to the surface. Lower the heat to a gentle simmer, cover partially, and cook for about 20 minutes. (The chicken will finish cooking later.) Lift out the chicken and set aside. Remove and discard the onion

- ½ teaspoon sea salt
- 1 cup hulled raw pumpkin seeds
- ½ cup roughly chopped white onion
- 6 green onions, green part only, roughly chopped
- 2 cloves garlic, roughly chopped
- 6 large romaine lettuce leaves, torn into pieces (about 3 cups packed)
- 10 large radish leaves, roughly chopped
- 3 chiles serranos, roughly chopped

and set the broth aside. Let the broth sit for a while, then spoon off as much fat as possible. (If you are cooking the chicken in advance, let the broth cool, cover, and refrigerate, then remove the congealed fat from the surface before using.)

FOR THE SAUCE: Heat 1 tablespoon of the oil in a *cazuela* or skillet over medium heat until shimmering. Add the *xoco-noxtles* and fry, stirring occasionally, until tender and somewhat brown, about 4 minutes. Using a slotted spatula, lift out the *xoconoxtles*, allowing any excess oil to drip back into the pan, and transfer to absorbent paper to drain. Sprinkle with the salt and set aside. Reserve the oil in the *cazuela*.

Finely grind the pumpkin seeds in a spice grinder or coffee grinder. Set aside.

Reheat the oil in the *cazuela* over medium heat. Add the white onion, green onion tops, and garlic and cook, stirring often and adding a little more oil if the pan seems dry, for 3 to 5 minutes. Using a slotted spoon, lift out the onions and garlic, allowing any excess oil to drip back into the pan, and transfer to a blender. Add the lettuce, radish leaves, chiles, and 3 cups of the reserved broth to the blender and blend until smooth.

Reheat the oil in the *cazuela* over medium-high heat, adding 2 to 3 tablespoons more oil. When the oil is hot, add the chicken and brown on both sides, about 8 minutes. When almost ready to serve, add the blended ingredients and the pumpkin seeds and mix well, then lower the heat to a gentle simmer. When the mixture just begins to bubble, stir in the *xoconoxtles* and heat through. Add more broth or water only if needed, as the sauce should be quite thick. Serve on warmed plates as quickly as possible.

PIPIÁN BLANCO
Chicken in White Almond Sauce

This unusual version of white *pipián* that Ricardo prepares with olives and capers is based on a traditional dish from around Xalapa, the capital of Veracruz, but the pronounced toasty flavor of nuts and seeds is more in the style of Mexico City. I suggest cooking the chicken up to one day in advance, which makes this dish an easy one to prepare for a special meal with guests. The pale yellow, or "blond," pickled *chile güero* can be found in the Mexican section of most well-stocked grocery stores. Serve Arroz Verde (page 225) for a colorful contrast.

Serves 6 . . . .

FOR THE CHICKEN
6 large chicken thighs, 2½ to 3 pounds

1 small white onion, quartered

6 cloves garlic, halved

3 sprigs fresh flat-leaf parsley

5 black peppercorns

1 tablespoon sea salt

FOR THE PIPIÁN
1¼ cups slivered blanched almonds, lightly toasted

1 cup unhulled sesame seeds, lightly toasted (page 18)

¼ cup canola or safflower oil

2 teaspoons sea salt

FOR THE GARNISH
6 chiles güeros en escabeche

30 pitted green olives, well rinsed

2 tablespoons small capers, rinsed

6 sprigs fresh flat-leaf parsley or cilantro

FOR THE CHICKEN: Put the chicken in a pot and add the onion, garlic, and 2 quarts water. Bring to a boil over medium-high heat, skimming off any foam that rises to the surface. Add the parsley, peppercorns, and salt, cover partially, and simmer over medium-low until the juices run clear when a thigh is pierced, about 25 minutes. Remove the chicken and set aside. Strain the broth through a fine-mesh sieve and set aside. Let it sit for a while, then spoon off as much fat as possible.

FOR THE PIPIÁN: Put the almonds, sesame seeds, and 2 cups of the reserved broth in a blender and process until a smooth puree forms. If you do not have a heavy-duty blender, you will need to grind the nuts and seeds in a spice grinder or coffee grinder before adding them to the blender.

Heat the oil in a *cazuela* or heavy skillet over medium heat until shimmering. Pour in the nut and seed mixture and fry, stirring constantly, until it starts to bubble. Reduce the heat to very low and continue to stir occasionally until the sauce has thickened, about 10 minutes. Gradually add 3 cups of the reserved broth and the salt while continuing to stir until the *pipián* becomes even thicker. Place the thighs in the sauce and reheat for 5 minutes.

You can serve this dish on warmed individual plates with each chicken piece topped with plenty of sauce and garnished with chiles, olives, capers, and a sprig of parsley, or you can serve it family style on a large platter.

PIPIÁN DE PUERCO ESTILO SAN FRANCISCO IXTACAMAXTITLÁN

Pork in a Sauce of Seeds, Nuts, and Chiles

One autumn, in the small Puebla village of Ixtacamaxtitlán, one of the local women, María Eugenia Bonilla Hernández, and her friends prepared a festive meal for a group of us. On the menu was this *pipián de puerco,* alongside another dish of tender beans and bits of nopales (page 23) and a seemingly endless quantity of freshly made tortillas. This is my adaptation of the savory *pipián* recipe that María served, still quite similar to the dish that her ancestors would have prepared, though they would have likely used small birds or wild turkeys. The *chiles chipotles* here, known as *chipotles mecos,* are the ones that look like wrinkled tan suede. María used a volcanic-rock *metate* and *mano* to grind her seed mixture into a smooth paste, but a heavy-duty blender will work. If you want to use a food processor to make the *pipían,* you will have to grind the spices, seeds, and nuts in a spice grinder or coffee grinder before you add them to the processor.

Serves 6 to 8 . . . .

▓ FOR THE MEAT

4 pounds boneless, meaty country-style pork ribs or pork shoulder, trimmed of excess fat and cut into 1½-inch squares, or a combination of ribs and shoulder

5 small cloves garlic

2 heaping teaspoons sea salt

▓ FOR THE PIPIÁN

2 chiles chipotles mecos, stemmed, then toasted (page 18)

3 cloves garlic, roasted (page 18), then peeled

¼ cup chile ancho seeds (from about 8 chiles), toasted (page 18)

2½ cups hulled raw pumpkin seeds, toasted (page 18)

¾ cup unhulled sesame seeds, toasted (page 18)

FOR THE MEAT: Put the meat in a wide *cazuela* or Dutch oven and add the garlic, salt, and water to cover by ½ inch. Bring to a boil over medium-high heat, skimming off any foam that rises to the surface. Lower the heat to medium, cover partially, and simmer until the meat is tender and the water begins to evaporate, about 40 minutes. Uncover and spoon out most of the broth into a container, leaving only enough liquid in the *cazuela* to come to the top of the meat. Set the broth aside. Reduce the heat and continue cooking the pork with the lid off, turning the meat often, until the broth has evaporated, the fat has rendered out of the meat, and the meat begins to brown, about 6 minutes. Do not overcook. Scoop the meat out into

½ cup skinned raw peanuts, toasted

½-inch stick Mexican true cinnamon bark (page 88)

2 whole cloves

1 tablespoon freshly rendered pork lard (page 24) or canola or safflower oil

Leaves from several fresh cilantro sprigs, finely chopped

a bowl and set aside. Leave the melted fat in the *cazuela* for cooking the *pipián* and set the *cazuela* aside.

FOR THE PIPIÁN: Soak the *chiles chipotles mecos* in a bowl in very hot water to cover until soft, about 20 minutes. Drain, tear into smaller pieces, and put in a bowl.

Add the garlic, chile seeds, 2 cups of the pumpkin seeds, the sesame seeds, the peanuts, the cinnamon, and the cloves to the chiles and stir well. Put half of the chile mixture in a blender along with enough of the reserved broth to release the blades and process until a slightly textured puree forms. Transfer to a bowl. Repeat with the remaining chile mixture and more broth and add to the puree in the bowl. (If you do not have a heavy-duty blender, you will need to process in small batches or you will need to grind the seeds, spices, and nuts in a spice grinder or coffee grinder before adding them to the blender.) To make a smoother sauce, pass the mixture through a medium-mesh sieve, pushing it through with the back of a wooden spoon.

Scrape off any shreds of meat adhering to the bottom of the *cazuela* and return it to medium-high heat. Add the lard and heat until shimmering. Quickly add the *pipián* mixture and stir slowly but constantly with a wooden spoon from the center to the edge for 5 minutes, adding more broth or water if needed. The *pipián* should be smooth and silky, rather like a heavy cream sauce. Add the pork and reduce the heat to low. Chile-rich dishes often require more salt than you might think, so taste and add more salt if needed. Continue cooking over low heat, stirring only two or three times, until the *pipián* is quite thick, 10 to 15 minutes.

Transfer to a warmed deep serving platter, sprinkle with the remaining ½ cup pumpkin seeds and the cilantro, and serve.

CHILES RELLENOS
AND OTHER REGIONAL SPECIALTIES

CHILES POBLANOS RELLENOS DE QUESO Y ENVUELTOS EN PASTA HOJALDRE
Poblano Chiles Stuffed with Cheese and Wrapped in Puff Pastry

The first time I was served these chiles encased in a puff of flaky pastry was at a small but very smart restaurant in the Zona Rosa in Mexico City, where Roberto Santibañez was the chef. They were delicious. I was there with my friend María Dolores Torres Yzábal, who confided in me that this was also one of her specialties, and she shared with me her recipe, which she serves with a tomato sauce.

The tangy-flavored *queso Chihuahua* that María Dolores uses is produced by the Mennonites in the northern Mexican state of Chihuahua and is almost impossible to find in the United States, but good substitutes exist.

These chiles can be prepared and stuffed a day in advance and kept covered in the refrigerator. The sauce can be made in advance as well, covered and refrigerated for up to 4 days, and reheated before serving. This is one of the most impressive dishes that I serve for dinner parties. I just put the chiles in the oven soon after my friends arrive. The earthy essence of Sopa de Hongos (page 79) is a good introduction to the chiles, and I like to finish the meal with something lighter, perhaps just a dish of Helado de Mango (page 248). For this celebratory meal, I often serve a dry Spanish Riesling. If you are serving fewer people, the recipe is easily reduced.

Serves 8

FOR THE CHILES

1 pound Muenster or Monterey Jack cheese, shredded

8 chiles poblanos, about 6 inches long, roasted and prepared for stuffing (page 18)

All-purpose flour for dusting

1 (1.1-pound) box frozen puff pastry (2 sheets), thawed according to package directions

1 egg, beaten

FOR THE TOMATO SAUCE

¾ pound ripe tomatoes (about 2 medium or 6 or 7 plum), roasted and peeled (page 18), then roughly chopped

½ white onion, finely chopped (about ⅓ cup)

2 cloves garlic, roughly chopped

½ chile serrano, stem, seeds, and membranes removed

2 tablespoons canola or safflower oil

1 bay leaf

1-inch stick Mexican true cinnamon bark (page 88), ground

½ teaspoon sea salt

FOR THE CHILES: Heat the oven to 375°F. Line a baking sheet with parchment paper.

Divide the cheese into 8 equal portions. One at a time, press each portion into an elongated shape that will fit inside a chile. Stuff the cheese into the chiles and press the slit edges to close tightly.

On a lightly floured work surface, roll out 1 pastry sheet about 1/16 inch thick. Cut the sheet into quarters. Put a stuffed chile, slit side down, onto the center of a quarter sheet and wrap the pastry around the chile, overlapping the edges, then seal the edges by dampening them with water and pressing together. You may need to trim the excess pastry off the ends. Repeat with the remaining 3 pastry quarters and 3 more chiles, then repeat with the remaining pastry sheet and chiles.

Place the pastry-wrapped chiles, seam side down, on the prepared baking sheet. If you are feeling creative and have pastry trimmings, make decorative cutouts from the trimmings and adhere them to the wrapped chiles with a little water. Lightly brush the wrapped chiles with the beaten egg. Bake until the pastry turns a deep gold, 50 to 60 minutes.

FOR THE SAUCE: While the chiles are baking, put the tomatoes and any juices, onion, garlic, and chile in a blender and process until fairly smooth but still with some texture.

Heat the oil in a saucepan or skillet over medium heat. When it is hot, pour in the tomato mixture and bring to a simmer. Stir in the bay leaf, cinnamon, and salt, reduce the heat to medium-low, and cook until the tomatoes have broken down and thickened and the flavors have blended, about 15 minutes. Remove and discard the bay leaf, then taste and add more salt if needed.

Transfer the chiles to warmed individual plates. Serve the sauce on the side to be added by everyone, as desired.

CHILES CHIPOTLES TAMARINDOS RELLENOS DE QUESO COTIJA

Chipotle Chiles Stuffed with Cheese

Here, the smoky flavor of the chiles delivers a subtle counterpoint to the rather bland *queso cotija* filling. This unusual recipe, which was given to Ricardo by Delia Muciño Cruz, who lives in the state of Mexico, is a palate-exciting main course.

What Delia calls *chiles chipotles tamarindos* are large (about 3 inches long) and puffy like a cushion. They are seldom found outside of central Mexico, but any other large, wine red *chile chipotle* will work if it has supple flesh. *Chiles pasillas de Oaxaca* can be used as well. If the only chiles you can find are smaller than 2½ inches, they will be hard to stuff, and you may need up to a half dozen more chiles to accommodate all of the stuffing.

This makes a savory meal when served with Arroz a la Mexicana (page 224) and with Ante de Coco Marquesote (page 258) for dessert.

Serves 4 to 6, depending on the size of the chiles . . . .

12 large, supple-fleshed chiles chipotles or chiles pasillas de Oaxaca, preferably about 3 inches long, with stems intact

2 cups whole milk

¼ cup grated piloncillo (page 42), azúcar morena or other unrefined brown cane sugar, or firmly packed dark brown sugar

1 teaspoon dried thyme

1 teaspoon dried marjoram

2 bay leaves

9 ounces queso cotija, queso añejo, or Muenster cheese, grated or crumbled

▮ FOR THE SAUCE

1½ pounds ripe tomatoes (3 or 4 large), peeled, seeded, and roughly chopped, or 2 (14½-ounce) cans diced tomatoes, drained

3 tablespoons finely chopped white onion

Cut each chile lengthwise from just below the stem to within ¼ inch from the bottom and open gently. With a small knife or spoon, scrape out the seeds and membranes. If the chiles are hard and dry, warm them on a *comal* or in a skillet over medium-low heat until they soften a bit.

Combine the milk, sugar, thyme, marjoram, and bay leaves in a wide saucepan over medium heat, stirring occasionally to dissolve the sugar. As soon as the milk comes to a boil, reduce the heat to low, add the chiles, and simmer until they begin to soften, about 15 minutes. Using a slotted spoon, transfer the chiles to absorbent paper and pat them dry. Discard the milk. When cool enough to handle, stuff

2 small cloves garlic

1 teaspoon sea salt

3 tablespoons canola or safflower oil

FOR THE BATTER AND FRYING

5 eggs, at room temperature, separated

½ teaspoon sea salt

½ cup sifted all-purpose flour

1½ cups canola or safflower oil

FOR THE GARNISH

½ cup Mexican crema (page 23), crème fraîche, or thick sour cream thinned with 1 tablespoon whole milk

½ pound Mexican manchego or Monterey Jack cheese, grated

the chiles with cheese, being careful to fill them just enough so they can still be easily closed.

FOR THE SAUCE: Put the tomatoes, onion, garlic, salt, and ¼ cup water in a blender and blend until a smooth sauce forms.

Heat the oil in a *cazuela* or heavy skillet over medium-high heat until shimmering. Pour in the tomato sauce, reduce the heat to medium-low, and cook, stirring occasionally, until you can see the bottom of the pan when scraped through the middle with the spoon and the sauce is very thick and almost pastelike, about 20 minutes. Remove from the heat and set aside.

FOR THE BATTER AND FRYING: Put the egg whites in a bowl, add the salt, and beat the whites with a whisk or an electric mixer until stiff peaks form. Add the yolks, one at a time, beating after each addition until combined. Fold in 1 tablespoon of the flour and set aside.

Put the remaining flour in a shallow bowl or other container. One at a time, roll the chiles in the flour, shake to remove the excess flour, and set aside.

Heat the oven to 350°F.

Pour the oil into a *cazuela* or heavy skillet and heat over medium-high heat until shimmering but not smoking. Holding a chile by its stem, quickly dip it into the batter, coating well, and then carefully place in the hot oil. Coat 1 or 2 more chiles the same way and add to the pan. Fry, turning as needed to cook on all sides, until golden. As the chiles cook, use a spoon or spatula to splash the hot oil over the top. Using a slotted spatula, lift out the chiles, allow any excess oil to drip back into the pan, and transfer to absorbent paper to drain. Repeat to cook the remaining chiles the same way. (If you have not used chiles with their stems intact, ladle some batter about the size of your chile into the hot oil, quickly add the chile, and then add more batter on top. The remainder of the cooking process is the same.)

Place the chiles in a single layer in a baking dish. Top each chile with some tomato sauce, a spoonful of the *crema*, and a sprinkle of the cheese. Bake just until the cheese melts, about 15 minutes. Transfer to warmed individual plates and serve right away.

CHILES POBLANOS RELLENOS DE PICADILLO NORTEÑO

Poblano Chiles Filled with Northern-Style Meat Stuffing

María Macías, a cook from the large northeastern state of Nuevo León, always prepared her *picadillo* by the traditional method of finely mincing (*picado*) boiled meat. Now, her granddaughter makes similar *chiles rellenos,* but she uses ground beef and pork in her filling. According to Ricardo, both grandmother and granddaughter reflect the regional practice of making the *picadillo* sweeter than cooks do in other parts of Mexico, creating a soothing contrast to the more raucous flavor of the chile.

Both the *picadillo* and the sauce can be made in advance. The chiles can also be stuffed and refrigerated in advance. Be sure to bring the stuffed chiles to room temperature before coating them with the batter. The sauce calls for *acitrón,* the sugary crystallized flesh of the spiny, large round *biznaga* cactus. It can be found in many Mexican markets in the United States. Don't mistake *acitrón* for candied citron peel.

It is also traditional to stuff these chiles with ¾ cup crumbled *queso fresco,* although grated Monterey Jack or white Cheddar will work as well. For a satisfying meal, serve Arroz a la Mexicana (page 224) as an accompaniment, and perhaps Rosca de Pasas (page 250), a typical northern Mexico dessert, to finish.

Serves 6

6 medium chiles poblanos, with stems intact

FOR THE SAUCE

2 pounds ripe tomatoes (about 6 medium), peeled and roughly chopped, or 4 cups drained diced canned tomatoes

1 cup crumbled crust-free French baguette bread (about 2 slices), or ½ French roll, crust removed

½ cup roughly chopped white onion

1 teaspoon roughly chopped garlic

1 teaspoon fresh marjoram leaves, or rounded ¼ teaspoon dried marjoram

Following the directions on page 17, roast and peel the chiles, then prepare them for stuffing. Set aside at room temperature.

FOR THE SAUCE: Put the tomatoes, bread, onion, garlic, marjoram, salt, sugar, and 1 cup water in a blender and process until smooth.

Heat the oil in a heavy skillet over medium heat until shimmering. Add the tomato mixture and fry, stirring frequently, until it turns dark orange and thickens slightly,

2 teaspoons sea salt

1 teaspoon sugar

¼ cup canola or safflower oil

▋ FOR THE PICADILLO

¼ cup canola or safflower oil

1 cup finely chopped white onion

2 cups peeled, seeded, and chopped ripe
   tomatoes (about 2 large), or 1 (14½-ounce)
   can diced tomatoes, drained

½ pound ground pork

½ pound ground beef

1¼-inch stick Mexican true cinnamon bark
   (page 88)

3 whole cloves

12 black peppercorns

¼ cup raisins

3 tablespoons minced fresh flat-leaf parsley
   (leaves only)

2 heaping teaspoons acitrón or candied
   pineapple, cut into ⅛-inch cubes

1 teaspoon sea salt

▋ FOR THE BATTER AND FRYING

5 eggs, at room temperature, separated and
   yolks slightly broken up

1 teaspoon sea salt

½ cup sifted all-purpose flour

Canola or safflower oil for frying

▋ FOR THE GARNISH

½ white onion, thinly sliced, then briefly
   blanched in boiling water and drained

about 5 minutes. Taste and if it is very acidic, add a little more sugar and maybe a pinch more salt if needed to bring out the flavor. The sauce can be made up to 5 days in advance, covered, and refrigerated.

FOR THE PICADILLO: Heat the oil in a *cazuela*, heavy skillet, or Dutch oven over medium heat. Add the onion and fry, stirring often, until golden, about 5 minutes. Add the tomatoes and cook, stirring frequently, for 30 minutes if using fresh tomatoes or 10 minutes if using canned tomatoes. Crumble in the pork and beef and continue to cook, stirring often so that nothing sticks and burns, until the sauce becomes quite dry, about 10 minutes.

Finely grind the cinnamon, cloves, and peppercorns in a spice grinder or coffee grinder. Stir the ground spices into the sauce, lower the heat to a gentle simmer, and cook for 5 minutes. Add the raisins, parsley, *acitrón,* and salt and continue to simmer for 5 minutes longer. Taste and adjust the seasoning with salt if needed. Remove from the heat and let cool. The *picadillo* can be made up to 2 days in advance, covered, and refrigerated. Bring to room temperature before using.

Spoon the *picadillo* into the chiles, packing it loosely and leaving room to close the chiles. They may have to be held together with toothpicks—just visualize stitching through thick satin cloth. The chiles can be stuffed a day in advance and refrigerated. Bring to room temperature before battering and frying.

FOR THE BATTER AND FRYING: Put the egg whites in a bowl, add the salt, and whisk until soft peaks form. Gradually whisk in the yolks and continue beating until stiff peaks form. Put the batter next to the stove.

Make sure the chiles are completely dry. Put the flour in a shallow bowl or pan. One at a time, roll the chiles in the flour, shake to remove the excess flour, and set aside.

Heat the oven to 200°F. Pour the oil to a depth of at least ½ inch into a large, heavy skillet and heat over medium-high heat to 375°F on a deep-frying thermometer. Holding a chile by its stem, quickly dip it into the egg batter and then immediately lay it in the oil. Coat 1 or 2 more chiles the same way and add to the pan. Fry, turning as needed to cook on all sides, until golden, about 2 minutes. (If there are any bare spots on the chiles, spoon on additional batter.) Using a slotted spatula, lift out the chiles, allowing any excess oil to drip back into the pan, and transfer to absorbent paper to drain. Keep the chiles warm in the oven. Repeat to cook the remaining chiles the same way, making sure the oil is always at 375°F before adding the next batch. Reheat the sauce.

Place the chiles on warmed plates. Spoon the hot sauce onto the chiles, top with the onion slices, and serve.

CHILES EN NOGADA
Poblano Chiles in Walnut Sauce

Along with *mole poblano,* no other dish in Mexico better represents the spectacular creations from the Puebla convents than *chiles en nogada,* large green chiles stuffed with a fruity meat *picadillo* studded with pieces of *acitrón,* the candied flesh of the *biznaga* cactus; cloaked with a creamy nut sauce; and topped with a scattering of ruby red pomegranate seeds. Its fame began when it was prepared by the Augustine nuns for a great feast in Puebla held in honor of Don Agustín de Iturbide, Mexico's short-term self-declared emperor, who assumed power shortly after the Mexican War of Independence.

In Puebla and throughout central Mexico, *chiles en nogada* are always served on Independence Day, September 16, with the vibrant green, white, and red of the dish symbolic of the colors of the Mexican flag. Another reason the dish is featured in early autumn is because pomegranates are red ripe and walnuts are fresh and milky tender, both considered essential to the perfect *chiles en nogada.* On a walk through a market in Puebla, Ana Elena Martínez, my assistant in Mexico, pointed out women kneeling over baskets of just-gathered walnuts persistently scraping off the dark peels with their fingernails. Not an easy task. One four-hour-long peeling and scraping experience was enough for me and now I just use the freshest peeled walnuts I can find.

In central Mexico, the pears, peaches, and apples used are quite different from those found in U.S. markets. They are from trees in the highlands and quite small and solid, so do your best to approximate them.

This dish requires many separate preparations, all of which can be made in advance. Although Ana Elena traditionally serves her chiles *en capeado,* or "battered then fried," which does require some last-minute effort, you can make them without the batter. Either way, the dish will impress dinner guests—even an emperor.

To start this meal, serve a light, elegant Sopa de Cilantro (page 78). After the main course, offer each guest a sliver of Flan de Leche (page 259) accompanied by a small glass of *tequila añejo.* I like to serve a full-bodied, oaky Chardonnay or Viognier during the meal.

Serves 10, with leftovers

▌ FOR THE NOGADA

25 shelled whole walnuts, the freshest possible

1½ cups whole milk

⅓ cup blanched sliced almonds

½ cup torn crust-free French bread or baguette

1½ cups Mexican crema (page 23), crème fraîche, or thick sour cream thinned with 1 tablespoon whole milk

2 tablespoons Spanish dry (fino) sherry

1 small clove garlic

½ teaspoon sea salt

⅛ teaspoon ground cinnamon (optional)

▌ FOR THE PICADILLO

¼ cup canola or safflower oil

½ cup finely chopped white onion

2 cloves garlic, finely chopped

1 pound ripe tomatoes (about 3 medium), peeled, cored, and finely chopped

2 tablespoons sea salt

2 pounds boneless pork shoulder, trimmed of excess fat and cut into ¼-inch cubes

FOR THE NOGADA: The day before you plan to serve the chiles, put the walnuts in a saucepan with water to cover, bring to a boil over high heat, and boil for 5 minutes. Drain and let the nuts cool until they can be handled, then peel or scrape off as much of the outer coating from each nut as possible. Place the nuts in a bowl, add the milk, cover, and soak overnight in the refrigerator.

The next day, drain the nuts, reserving the milk, and put in a blender or food processor. Add the almonds, bread, *crema,* sherry, garlic, salt, cinnamon (if using), and enough of the walnut soaking milk to make a thick sauce and process until smooth. Cover and refrigerate until ready to use, then bring to room temperature before using.

FOR THE PICADILLO: Heat the oil in a *cazuela,* Dutch oven, or large, heavy skillet over medium-high heat until shimmering.

1 pound slightly underripe pears (3 or 4), preferably Seckel, though Bosc or other cooking pears will do

1 pound firm peaches (3 or 4)

1 pound apples (3 or 4), preferably crisp Rome Beauty, McIntosh, or Gravenstein

1 partially black plantain (page 103)

½ cup roughly chopped raisins

½ cup roughly chopped blanched almonds

⅓ cup roughly chopped acitrón or candied pineapple

1-inch stick Mexican true cinnamon bark (page 88)

½ teaspoon sugar

½ teaspoon freshly ground black pepper

FOR THE CHILES

12 chiles poblanos, stems intact if using with batter

FOR THE OPTIONAL BATTER AND FRYING

6 eggs, at room temperature, separated

1 teaspoon sea salt

½ cup plus 2 tablespoons all-purpose flour

Peanut or safflower oil for frying

FOR THE GARNISH

Seeds from 1 pomegranate

Leaves from 1½ bunches fresh flat-leaf parsley (about 20 sprigs), chopped

Add the onion and sauté until translucent, about 5 minutes. Add the garlic and stir for several minutes. Add the tomatoes and cook, stirring frequently, until the mixture is almost dry, about 15 minutes. Sprinkle with the salt, then stir in the meat and cook, stirring occasionally, for 30 minutes. Meanwhile, peel the pears, peaches, apples, and plantains. Halve and core the pears and apples, and halve and pit the peaches. Cut all of the fruits into ¼-inch cubes. This should not be done in advance, as the fruit will darken.

Add the cubed fruit, raisins, almonds, *acitrón*, cinnamon, sugar, and pepper to the meat and mix well. Cook, stirring occasionally, until the meat is tender, about 30 minutes. Taste and add more salt and sugar if needed. Remove from the heat and set aside until ready to stuff the chiles. Barely reheat before using, if not warm.

FOR THE CHILES: Following the directions on page 18, roast and peel the chiles, then prepare them for stuffing.

Stuff the *picadillo* into the chiles, packing it loosely until the chiles are plump and just barely closed.

FOR THE OPTIONAL BATTER AND FRYING: Put the egg whites in a bowl and beat with an electric mixer until soft peaks form. In a separate bowl, lightly beat the egg yolks with a whisk. Fold the yolks, 2 tablespoons of the flour, and the salt into the whites. Put the batter next to the stove.

Put the remaining ½ cup flour in a shallow bowl or pan. Make sure that the chiles are perfectly dry. One at a time, roll the chiles in the flour, shake to remove the excess flour, and set aside.

Heat the oven to 200°F. Pour the oil to a depth of 2 inches into a large, heavy skillet and heat over medium heat until shimmering. Holding a chile by its stem, quickly dip it into the batter and then immediately lay it in the hot oil. Coat 1 or 2 more chiles the same way and add to the pan. Fry, turning as needed to cook on all sides, until golden, about 2 minutes. As the chiles cook, use a spoon or spatula to splash the hot oil over the top. Using a slotted spatula, lift out the chiles, allowing any excess oil to drip back into the pan, and transfer to absorbent paper to drain. Keep the chiles warm in the oven. Repeat to cook the remaining chiles the same way, making sure the oil regains its temperature before adding the next batch and adding more oil if necessary.

Arrange the chiles on a warmed platter or on individual plates. Spoon the *nogada* sauce over the top and decorate with the pomegranate seeds and parsley. Or, if you decided not to cloak the chiles in batter, you can served the stuffed chiles at room temperature topped with the sauce and pomegranate seeds.

SOPA DE PAN
Festive Bread Soup

This unusual and bedazzling celebratory dry soup of Spanish origin is served throughout the regions of Tuxtla Gutiérrez and San Cristóbal de las Casas in Chiapas. *Sopa de pan* is one of Alty Orantes de Fernández's favorite dishes for fiestas, where she usually serves it as a main course. Alty worked at her mother's restaurant in Tuxtla Gutiérrez, the capital of Chiapas, for over twenty-five years and finally said "no more." But then her son, a lawyer, decided to open a taquería. According to Alty, he was a better lawyer than he was a cook and so she helped him out. Soon she took over the taquería and then ran it for the next twenty years.

I like to start the meal with a bowl of "wet" Caldo de Tichindas (page 76).

Serves 4 to 6

1 long baguette, preferably sourdough, cut into ½-inch-thick slices

1½ cups canola or safflower oil, plus more if needed

4 tablespoons unsalted butter

1 black-ripe plantain (page 103), peeled, quartered crosswise, and then sliced lengthwise into ¼-inch-thick strips

Arrange the bread slices in a single layer on a work surface and let dry for an hour or so. Alternatively, arrange the slices on a large baking sheet and put in a 200°F oven for 15 minutes, then remove from the oven and reserve.

Heat 1 cup of the oil and 2 tablespoons of the butter in a large skillet over medium

6 black peppercorns

2 whole allspice

2 whole cloves

½-inch stick Mexican true cinnamon bark (page 88)

¼ white onion, sliced

4 tomatoes, thickly sliced, plus 2 plum tomatoes, chopped

6 cups chicken broth (page 25)

1 sprig fresh flat-leaf parsley, chopped

½ teaspoon dried oregano, preferably Mexican

½ teaspoon dried thyme

½ teaspoon sea salt

½ teaspoon freshly ground black pepper

Large pinch of saffron threads, crushed between your fingers

¼ cup raisins

2 hard-boiled eggs, peeled and sliced

heat. When the oil is quite hot, add half of the baguette slices and brown lightly on both sides. Using a slotted spatula, lift out the slices, allowing any excess oil to drip back into the pan, and transfer to absorbent paper to drain. Add the remaining ½ cup oil and remaining 2 tablespoons butter to the skillet and fry the remaining baguette slices the same way, then drain on absorbent paper.

Add the plantain strips to the oil remaining in the pan and fry over medium heat, turning once, until speckled with brown on both sides. If the strips begin to stick, add a little more oil to the pan. Using the slotted spatula, transfer the strips to absorbent paper to drain. Add the peppercorns, allspice, cloves, and cinnamon to the hot oil and fry just until the oil is very aromatic. Then, using the slotted spatula, transfer the spices to the center of a small square of cheesecloth. Gather the corners of the cheesecloth together and tie securely with kitchen string.

Add the onion slices to the oil remaining in the pan and fry over medium heat until pale yellow, adding more oil if they begin to stick. Using the slotted spatula, transfer the onion to a plate and set aside. Add the sliced tomatoes to the pan and fry briefly until they are softened but still hold their shape. Using the spatula, transfer to a plate and set aside.

Bring the broth to a simmer in a saucepan over medium heat. Stir in the chopped tomatoes and the bundle of fried spices, then add the parsley, oregano, thyme, salt, pepper, and saffron. Simmer for 30 minutes to blend the flavors, then taste and add more salt if needed.

Heat the oven to 350°F. Lightly butter a shallow 9-by-11-inch baking pan.

Layer half of the bread slices in the bottom of the prepared pan. Top with the slices of tomato, onion, and plantain and sprinkle with the raisins. Layer the remaining bread slices on top. Remove the bundle of spices from the broth and pour the broth evenly over the surface. Bake until thoroughly heated, about 20 minutes.

Remove from the oven and garnish with the egg slices. Serve in warmed shallow bowls.

QUESO RELLENO
Stuffed Edam Cheese

For as long as Ricardo can remember, the large red-waxed balls of Edam cheese from the Netherlands have been arriving in great quantities to the free ports of Chetumal and Cozumel in the state of Quintana Roo. But the tasty and impressive *queso relleno*, a signature dish of the region, is a rather recent addition to Yucatán's table, said to have been created in the 1950s to honor visiting dignitaries from the Netherlands. The cheese is stuffed with ground pork and a savory mélange of Spanish olives and capers and local tomatoes and chiles and then served with various sauces. Small Edams are readily available, but the four-pound one you need for this recipe may have to be special ordered from a cheese shop or online (see Sources). Make certain that you are using the almost-round Edam cheese for this dish, and not the flatter Gouda, which also comes sealed in red wax and has a higher butterfat content. The latter will not work for this recipe.

Ricardo's friend Fernando Escalante bragged about his special *queso relleno* for many years, and although his recipe looks long and formidable, don't be daunted. Almost all of the components can be prepared ahead of time and assembled the day of serving. We recommend making the special seasoning paste, *recado de especie,* and the *picadillo yucateco* a day in advance, as well as beginning the preparation of the cheese. The *picadillo de jitomate, chiltomate* sauce, and *kol,* a saffron-flavored gravy, are best made early on the day of serving. Make sure that everything is ready and put in serving bowls, as the dish requires some synchronized movements.

Fernando traditionally starts the meal with bowls of sizzling *sopa de lima* (page 86) and has a seemingly endless supply of freshly made corn tortillas (page 19) close by for enfolding the cheese, filling, and sauces. He also accompanies the *queso* with *arroz blanco* (page 223) and serves *horchata* (page 275) and a choice of local beers to drink.

Serves 8

FOR THE CHEESE
1 (4-pound) Edam cheese, about 5½ inches in diameter

FOR THE RECADO DE ESPECIE
6 cloves garlic, roasted (page 18), then peeled

3 whole cloves

FOR THE CHEESE: Pare off the red wax from the cheese. With a very sharp knife, cut a ¾-inch-thick slice from the top of the cheese; reserve for the lid.

Stand the cheese upright. Measure in ¾ inch from the edge of the rim and trace a line around the top. Then, carefully

1½-inch stick Mexican true cinnamon bark
(page 88)

½ teaspoon black peppercorns

½ teaspoon dried oregano, preferably Mexican,
or 12 dried Yucatecan orégano leaves

▌ FOR THE PICADILLO YUCATECO

1 tablespoon recado de especie

1 tablespoon freshly squeezed bitter orange
juice (page 26) or diluted unseasoned rice
vinegar (page 50)

2 pounds coarsely ground pork

⅔ cup plus 2 tablespoons freshly rendered
pork lard (page 24) or canola or safflower oil

½ cup finely chopped white onion

2 teaspoons minced garlic

2 green chiles dulces or ½ green bell pepper,
seeds and membranes removed and finely
chopped

1 xcatic, Anaheim, banana, or similar blond
chile, seeds and membranes removed and
finely chopped

1 cup small capers, rinsed

⅓ cup roughly chopped pitted green olives

⅓ cup raisins

Sea salt

2 pounds tomatoes (about 6 medium),
peeled, seeded, and roughly chopped, or
2 (16-ounce) cans diced tomatoes, drained

▌ FOR THE PICADILLO DE JITOMATE

6 tablespoons freshly rendered pork lard
(page 24) or canola or safflower oil

½ cup finely chopped white onion

1 green chile dulce or ½ small green bell
pepper, seeds and membranes removed and
finely chopped

1 xcatic, Anaheim, banana, or similar blond
chile, seeds and membranes removed and
finely chopped

carve a hole in the ball of cheese, removing the center little by little, first with a short, curved knife and then with a sharp-tipped spoon such as a grapefruit spoon. Take care not to carve out too much of the interior; the walls of the hollowed-out cheese should be about ¾ inch thick. If they are too thin, the cheese can break or lose shape. If they are too thick, there will be no room for the filling. Hollow out the lid in the same manner. Any removed cheese can be wrapped and refrigerated and used for cooking.

Some cheeses are fresher than others. If the shell is soft, leave the cheese at room temperature as long as possible—for hours, or even a day. If the shell is very dry, it should be completely submerged in cold water for an hour or so to soften slightly. What you want is a shell that is firm and a little hard but not leathery.

FOR THE RECADO: Smash the garlic in a *molcajete* until very smooth. Finely grind the cloves, cinnamon, peppercorns, and oregano in a spice grinder or coffee grinder. Add the ground mixture to the garlic and mix together until a paste forms. Cover tightly and set aside until ready to use.

FOR THE PICADILLO YUCATECO: Put the *recado* in a large bowl and dilute with the orange juice. Add the meat and squish together the meat and seasoning with your hands. Pour 3 quarts water into a large pot, place over high heat, and bring to a boil. Add the pork, lower the heat to medium, and simmer until the meat is no longer pink, about 10 minutes. The meat

¼ cup roughly chopped green olives

3 tablespoons raisins

2 tablespoons small capers, rinsed

½ teaspoon sea salt

2 pounds ripe tomatoes (about 6 medium), peeled, seeded, and roughly chopped, or 2 (14½-ounce) cans diced fire-roasted tomatoes, drained

▓ FOR THE CHILTOMATE

2 pounds ripe tomatoes (about 6 medium), roasted and peeled (page 17), or 1 (28-ounce) can diced fire-roasted tomatoes, drained

¼ cup minced white onion

½ teaspoon sea salt

1 chile habanero, roasted (page 17)

▓ FOR THE KOL

Reserved meat broth

Large pinch of saffron threads, crushed between your fingers

⅓ cup freshly rendered pork lard (page 24) or canola or safflower oil

1 cup all-purpose flour

1 teaspoon sea salt

▓ FOR THE ASSEMBLY

2 hard-boiled eggs, cut crosswise into ½-inch-thick slices

2 (18-inch) squares banana leaf, softened (page 22)

2 tablespoons freshly rendered pork lard (page 24) or canola or safflower oil

tends to mass together; this is normal. Let cool in the broth, then strain the meat, reserving the broth for the *kol*. Set the meat aside.

Heat 2 tablespoons of the lard in a *cazuela* or heavy skillet over medium heat until shimmering. Stir in the onion, garlic, *chile dulce*, and *chile xcatic* and sauté without browning until soft. Lower the heat and stir in the capers, olives, and raisins, mixing well. Season to taste with salt, then remove from the heat and reserve.

In another *cazuela* or a heavy saucepan, heat ⅓ cup of the lard over medium-high heat until very hot. Add the tomatoes and stir constantly with a wooden spoon until the color deepens, about 6 minutes. Stir in the onion mixture, reduce the heat to medium, and cook for 2 more minutes to meld the flavors. Remove from the heat and reserve.

In a large, heavy skillet or *cazuela*, heat the remaining ⅓ cup lard over medium-high heat until it is very hot. Break up any clumps of the simmered meat and add the meat to the pan, stir well, and fry until lightly golden. Add the tomato mixture and mix well, then taste and add more salt if needed. Lower the heat to medium-low and cook, stirring occasionally, for 5 minutes. Remove from the heat and let cool.

FOR THE PICADILLO DE JITOMATE: Heat 2 tablespoons of the lard in a skillet over medium-high heat. Add the onion and fry until golden. Stir in the *chile dulce* and *chile xcatic* and cook for just a moment, then mix in the olives, raisins, capers, and salt. Remove from the heat and reserve.

In a large pot or *cazuela*, heat the remaining 4 tablespoons lard over medium-high heat until very hot. Add the tomatoes and stir constantly with a wooden spoon until the color deepens, about 6 minutes. Stir in the chile mixture, and when it begins to simmer, lower the heat and keep the mixture warm until serving. Or, remove from the heat and serve at room temperature.

FOR THE CHILTOMATE: Put the tomatoes and onion in a blender or food processor and pulse for about 5 seconds until a textured sauce forms. Pour into a saucepan or *cazuela* over medium heat, stir in the salt, and cook, stirring occasionally, for 15 minutes. Add the whole *chile habanero,* taking care not to tear it (if you do, the salsa will be extremely *picante*). Stir in 1 cup water and continue to cook until the sauce reduces and is somewhat thick, about 10 minutes. Remove from the heat and set aside to cool, leaving the whole chile in the salsa. Serve at room temperature.

FOR THE KOL: Heat the reserved broth in a saucepan over medium heat and simmer until reduced to 2 quarts. Keep hot.

In a small bowl, soak the saffron in 2 tablespoons hot water. Set aside.

Heat the lard in a deep skillet over medium-high heat until shimmering. Stir in the flour and cook, stirring constantly, just until it becomes pastelike. Do not allow the flour mixture to change color. Dribble in the hot broth, a little at a time, while stirring constantly. When all of the broth has been added, you should have a thick, heavy sauce. Add the saffron mixture and salt, lower the heat to a gentle simmer, and cook, stirring occasionally, until the sauce has reduced, about 10 minutes. Taste and add more salt if needed. Keep the sauce quite warm on the stove top, or remove from the heat, cover, and set aside, then reheat just before ready to serve.

FOR THE ASSEMBLY: Rewarm the *picadillo yucateco.* Spoon 1½ cups of the mixture into the hollowed-out cheese and press with a spoon to compact it. Arrange the egg slices in a single layer on top of the *picadillo,* and then add more *picadillo,* filling the cheese. Spoon ½ cup of the *picadillo* into the hollow in the lid and press firmly so that it won't fall out when turned over to close the cheese. You will have about 5 cups of *picadillo* left over; reserve to serve later, then reheat just before serving.

Crisscross the banana leaves, shiny side up, on a work surface, making sure they are large enough to enclose the cheese. With a brush or by hand, rub the lard on the part of the banana leaves that will be touching the cheese. Fold the leaves up around the cheese and tie securely with kitchen string.

Cut a piece of cheesecloth large enough to cover the cheese completely. Dampen and then wring out the cloth and lay it on a flat surface. Place the wrapped cheese in the middle of the cloth, gather the corners of the cloth at the top of the cheese, and tie securely on top with kitchen string, leaving a "tail" to use for pulling the cheese out of the pot.

For the final step you will need a pot for steaming, at least 10 inches in diameter and 6½ inches deep. Pour water to a depth of about 1 inch into the bottom and place a rack or an inverted pie pan in the pot. The water should not touch the cheese once it is set on the rack or pie pan. Bring the water to a boil, lower the heat to a simmer, and carefully lower the cheese onto the rack. Cover tightly and steam for 15 to 30 minutes. Care must be taken not to overcook the cheese as it will melt. It is ready when it feels just soft to the touch. Remove the pot from the heat. Using the tail of the string, carefully lift out the cheese. Let the cheese rest for several minutes before serving.

When ready to serve, remove the cheesecloth and carefully lift the cheese, still wrapped in banana leaves, onto a warmed large platter. Untie the banana leaves and let them open onto the platter. Traditionally, the cheese is sliced into wedges like a cake and everyone is served a piece in a shallow bowl drowned in the warm *kol* and then topped with the *chiltomate* sauce. Put the *picadillo de jitomate* and the extra *picadillo yucateco* in small bowls for guests to add to their *queso relleno*. It helps if everyone has a spoon to scrape out all the cheese and to eat the sauces.

CAPÓN CHICHIMECA
Stew of Prickly Pear with Potatoes and Cabbage

In the highlands of northeastern Guanajuato, the Misión de Chichimecas is the last remaining settlement of the once marauding Chichimec group of indigenous people. It was in this region in 1552 that they finally succumbed to the Otomí, allies of the Spanish who were threatened by the presence of the Chichimec on the route linking the nearby silver-producing mines to Mexico City. Here at the mission, the Chichimec still preserve the deeply rooted traditions of their ancestors, including their way of eating. This stew using the abundant *xoconoxtles* (page 211), the prized, quite sour fruit of one type of the opuntia cactus, is one such example. The fruits are often found at well-stocked Mexican markets. Make sure you do not buy the sweeter, similar *tuna*. The *xoconoxtle* is so important to the Chichimec and others in this part of Guanajuato that it tends to be the central ingredient in many different sauces, often becoming the main part of a rural meal, as in this dish served to Ricardo by Ofelia Rizo de Galindo.

Chicharrones, huge pieces of thin pork rind, deep-fried in lard until crackling and then sold in large, golden sheets, should be purchased at a Mexican *tienda* (market), as the packaged version sold in regular grocery stores is not an acceptable substitute. If you cannot find *chicharrones* anywhere, diced, crisply fried thick-cut bacon, although not traditional, would be an adequate substitute. At least it will provide a welcomed hit of pork flavor. The Chichimec would add catfish, if available, or even chicken to the stew for added protein and flavor.

Serves 6

1½ pounds ripe tomatoes (about 12 or 13 plum or 3 large), roughly chopped

2 cloves garlic

12 xoconoxtles, the pinker the better, peeled, halved vertically, seeded, and cut into ¼-inch cubes

¼ pound tomatillos (about 3), husked, well rinsed, and finely chopped

2 cups ¼-inch-cubed, peeled red or Yukon Gold potatoes (about 3 medium)

1 cup chopped white onion

4 cups finely chopped cabbage

3 chiles de árbol, toasted (page 18)

½ teaspoon sea salt

1 ripe Hass avocado, halved, pitted, peeled, and sliced

1 cup slightly crumbled chicharrón

Put the tomatoes and garlic in a blender and process until smooth. Set aside.

Put the *xoconoxtles,* tomatillos, potatoes, onion, and 2 cups water in a large saucepan over medium-high heat and bring to a boil. Cook just until the potatoes are almost soft, about 10 minutes. Stir in the pureed tomatoes, cabbage, and chiles and add more water if needed to cover the cabbage. Season with the salt and cook until the cabbage and potatoes are tender, about 5 minutes longer. Taste and add more salt if needed. (If desired, remove from the heat, let cool, cover, and refrigerate for a few days to allow the flavors to intensify.)

Before serving, remove the chiles. Ladle the stew into warmed wide, shallow bowls, top with the avocado and *chicharrón,* and serve.

Tunas y Xoconoxtles

Fruits of the Nopal Cactus

When you drive along almost any back road in central Mexico, you may see colonies of the nopal, or prickly pear cactus, on both sides. Some of the cacti are branched like small trees with light rose to apple green globular fruits, or *tunas*, emerging from the margins of flattened paddles, or nopales.

There are two main edible species of this prized fruit. The fruit of the *Opuntia ficus-indica* has prickle-studded skin, a myriad of tiny seeds scattered throughout its pale green flesh, and a sweet flavor. It is used primarily in drinks and refreshing ices. The *tunas agrias*, or *xoconoxtles* (*O. lasiacantha*), are similar in appearance but have smoother skin, and when they are cut open, the seeds are snuggled together in the center. What is exceptional about the *xoconoxtle* is the sour flavor of the flesh, which is relished as an ingredient in stews and other savory dishes.

Although both types of *tuna* flourish in the southwestern part of the United States and now in many hot, arid countries around the world, they are only recently finding their way into U.S. supermarkets.

GUARNICIÓNES Y ENSALADAS

Accompaniments and Salads

Have a meal in Mexico without beans? Forget it. Beans were one of the area's first domesticated crops, and along with corn have been central to the Mexican diet for centuries, the two consumed together providing a much-needed complete protein. No matter where you are in the country you will be served a savory portion of red, black, mottled brown, white, soft pink, yellow, saddle tan, or speckled beans in one form or another.

Although rice is a relative newcomer to Mexican cuisine, having arrived with the Spanish and the Africans in the 1500s, it is now a common component of the everyday diet. For example, during a leisurely midafternoon meal, it may be served as a "dry" soup, much like the pasta course in a traditional Italian meal. I remember well my surprise many years ago on ordering *sopa de arroz* at a popular restaurant in Mexico City and being served a plate of pilaf-like savory white rice flecked with vegetables rather than a bowl of broth and rice. At formal meals in the past, and occasionally even today, the traditional "wet" soups are followed by *sopas secas*, or "dry soups," perhaps a plate of colorful rice, pasta, or even French-influenced crepes. All are still an important part of Mexican cuisine but are now often served as a separate course or as an accompaniment—maybe rice red with tomatoes or green with chiles or even black rice.

Vegetables are everywhere in Mexican markets. An older woman, her face gouged with age, sitting on the ground with legs folded under her, may hesitantly smile at you and with her wrinkled hand offer a slice of the small native avocado. Carefully balanced pyramids of these avocados, of tiny tomatillos, and, in the rainy season, of wild mushrooms are stacked here and there. Nearby, a younger woman with several small children, including one baby tightly swaddled and asleep in a wooden crate, offers wild herbs, perhaps the fleshy purslane that she and her family foraged to bring to the market.

Red ripe tomatoes, tomatillos encased in their papery wrappings, squashes, carrots, onions, little potatoes, and chayotes, some smooth skinned and some with spines, will be tantalizingly arranged in the regular stalls, along with the familiar green beans, favas, and, in Yucatán, little white beans known as *ibes*. There will be enormous mounds of fresh and dried chiles, huge cabbages, bundled radishes, and, especially in Chiapas, an abundance of beets. Often overlooked by the casual visitor are the displays of rather unappealing elongated, starchy tubers and corms, including yuca and malanga (page 232) and sweet potatoes (*camotes*) in the Caribbean states. Many of these vegetables are combined to make everyday dishes or are used in salsas.

The crisp green salad with a choice of dressing common in the United States is not traditional in Mexican meals. Lettuce, cabbage, tomatoes, and radishes are more apt to be used as condiments. These days, however, customs are changing. If you wander through markets, you will see salad makings displayed, such as nopales, favas, and green beans. At restaurants, the classic Caesar salad, reportedly created in Tijuana by an Italian chef, may be offered, or perhaps a salad of watercress and blue cheese will be on the menu.

FRIJOLES DE LA OLLA
Brothy Beans

Sólo la olla sabe de sus frijoles" states the wooden sign hung on the wall of a *fonda* in Veracruz. "It is only the pot that knows its own beans." In homes and small *fondas* throughout Mexico, beans simmer in large ollas, bulbous-shaped clay pots, their earthy aroma filling the air. Traditionally, a smaller olla filled with water placed on top of the pot serves as both a lid and a way to heat the water that occasionally needs to be added to the beans. Fuel is often scarce and this is a practical way to conserve precious wood.

These brothy beans, cooked with lots of water and just a scattering of herbs, onion, and garlic, are the classic bean dish of Mexico. They are often served as soupy *frijoles caldos*, ladled into small bowls, the beans submerged in their broth, and offered toward the end of a meal so no one leaves the table hungry. Or, they are served as *frijoles cocidos*, the beans drained slightly to accompany grilled meats or tacos.

No matter whether the beans are cooked in an olla, Dutch oven, or other heavy pot, the procedure will be the same. All that needs to be adjusted is the length of the cooking time. The fresher the beans are, the less cooking time is needed, but 2½ to 3 hours is a reasonable estimate, although 4 hours or more is not unusual.

Makes 3 to 4 cups cooked beans and at least 4 cups broth; serves 6 to 10, depending on use

1 pound dried beans (2⅔ cups large beans or 3 cups small beans)

¼ white onion

1 head garlic, outer papery skin removed and halved crosswise

1 tablespoon freshly rendered pork lard (page 24) or canola or safflower oil

3 sprigs fresh epazote, or 6 sprigs fresh cilantro (epazote is the herb of choice for black beans)

1 teaspoon sea salt

Salsa Negra con Chipotles (optional; page 41)

Rinse and sort the beans, discarding any broken pieces. Put in an olla (page 15) or large, heavy pot, add 3 quarts water, and bring to a boil over high heat. This may take from 10 minutes in an enameled cast-iron Dutch oven to 30 minutes in the traditional clay pot. When the water begins to bubble, immediately lower the heat to a gentle simmer and add the onion, garlic, and lard. Cover partially and simmer, stirring occasionally, for 1 to 2 hours. If the beans are not covered by at least 1 inch of water, add hot water. Add the epazote or cilantro, stir in the salt, and continue to simmer until the beans are almost soft, maybe 2 hours more. The centers of these beans should not be al dente.

Taste and add more salt if needed, then remove the pot from the heat and spoon out and discard the onion, garlic, and herb sprigs. The beans are now ready to eat, though they will have even better flavor if allowed to sit for at least a few hours—or better yet, overnight—before reheating and serving. (They should be transferred to a storage container with the broth, covered, and stored in the refrigerator, where they will keep for at least 4 days.)

Serve the beans in small bowls with plenty of the soupy broth and a dollop of the salsa, if desired. These beans can also be used to prepare other bean dishes, such as Frijoles Chinos o Fritos (page 216), Frijoles Puercos (page 105), or Frijoles Charros (page 220).

VARIATION: FRIJOLES DE LA OLLA MUY RICOS (RICH BROTHY BEANS)

Most Mexican home cooks, to make their *frijoles de la olla* richer and tastier, routinely go one step further. The day after making them they add more onions, which they fry until they glisten like black silk. The other difference is that on the second day the beans have a much thicker consistency, which is often the preferred way to enjoy them.

To enrich the beans, heat 2 tablespoons freshly rendered pork lard (page 24) or canola or safflower oil in a *cazuela*, large, heavy skillet, or Dutch oven over medium-high heat. Add ⅓ cup chopped white onion and fry, stirring often, until very dark brown—almost black—8 to 10 minutes. Stir in 2½ cups drained beans from Frijoles de la Olla and fry, stirring often, until they start to dry out, 2 to 3 minutes. Stir in 3 cups of the bean broth, smash down some of the beans, and stir together. Bring to a boil, then taste and add salt if needed.

Serve in warmed bowls that hold about 1 cup beans and an abundant amount of the broth (serves 6, about ¾ cup beans per serving). Think of the beans and broth as a type of sauce to serve on the same plate with most egg dishes or with grilled meats. The beans can also be more thoroughly smashed, a bit more liquid added, and then used as a satisfying filling for Tortas Ahogadas (page 74) or as a topping for tostadas (page 21).

FRIJOLES CHINOS O FRITOS
Fried Beans

When Ricardo first came to Mexico City, he ordered beans in a small *fonda* and the cook asked, "Fritos o refrito?" (Fried or refried?) That was when Ricardo began to understand the various stages of bean cookery. The first stage, *frijoles chinos*, is a common way of cooking beans in and around Mexico City. The name confusingly refers to the way the bean texture resembles the tightly curled hair of African slaves brought to Mexico in the middle of the sixteenth century.

This same preparation is typically called *frijoles fritos* by cooks in central Mexico, though it differs somewhat as the beans are served before they have absorbed all of the broth and are still somewhat runny.

You can make fried beans from almost any type of dried bean. The diminutive black bean is commonly used in southern Mexico and red or brown beans are popular in the rest of the country. If you are in a hurry, an equal amount of canned beans may be substituted with additional water added to the can liquid if needed.

These tasty beans are served in homes and in small market *fondas* almost any time of the day. They partner perfectly with grilled meat and egg dishes, such as Huevos al Albañil (page 78). Serve them in a separate small, flat dish or as a side on the main plate. A light sprinkle of fresh cheese will provide a color and taste contrast.

Serves 6 . . . .

¼ cup freshly rendered pork lard (page 24), bacon fat, or canola or safflower oil

¼ cup finely chopped white onion

½ teaspoon finely chopped garlic

2½ cups drained Frijoles de la Olla (page 214), plus 1 cup bean broth

½ teaspoon sea salt

FOR THE OPTIONAL TOPPING
½ cup crumbled queso fresco

Heat the lard in a skillet over medium-high heat. Add the onion and fry, stirring often, until lightly browned, 4 to 5 minutes. Add the garlic and beans and begin to smash the beans with a bean or potato masher until they are pastelike but still have some lumps. Stir in the broth and salt and continue to smash and stir occasionally, for about 5 minutes. When the bean mixture begins to spew and sputter, lower the heat and cook, stirring occasionally, until the bottom of the pan stays clear for a moment when scraped with a spoon, another 5 to 7 minutes. Serve hot, and, if you want, sprinkle on the cheese.

FRIJOLES REFRITOS
Well-Fried Beans

To make the traditional Mexican well-fried beans, or *frijoles refritos*, you carry *frijoles chinos* (page 216) one step further and fry them again in oil until they are even thicker. This is often done as the last part of a continuous process, or the beans are set aside for a day or two and then finished just before serving. In central Mexico, they are cooked until they are quite dry, but in the states bordering the Gulf of Mexico, they are cooked even more—to the point that they can be flipped over and shaped into a roll. These beans, perhaps with a topping of *queso fresco*, are a perfect partner for Enchiladas San Luis Potosí (page 111) and similar enchiladas, soft tacos, or innumerable other dishes. The bean roll is often served as a *botana* for a casual gathering.

Serve the beans as a side on the main plate. If they are shaped into a roll, transfer the roll to a warmed platter, sprinkle with *queso fresco*, and garnish with chopped white onion. Push some *totopos* in the top as a decoration and for scooping up the beans and then cluster more around the sides.

Serves 6

2 tablespoons freshly rendered pork lard (page 24), bacon fat, or canola or safflower oil

Frijoles Chinos (page 216)

▮ FOR THE OPTIONAL TOPPING

¼ cup crumbled queso fresco or queso añejo

¼ cup chopped white onion, if serving in a roll

Totopos (page 21), if serving in a roll

Heat the lard in a skillet over low heat, add the beans, and cook, mashing and stirring, until quite dry and a wooden spoon pulled through the center of the beans forms a long canyon, 15 to 20 minutes.

If preparing the beans central Mexico–style, serve immediately, topped with a little cheese, if desired. If preparing rolled beans, continue to cook until the mass of beans pulls away from the side of the skillet. Shake the pan back and forth, sliding the beans to one side, then tilt the pan so the mass of beans flips over into a roll, like an omelet. A spatula may be used to help turn it. Transfer to a platter, sprinkle with the cheese and onion, and accompany with the *totopos*.

FRIJOLES NEGROS COLADOS A LA YUCATECA
Yucatecan-Style Strained Black Beans

These velvety black beans are an indispensable part of many meals in Yucatán, especially as an accompaniment to the famed *pescado tikin xik* (page 174). *Frijoles colados,* or "strained beans," are very smooth, almost like a heavy soup, and when well fried, they develop a pastelike texture. They are usually served on a separate plate as part of a meal, topped with fried slices of ripe plantain (page 103) or garnished with crumbled *queso fresco* or *queso panela* and accompanied with *totopos* (page 21) for scooping up the beans.

Serves 8

3 cups drained Frijoles de la Olla (page 214), made with black beans, or drained canned black beans similarly seasoned with garlic and onion, plus 3 cups bean broth or liquid from can with water added if needed

⅓ cup freshly rendered pork lard (page 24) or canola or safflower oil

Put half of the beans and half of the broth in a blender and process until smooth. Set aside in a bowl. Repeat this step with the remaining beans and broth. If the puree is not perfectly smooth, use a large spoon to push the puree through a wide-mesh sieve.

2 tablespoons finely chopped white onion

1 chile habanero, roasted and stemmed
(optional; page 17)

½ teaspoon sea salt

Heat the lard in a large, heavy skillet or *cazuela* over medium-high heat. Add the onion and fry, stirring often, until it turns dark gold, about 6 minutes. Add the pureed beans and chile (if using) and stir frequently with a wooden spoon to prevent the beans from sticking, being careful not to smash up the chile. When the mixture begins to thicken and starts to draw away from the sides of the pan, after about 15 minutes, remove from the heat. Season with the salt, then taste and add more salt if needed. Remove the chile before serving. Serve the beans hot or at room temperature.

FRIJOLES MANEADOS
Rich Sonoran Pureed Beans

This traditional way of transforming the humble bean into a rich, sensuous dish is a specialty of the dairy-rich northern state of Sonora. The name *manea* refers to a thin strip of leather used to bind the legs of cattle as they are roped and tied, and the term *maneados* is descriptive of the binding of the beans by incorporating cheese and milk. The first time I had this dish, now a family favorite, it was prepared by María Dolores Torres Yzábal. This version is a slight adaptation of her recipe by our mutual friend Ricardo, with additional suggestions by Morelia restaurateur Alma Cervantes Cota. In Mexico, the hard-to-find authentic *queso Chihuahua* made by the Mennonite community would be used, although adequate substitutes exist. It is important to have all of the ingredients ready before you start the final preparation.

Serve with flour tortillas or *totopos* (page 21). The beans can be prepared ahead and reheated. Add an additional ¼ cup whole milk when reheating.

Serves 6

1 large chile ancho, with membranes intact,
toasted (page 18)

¼ cup plus 1 tablespoon freshly rendered pork
lard (page 24) or canola or safflower oil, plus
more if needed

½ cup finely chopped white onion

In a bowl, soak the chile in ¼ cup very hot water until almost soft, about 5 minutes. Drain, pat dry with absorbent paper, and tear into very small pieces or thinly slice. Set aside.

2½ cups drained Frijoles de la Olla (page 214), made with yellow, pinto, or other light pink beans

¾ cup whole milk

1 tablespoon unsalted butter

1 teaspoon sea salt, if needed

½ pound Mexican manchego, medium-sharp white Cheddar, Muenster, or Monterey Jack cheese, coarsely shredded or cut into small chunks

Heat ¼ cup of the lard in a large, heavy skillet over medium-high heat until shimmering. Add the onion and fry, stirring often, just until it starts to brown, about 4 minutes. Remove from the heat. Using a slotted spoon, remove half of the onion from the pan, allowing any excess fat to drip back into the pan, and put in a blender. Add half each of the beans and milk and blend until smooth. Transfer to a bowl. Repeat with the remaining onion, beans, and milk and add to the bowl.

Reheat the skillet over medium-high heat, adding a little more lard or oil if the pan is dry. Scrape in the bean mixture and the butter and stir, making sure nothing sticks and burns, until the bean mixture is very thick and stands in soft peaks when lifted with a spoon. The beans should pull away from the sides of the pan and be almost dry. Taste and add the salt only if needed. The beans may already be well seasoned. Stir in the chile and cheese until the cheese melts. Serve immediately.

FRIJOLES CHARROS
Cowboy Beans

The word *charros* refers to the skilled and elaborately costumed horsemen from Jalisco and other far northern ranching states. They enjoy their beans just as dressed up as they are, so a profusion of embellishments is added to these soupy cooked beans, creating a macho dish that became especially popular in Nuevo León, Tamaulipas, Chihuahua, and Jalisco in the 1970s. Hearty bowls of these tasty beans and the "drunken" version that follows are traditionally matched with every conceivable type of grilled meat, which is cooked on poles in huge pits of smoldering charcoal at open-air *campestros* throughout the region. You can cook beef, pork, chicken, or tiny quail on your own grill to serve alongside the beans.

Serves 8 to 10 . . . .

½ pound thick-cut bacon slices, cut into ¼-inch pieces

½ cup finely chopped white onion

2 teaspoons minced garlic

3 ripe tomatoes (about 1 pound), roasted and peeled (page 18), then chopped, or 1 (14½-ounce) can diced fire-roasted tomatoes, drained

1 tablespoon finely chopped chile serrano

2½ cups drained Frijoles de la Olla (page 214), made with the local bayo, peruano, or flor de mayo beans (see Sources), though pinto beans can be reluctantly substituted, plus 3 cups bean broth

¼ cup finely chopped fresh cilantro, thick stem ends removed

Sea salt

FOR THE GARNISH

¼ cup finely chopped fresh cilantro, thick stem ends removed

2 tablespoons roughly chopped white onion (optional)

2 limes, quartered

Fry the bacon in a *cazuela* or heavy pot over medium-low heat until slightly crisp, about 10 minutes. Stir in the onion and cook, stirring occasionally, until the onion is soft and golden, about 3 minutes. Add the garlic and cook for a few seconds longer. Stir in the tomatoes and chile, raise the heat to medium-high, and continue cooking, stirring occasionally, until the flavors are well mingled, about 4 minutes more.

Add the beans, broth, and cilantro and stir well. When the beans return to a slow boil, lower the heat and simmer, stirring occasionally, for 10 minutes. Mix well, taste, and season with salt if needed.

Serve the beans in warmed bowls. Garnish with the cilantro and with some onion if you like, and suggest everyone add a squeeze of lime juice to intensify the flavor. If you have made the beans ahead, you will need to add more bean broth or some water for reheating them, as they readily absorb liquid.

VARIATION: FRIJOLES BORRACHOS (DRUNKEN BEANS)

Prepare the beans as directed. Add 1 cup Mexican dark beer or 2 tablespoons 100 percent agave *tequila blanco* or *reposado* to the finished beans and simmer for an additional 5 minutes. The alcohol disappears, leaving behind only the lusty flavor. It is not surprising that these beverages found their way into bean pots, as Monterrey is not only the capital of the state of Nuevo León but also the brewery capital of Mexico, and Jalisco is the center of tequila production.

MOROS Y CRISTIANOS
Black Beans with White Rice

For hundreds of years, Moors from North Africa controlled most of Spain and brought with them many new culinary ingredients, including rice. The Spanish eventually brought the Moorish centuries to an end in Iberia, but the Moors' culinary contributions remained. This provocatively titled dish, Moors and Christians, which combines the white rice of the Moors with the black beans of the newly acquired lands in Mexico, is part of that culinary legacy. As with most Mexican dishes, there are many variations: some versions are soupy and some are quite dry; some taste primarily of the earthy black beans and others are well seasoned. This is my version based on notes I made in Veracruz while eating the dish for the first time.

I like to pair this side dish with Camarones al Mojo de Ajo (page 176) or Mone de Robalo (page 172), both made with seafood from the lapping waters of the Gulf of Mexico.

Serves 4 to 6

1½ recipes Frijoles de la Olla Muy Ricos (page 214), made with black beans, plus 3 cups bean broth

4 bay leaves

4 thick-cut bacon slices, diced

½ white onion, finely chopped

2 cloves garlic, finely chopped

1 teaspoon ground coriander

1 teaspoon dried thyme leaves, crushed between fingers

1½ cups medium-grain white rice

½ teaspoon sea salt

½ teaspoon freshly ground black pepper

Put the beans and broth in a saucepan, add the bay leaves, and bring to a simmer over low heat. Cover and cook for 30 minutes, adding water if needed to maintain the original level of broth. Remove from the heat and set aside.

Heat the oven to 350°F. Heat a large *cazuela* or Dutch oven over medium-low heat. Add the bacon and fry, stirring often, until crisp, about 6 minutes. Using a slotted spoon, transfer to absorbent paper to drain briefly, then add the bacon to the beans.

Pour out all but 1 tablespoon of the fat from the pan and reheat over medium heat. Add the onion and garlic and stir until soft and a deep shade of yellow, about 8 minutes. Add the coriander, thyme, and rice and stir until the rice is well coated and shiny with the bacon fat. Pour in the beans and their broth, season with the salt and pepper, and then taste and add more salt and pepper if needed.

Cover tightly and bake until the liquid has been completely absorbed, about 30 minutes. Remove from the oven and let sit for 5 to 10 minutes. Remove and discard the bay leaves and serve.

Alternatively, the beans and rice can be packed into an 8-inch ring mold and returned to the oven for 2 minutes, then inverted onto a warmed platter.

ARROZ BLANCO
Seasoned White Rice

Over the years, I have tried many different methods for cooking the pilaf-style white rice of Mexico. Although all of the methods are quite similar, I always return to the way that Ricardo first showed me, which I included in my earlier book *Savoring Mexico*.

When cooking rice in Mexico, it is important to rinse the raw rice well under cold running water before you put it in the pot. This step is usually not necessary for rice purchased in the United States.

Serve the rice in a large bowl, or make individual servings by pressing it into small, rounded individual molds and then inverting the molds onto plates. This is especially attractive if the rice is accompanying a mole or a similar saucy dish.

Serves 6 to 8

¼ cup roughly chopped white onion

2 small cloves garlic, roughly chopped

2 tablespoons canola or safflower oil

1½ cups medium- or long-grain white rice

3 cups chicken broth (page 25), heated, or hot water

½ teaspoon freshly squeezed lime juice

1 teaspoon sea salt

4 sprigs fresh flat-leaf parsley, tough stem ends removed and roughly chopped

Put the onion, garlic, and ¼ cup water in a blender and process until quite smooth.

Heat the oil in a 2- to 3-quart saucepan over medium heat. Add the rice and cook, stirring constantly, until it becomes translucent and begins to crackle. Reduce the heat to low and stir in the onion mixture until well mixed. Add the broth, lime juice, and salt, stir once or twice, and when the mixture begins to boil, lower the heat, cover, and cook for about 15 minutes.

Take a quick peek to see if all of the liquid has been absorbed. If it hasn't, re-cover and continue to cook over low heat for another few minutes.

Remove from the heat, and without opening the lid, ignore the pan for about 10 minutes while the rice grains continue to expand. Stir with a fork to fluff the grains, then spoon into a warmed serving bowl or directly onto individual plates. Sprinkle with the parsley and serve immediately.

VARIATION: ARROZ CON PLÁTANOS (WHITE RICE WITH PLANTAINS)

This favorite combination of white rice and plantains (page 103) is found throughout the Gulf Coast region. Melt 2 teaspoons butter or heat a drizzle of canola or safflower oil in a heavy skillet over medium-high heat. Add cubes of black-ripe or mostly black plantain and fry until almost crispy brown, about 2 minutes. When the rice is ready to serve, stir in the plantain cubes and ½ cup crumbled *queso fresco*. Sometimes *rajas* made from *chiles poblanos* (page 18) are cooked in the rice for additional flavor and color.

ARROZ A LA MEXICANA
Mexican Red Rice

This classic red rice with its flavors of Mexico is often called Spanish rice in the United States, though I don't know why. I have never encountered anything similar to it in Spain, except perhaps the rice you find in paella. This dish has as many variations as there are Mexican cooks, and for this recipe I have combined some of my favorites, leaving out the usual peas and carrots in favor of corn. To deepen the red color and brighten the flavor, I have included both *chiles guajillos* and pureed tomato in the sauce.

Serves 4 to 6 . . . .

FOR THE SAUCE

2 chiles guajillos, stems, seeds, and membranes removed

1 medium ripe tomato, roughly chopped, or ¾ cup drained diced canned tomatoes

3 tablespoons chopped white onion

2 small cloves garlic

Pinch of dried oregano, preferably Mexican

FOR THE SAUCE: Soak the chiles in a bowl in hot water to cover until soft, about 30 minutes. Drain, tear into smaller pieces, and put in a blender. Add the tomato, onion, garlic, and oregano to the blender and process until quite smooth.

FOR THE RICE

2 tablespoons canola or safflower oil

1 cup medium- or long-grain white rice

1¾ cups chicken broth (page 25) or water

½ cup fresh or frozen corn kernels

Sea salt

1 ripe plum tomato, halved, seeded, and cut into ½-inch pieces

3 sprigs fresh cilantro, thick stem ends removed and finely chopped

FOR THE RICE: Heat the oil in a heavy saucepan over medium-high heat until shimmering. Add the rice and stir until the kernels turn ivory, 2 to 4 minutes. Do not let it color. Pour the pureed chile mixture through a medium-mesh sieve into the rice, pressing and scraping it through with the back of a spoon. Add the broth and corn, and stir gently to blend all of the ingredients together. Bring to a boil, then reduce the heat to medium-low. Taste the sauce and season with salt. You will need about ½ teaspoon if the broth was unsalted and less if it was salted. Cover tightly and cook until most of the broth is absorbed and small air holes appear on the surface, about 15 minutes. Remove from the heat and let steam, covered, for about 20 minutes so the rice kernels continue to expand.

When ready to serve, scatter the tomato pieces over the top, then fluff the rice and mix together with a fork. Transfer to a warmed platter, garnish with the cilantro, and serve hot. The rice can be cooked ahead, omitting the tomato pieces and cilantro, and set aside at room temperature. Reheat over boiling water in a steamer until hot, then mix in the tomato pieces and garnish with the cilantro.

ARROZ VERDE
Green Rice

In Mexico, rice dishes come in four different colors: white; red; black, which is made with black beans in Veracruz and sometimes with squid ink in Campeche; and green, which is my favorite and which is seldom found except in central Mexico. This classic rice dish is a great accompaniment to a plate of grilled fish for a simple supper or to Almendrado Huasteco (page 133) for a party.

Serves 6

4 chiles poblanos, roasted, peeled, and seeds and membranes removed (page 17), then roughly chopped

½ cup minced fresh cilantro leaves, thick stem ends removed

¼ cup chopped white onion

2 tablespoons minced fresh flat-leaf parsley (leaves only)

2 teaspoons chopped garlic

¼ cup canola or safflower oil

2½ cups medium- or long-grain white rice

2¼ cups chicken broth (page 25) or water

1½ teaspoons sea salt

▌ FOR THE GARNISH

2 chiles poblanos, roasted, peeled, seeds and membranes removed, and cut lengthwise into ⅛-inch-wide strips (page 17)

½ cup Mexican crema (page 23), crème fraîche, or thick sour cream thinned with 1 tablespoon whole milk

½ cup cooked fresh or frozen corn kernels

Put the chiles, cilantro, onion, parsley, garlic, and ½ cup water in a blender and process until smooth.

Heat the oil in a heavy pot over medium-high heat. Add the rice and stir until the grains are ivory colored and emit a nutty aroma, about 8 minutes. Stir in the pureed chile mixture and fry for 1 minute longer. Add the broth and salt, lower the heat to medium-low, cover tightly, and cook for 15 minutes without lifting the lid. Uncover and stir quickly to make sure the rice kernels are not sticking to one another and the color is uniform, as the herbs tend to cling to the sides of the pan, leaving the rice in the center white. Re-cover and finish cooking for just a few minutes until all the liquid has been absorbed. Remove from the heat and let rest, covered, for about 15 minutes.

Before serving, fluff up the rice from the bottom with a fork. Spoon onto a heated platter. Garnish with the chile strips, *crema*, and corn kernels and serve hot.

CREPAS DE NATAS
Crepes with Clotted Cream

When you think of Mexican food, crepes do not usually come to mind. But ever since 1861, when Mexico was invaded by the French army of Napoleon III, and Austrian archduke Ferdinand Maximilian and his wife, Princess Charlotte of Belgium, were later imposed as rulers, the influence of French and central European cuisine has been strong. Well into the 1930s, most of the Mexican aristocracy had French chefs, or their Mexican cooks learned to cook French food, and up until recently, the top Mexico City restaurants served primarily French dishes.

This dish, rather like lasagna, is made with crepes and thick cream and served as a *sopa seca*, or "dry soup," at the Vázquez Nava family's delightful Nico's restaurant, outside of Querétaro. I like to use it as part of a festive buffet, with Conejo en Adobo (page 139), a savory rabbit dish.

In Mexico's dairy-rich north-central region, in states such as Michoacán, Guanajuato, and Querétaro, *natas*, or clotted cream, is a common ingredient. For those not able to get true *natas*, a thick Mexican *crema* or crème fraîche is an adequate substitute.

To save time, you can purchase 15 to 25 thin crepes, 7 to 8 inches in diameter. All of the components can be prepared, then assembled and baked just before serving.

Serves 12 . . . .

▮ FOR THE CREPES

4 tablespoons unsalted butter, melted and cooled

2½ cups all-purpose flour

6 eggs

1⅓ cups whole milk or beer, or more if needed

3 tablespoons minced fresh cilantro, thick stem ends removed

1 teaspoon sea salt

Melted unsalted butter, cooled slightly, or canola or safflower oil for cooking

▮ FOR THE FILLING

4 tablespoons unsalted butter, cut into small pieces, plus more for the pan

3½ cups tomato puree, or 1 (28-ounce) can tomato puree

2 cups natas, Mexican crema (page 23), crème fraîche, or thick sour cream thinned with 1 tablespoon whole milk

1 teaspoon granulated chicken bouillon

1 teaspoon sea salt

½ teaspoon freshly ground black pepper

2 chiles poblanos, roasted, peeled, seeds and membranes removed, and cut lengthwise into ⅛-inch-wide strips (page 18)

FOR THE CREPES: Put the butter, flour, eggs, milk, cilantro, and salt in a blender or food processor and process until smooth, adding more milk if needed to ensure a very light batter. Cover with plastic wrap and set aside at room temperature for at least 30 minutes.

Heat an 8- to 9-inch crepe, omelet, or similar pan with sloping sides, preferably nonstick, over medium heat. Lightly brush the bottom of the pan with a little melted butter. This does not have to be repeated for each crepe, but if the crepes begin to stick, add a little more butter.

Stir the batter, and if it is has thickened, add more milk until it is once again light. Using a ladle or large spoon, scoop up 3 tablespoons of the batter, pour it into the middle of the pan, and then immediately remove the pan from the heat and quickly tilt and rotate it, swirling the batter to form a thin crepe. Return the pan to the heat and cook until the bottom of the crepe is very lightly browned, about 1 minute. The crepe should slide around

1 whole chicken breast, poached, skinned, boned, and meat shredded (page 25)

FOR THE TOPPING

¾ cup Mexican crema (page 23), crème fraîche, or thick sour cream thinned with 1 tablespoon whole milk, if needed

2 tablespoons finely chopped fresh cilantro, thick stem ends removed

in the pan when the pan is sharply jerked. To turn the crepe, shake the pan to free the edges of the crepe, then jerk the pan so the crepe flips over. This move takes practice; use a spatula until you master it. Very lightly brown the second side for about 30 seconds, then invert the pan over a large plate, dropping the crepe onto it. Repeat until you have used up all of the batter. As the crepes are ready, stack them, separating them with squares of waxed paper or aluminum foil.

The crepes can be used immediately, or they can be made in advance, placed in a resealable plastic bag, and refrigerated for up to 1 day or frozen for up to 1 month. To thaw the crepes, heat them, covered, in a 300°F oven or in a microwave just until soft and pliant.

FOR THE FILLING: Heat the oven to 350°F. Butter a 9-by-11-inch or 10-by-12-inch pan with 2½- to 3-inch sides.

Put the tomato puree and *natas* in a blender and process until combined. Pour into a saucepan and bring to a low boil over medium heat. Reduce the heat to low and simmer, stirring occasionally, until the sauce is reduced, about 15 minutes. Add the bouillon granules, salt, and pepper and stir until the granules have dissolved. There should be about 4½ cups sauce.

Spoon a thin layer of the tomato sauce into the bottom of the prepared pan. Top with a layer each of crepes, chile strips, chicken, and more sauce, then repeat the layers, starting with the crepes. Continue to repeat the layers until all of the crepes, chile strips, and chicken are used up, ending with a layer of crepes. You should have about 10 layers of crepes. Pour the remaining sauce evenly over the top, then dot the top with the butter.

Cover and bake for 30 minutes. Top each serving with a generous portion of the *crema* and a sprinkling of cilantro.

CALABAZA CON ELOTE
Zucchini with Corn

Arminda Flores, an indigenous Purépecha from Michoacán near Lake Pátzcuaro, was born in her grandmother's kitchen, and kitchens seem to have been her natural world ever since, even though she works most days advising women awaiting childbirth. I have had many soul-satisfying meals at her table. This very simple vegetable dish from her collection is a good accompaniment to grilled meats or fish.

Serves 6 to 8

3 plum tomatoes, roasted and peeled (page 18), or 1 cup drained diced fire-roasted canned tomatoes

2 chiles serranos, stems, membranes, and seeds removed

4 ears corns, husks and silk removed

1 tablespoon olive oil

½ white onion, finely chopped

1 clove garlic, minced

2 pounds medium zucchini, roughly chopped

½ teaspoon sea salt

1 cup Mexican crema (page 23), crème fraîche, or thick sour cream thinned with 1 tablespoon whole milk, if needed

Put the tomatoes and chiles in a blender and process until smooth but still with some texture. Set aside. With a sharp knife, slice the kernels from the ears of corn and set aside.

Pour the oil into a heavy skillet or *cazuela* over medium heat. When it is hot, add the onion and garlic and sauté just until the onion starts to turn yellow. Mix in the corn and pureed tomato mixture and cook, stirring occasionally, for 5 minutes. Add the zucchini, lower the heat, cover, and simmer just until the zucchini are tender, about 8 minutes. Do not overcook. Add the salt and *crema* and stir just until warm. Serve immediately.

BISTECES DE CHAYOTE
Fried Chayote Slices in Tomato Sauce

In Veracruz, there are large fields of the native chayote, the plants climbing and sprawling on tall crossed poles with nets eight feet above the ground—an elevated green tapestry. A pear-shaped member of the gourd family, the chayote has long been a staple of both the state's indigenous people and the descendants of African slaves, though now it is popular with everyone and is a familiar food throughout Mexico.

Rosita Potey de Castagne, who lives in the town of San Rafael, Veracruz, prepares chayote in various guises, but because of its bland taste, she always prefers to combine it with a more assertive flavor. Her favorite way is to cut it into small "steaks," fry them, and then smother them with a *picante* tomato sauce. In Mexico, a dangerously spiny chayote is prized, but both smooth and spiny varieties have a thick, nutlike seed in the center—a tasty morsel always claimed by the cook. This is just the dish to pair with Pierna de Cerdo al Horno (page 140), a succulent pork dish. It also makes a light vegetarian main course, served with a salad.

Serves 4 to 6 . . . .

FOR THE CHAYOTES

- 4 chayotes (about ½ pound each)
- 2 teaspoons sea salt
- 2 tablespoons canola or safflower oil

FOR THE SAUCE

- 2 medium, ripe tomatoes, chopped, or 1 (14½-ounce) can diced tomatoes, drained
- ½ cup roughly chopped white onion
- 2 cloves garlic, roughly chopped
- 1 chile serrano, stemmed and roughly chopped
- 1 tablespoon canola or safflower oil
- 1 teaspoon sea salt
- ¼ teaspoon freshly ground black pepper

FOR THE CHAYOTES: Put the chayotes in a large pot with water to cover, add the salt, cover, and bring to a boil over medium heat. Cook just until tender when pierced with a fork, 30 to 60 minutes. Remove the chayotes from the water and discard the water. Let cool, then peel, cut in half lengthwise, and scoop out the large seed from the middle. Cut each half lengthwise into ⅓-inch-thick slices and pat dry. Set aside.

FOR THE SAUCE: Put the tomatoes, onion, garlic, and chile in a blender and process until smooth.

Heat the oil in a *cazuela* or heavy skillet over medium-high heat until shimmering. Pour in the tomato mixture and fry, stirring frequently, for about 6 minutes. Add the salt and pepper, then simmer for a few minutes to blend the flavors. Taste and add more salt and pepper if needed. Keep warm.

To fry the chayote slices, heat the oil in a *cazuela* or large, heavy skillet over medium heat until it ripples. Working in batches, add the chayote slices and fry, turning once, until browned on both sides. Remove with a slotted spatula, allowing the excess oil to drip off, and drain on absorbent paper.

Arrange the fried chayote slices on a warmed platter, drench with the hot sauce, and serve.

VERDOLAGAS A LA MEXICANA
Purslane with Tomatoes and Chiles

There is hardly a gardener who doesn't complain about two spreading plants that they consider real pests, crabgrass and purslane. I agree about the crabgrass, but purslane (*Portulaca oleracea*), or *verdolagas* as it is known in Mexico, should be harvested for its small, fleshy acidic leaves. If you find it growing in your garden, you will have a ready source of a tasty and nutritious green. It is also available at many farmers' markets.

Purslane imparts a great taste accent to pork, and adding it to pork stew is the traditional way of preparing it in Mexico. But Arminda Flores, who lives in Michoacán, often prepares this simple side dish as an accompaniment to all kinds of pork dishes.

Serves 4

¾ pound purslane

1½ teaspoons sea salt

1 tablespoon freshly rendered pork lard (page 24) or olive oil

¼ white onion, chopped

1 clove garlic, slivered

2 large, ripe tomatoes, chopped (about 2 cups)

1 chile serrano, stemmed and minced

¼ teaspoon dried oregano, preferably Mexican

Cut off the roots and thick, darker stems of the purslane and discard. Rinse the leaves and thinner stems thoroughly to dislodge any trapped grit and chop roughly. You should have about 4 cups.

Put the purslane in a pot, add 1 teaspoon of the salt and water to cover, and bring to a boil over high heat. Lower the heat to a gentle simmer, cover, and cook for 5 minutes. Drain and set aside.

Heat the lard in a skillet over medium heat. When it is hot, add the onion and garlic and sauté just until the onion starts to turn yellow. Add the tomatoes, chile, and oregano and cook for several more minutes. Stir in the purslane, add the remaining ½ teaspoon salt, and cook over low heat until the tomatoes have softened and the flavors are blended, about 15 minutes. Serve immediately in a warmed bowl.

Yuca and Malanga

According to food historian Sophie D. Coe, yuca (*Manihot esculenta*), a swollen-looking, very starchy 10- to 15-inch-long root, was carried to Africa from Brazil hundreds of years ago by the Portuguese, and then to the West Indies and Mexico by the Spaniards to feed their slaves. Yuca (pronounced yoo-ka), not to be confused with yucca, an entirely different plant, looks somewhat like a skinny sweet potato. It is now grown in at least eighty-five countries and is the source of tapioca, which gives you an idea of its bland flavor. It cries out for a dominant seasoning such as chiles or garlic. Sometimes labeled cassava, yuca can be found in many Latin markets, especially in Florida, Texas, and California, but it may require a search. I've heard that it is sometimes available frozen, too, and I was able to find a few fresh roots in several western Washington supermarkets, so it is out there.

Malanga (*Xanthosoma* sp.), another native of the tropical New World, goes by an extremely confusing number of different names in other countries, where it is a staple food source. It is similar to taro in that they both have large elephant ear–like leaves and are starchy corms rather than tubers or roots. The malanga corms that I have seen in Veracruz markets, and occasionally in the southern United States, have a white interior, with the texture of a water chestnut and a rather earthy flavor. Some species have yellow or lavender flesh. With its potato-like consistency, malanga is used in much the same way as yuca, and is just as ideal for slicing and deep-frying for chips (page 233). It is a particular favorite of the African Mexicans in Veracruz.

YUCA FRITA
Fried Yuca Strips

If you like French fries, you may become addicted to Ricardo's mother's crisp slices of yuca. No ketchup, please, but Salsa de Cuaresmeños (page 32) or Salsa Verde Cocida con Aguacate (page 31) is welcomed for this dish common in both Tabasco and adjacent Veracruz.

It is important that the bulbous root of the yuca (page 232) be hard and fresh, with no dried-out or soft portions. Malanga (page 232) is also often substituted for the yuca.

Serves 4

1½ pounds yuca

Peanut oil for deep-frying

1 teaspoon sea salt

Using a sharp, heavy knife, peel the yuca, paring away the heavy skin and the pink layer beneath it. Using a mandoline or a sharp knife, cut the yuca into strips about 4 inches long and ⅜ inch thick, avoiding the tough central core of the root. As the strips are cut, immerse them in a bowl of cold water. Just before you are ready to begin frying, drain the strips and pat them dry.

Heat the oven to 200°F. Pour the oil to a depth of 3 inches into a deep, heavy pot and heat to 375°F on a deep-frying thermometer or until a cube of bread dropped into the oil turns crispy brown in 3 seconds. Carefully place about 1 cup yuca strips into the hot oil and fry until lightly golden, about 3 minutes. Using a slotted spoon, lift out the strips, allowing any excess oil to drip back into the pot, and drain on absorbent paper, then put on a baking sheet and keep warm in the oven. Repeat to cook the remaining strips the same way, making sure the oil is always at 375°F before adding the next batch. (If you have fried the strips 30 minutes or more in advance, you can recrisp them in hot oil for about 1 minute.)

Season the yuca strips with the salt and serve hot.

ENSALADA DE PIÑA CON LECHUGAS
Pineapple Salad with Lettuce

Salads are not traditionally part of a Mexican meal, but they are becoming increasingly popular, especially those similar to this colorful and refreshing creation of Ricardo's. It is the perfect complement to any seafood dish, especially Camarones al Mojo de Ajo (page 176). To serve the salad as a vegetarian main course, omit the crumbled *queso fresco* and add cubes of your favorite cheese.

Serves 6

3 cups ⅓-inch-cubed fresh pineapple

1 cup bite-size jícama pieces

1 cup crumbled queso fresco or shredded low-moisture mozzarella cheese (optional)

½ cup thinly sliced red onion, cut in half into crescent moons

¾ cup extra virgin olive oil

3 tablespoons white wine vinegar or freshly squeezed lemon juice

½ teaspoon sea salt

Pinch of freshly ground black pepper

⅓ cup chopped fresh flat-leaf parsley (leaves only)

⅓ cup chopped fresh cilantro, thick stem ends removed

⅔ pound torn mixed lettuces

2 firm but ripe Hass avocados, halved, pitted, peeled, and thickly sliced

1 cup pecan halves

Mix together the pineapple, jícama, cheese, and onion in a bowl and set aside.

Put the olive oil and vinegar in a large bowl and whisk until emulsified. Stir in the salt and pepper, then taste and add more salt and pepper if needed. Add the parsley, cilantro, and pineapple mixture and toss to coat evenly.

Divide the lettuce among individual plates. Spoon the salad onto the lettuce, dividing it evenly. Garnish with the avocado slices and pecans and serve.

ENSALADA CLÁSICA DE NOPALES
Classic Cactus Salad

In central Mexico, cactus salad is prepared in innumerable ways. In the local markets, rows of women sitting cross-legged on mats or in small chairs tediously scrape prickles from the cactus paddles and then cut them into cubes—the first step in making this traditional salad. It is often served alongside enchiladas or with grilled meats.

Serves 6

1 pound nopales (4 small to medium paddles), cleaned as directed on page 23

Sea salt

4 ripe plum tomatoes, cut into ¼-inch-thick slices

6 thin slices white onion, separated into rings

5 ounces queso panela or moist, acidic mozzarella cheese, cut into ¼-inch cubes

¼ cup olive oil

¼ cup chopped fresh cilantro, thick stem ends removed

1 teaspoon dried oregano, preferably Mexican

¼ teaspoon freshly ground black pepper

Cut the nopales into 2-by-¼-inch strips. Put the strips and 2 teaspoons salt in a saucepan, add water to cover, and bring to a boil over medium-high heat. Cook until the strips are tender, about 10 minutes. Using a slotted spoon or wire skimmer, scoop the nopales out of the water into a sieve or colander and rinse off any remaining viscous residue under cold running water. Drain well and pat dry.

Toss together the nopales, tomatoes, onion, and cheese. This can be done in advance, with the mixture covered and kept cool in the refrigerator for several hours. Bring to room temperature before serving.

Divide the nopal mixture among small individual plates. Whisk together the oil, cilantro, oregano, and pepper, and a pinch of salt in a small bowl. Taste and add more salt and pepper if needed. Drizzle the dressing on the salads just before serving.

ESCABECHE DE VERDURAS
Tangy Vegetable Salad

This lightly pickled, green-and-white vegetable salad, punctuated with orange carrots, is a favorite of Yolanda Ramos, and as a girl growing up in Tlaxcala, she often went into the garden with her grandfather to choose the vegetables for making it.

The vegetables and the amounts can vary. Whatever you find growing in your garden or at the farmers' market will work, but try for a variety of colors, shapes, and textures for a total of 3 to 4 cups vegetables. It is important that the vegetables be crisp and tender when cooked. This salad makes a colorful contrast to grilled meats or chicken.

Serves 4 to 6

▌ FOR THE SALAD
Sea salt

½ small cauliflower, broken into small florets (about ¾ cup)

¼ pound green beans, trimmed but left whole if small or cut on the diagonal into 1-inch pieces if large (about ½ cup)

¾ pound small green peas in the pod, shelled (about ¾ cup)

1 small zucchini (about ¼ pound), cut crosswise into ⅓-inch-thick slices (about ½ cup)

¼ pound baby or small carrots, peeled and left whole if baby or halved lengthwise if small (about ½ cup)

4 large green onions or 2 spring onions, white part only, cut on the diagonal into ⅛-inch-thick slices

½ cup chopped, peeled cucumber or jícama

1 chile jalapeño, stem, seeds, and membranes removed and finely chopped

▌ FOR THE DRESSING
2 cups mild white vinegar such as vinagre de piña or diluted unseasoned rice vinegar (page 50)

FOR THE SALAD: Have ready an ice-water bath. Pour water to a depth of 1½ inches into a 2-quart pot. Add ½ teaspoon salt and bring to a boil. Drop in the cauliflower florets and cook just until barely tender, about 6 minutes. Remove with a slotted spoon and immediately dunk in the ice-water bath to halt the cooking. Remove from the ice water and drain well. Replenish the ice in the water bath.

Return the water in the pot to a boil. Plunge in the green beans and cook until crisp tender, about 7 to 10 minutes. Drain the beans and immediately dunk them in the ice-water bath to halt the cooking. Remove from the ice water and drain well. Replenish the ice in the water bath.

Refill the pot with no more than 1 cup water and bring to a boil. Add the peas and cook until barely tender, 3 to 5 minutes. Remove with a slotted spoon and immediately dunk in the ice-water bath to halt the cooking. Remove from the ice water and

3 bay leaves

2 sprigs fresh thyme, or ½ teaspoon dried thyme

2 sprigs fresh oregano, preferably Mexican, or ½ teaspoon dried oregano

5 black peppercorns

3 whole cloves, ground, or ⅛ teaspoon ground cloves

Leaves from 2 sprigs fresh mint, roughly chopped

drain well. Replenish the ice in the water bath.

Return the water in the pot to a boil and add the zucchini. When the water returns to a boil, add ¼ teaspoon salt, cover, and cook until tender, no more than 5 minutes. Remove with a slotted spoon and immediately dunk in the ice-water bath to halt the cooking. Remove from the ice water and drain well. Replenish the ice in the water bath.

Add another cup or so of water to the pot and bring to a boil. Add a pinch of salt and the carrots; the water should barely cover them. Cover tightly and cook just until tender, 8 to 10 minutes. Drain and immediately dunk in the ice-water bath to halt the cooking, then drain again.

FOR THE DRESSING: Pour the vinegar into a small pot, add the bay leaves, thyme, oregano, peppercorns, cloves, and mint, and bring to a boil. Remove from the heat and let cool completely.

Strain the dressing through a fine-mesh sieve into a large bowl. Carefully spoon in all of the cooked vegetables and the onions, cucumber, and chile and sprinkle with salt. Toss well to coat evenly, then cover and marinate at room temperature until the vegetables are well seasoned, about 1 hour.

Just before serving, pour off any excess dressing and spoon the salad onto a platter or into a large, shallow bowl. The salad tastes best served at room temperature, though it can also be slightly chilled.

ENSALADA DE HABAS DESCALZAS
Barefoot Fava Bean Salad

I ate my first fresh fava beans many years ago when my husband and I were living in Spain, and I liked their rather nutty and bittersweet flavor right away. Now I look for them every late spring in Seattle's Pike Place Market and in other farmers' markets.

Fava beans are prized in Mexico, particularly in the central states. I sometimes see older men, their shoulders bent, pushing wheelbarrows full of the plump pods through congested market aisles, with villagers stopping them along the way to buy what they need. On the surrounding streets, one or two pickup trucks loaded with freshly picked favas serve as alternative sources.

In Mexico, shelled favas are prepared two different ways: "with shoes" or "barefoot." The ones "with shoes" have their inner skins intact and are eaten only when very young and tender. The "barefoot" beans have their inner skins peeled away. Peeling the beans is a tedious, mindless, time-consuming task but well worth the effort to create this simple, colorful, nutty-tasting salad. If you have a favorite television show, this is the time to watch it.

Serve this salad as an accompaniment to any simple chicken or meat dish.

Serves 4 . . . .

FOR THE DRESSING
- ¼ cup extra virgin olive oil
- 1 tablespoon sherry vinegar or white wine vinegar
- 1 teaspoon dried oregano, preferably Mexican
- 1 teaspoon sea salt
- ¼ teaspoon freshly ground black pepper

FOR THE FAVA BEANS
- 3 cups small to medium shelled fresh or frozen fava beans (about 3½ pounds in the pod)
- 2 teaspoons sea salt
- 1 sprig fresh mint

FOR THE DRESSING: Put all of the ingredients in a jar, cover tightly, and shake vigorously until the dressing emulsifies. Set aside.

FOR THE FAVA BEANS: If using frozen fava beans, you can skip this step. If using fresh fava beans, first pry them out of their cozy, fuzzy pods. Have ready an ice-water bath. Bring a large pot of salted water to a boil, add the beans, and blanch briefly—less than 1 minute. Drain the beans, immediately dunk them in the ice-water bath to halt the cooking, and then drain again.

FOR THE SALAD

FOR THE SALAD

2 large, firm but ripe tomatoes, each cut into 6 slices or roughly chopped

½ cup finely chopped white onion

¼ cup finely chopped fresh mint or cilantro, thick stem ends removed

Now begins the tedious and necessary step of removing their "shoes." With your fingernails, pinch off a bit of the tough skin at the top of each bean—the end that looks as if it may sprout. With your other hand, squeeze the skin at the bottom of the bean to free the bean from its skin.

If it does not slip freely, peel off a little more of the tough skin at the top of the bean, then squeeze again.

Put the beans in a saucepan, add the salt, mint, and 2 cups water, and bring to a boil over high heat. Lower the heat to a gentle simmer and cook just until tender, about 4 minutes. Drain into a colander and place under cold running water until cool, then drain again. Frozen favas may take up to 8 minutes to cook.

FOR THE SALAD: Transfer the beans to a bowl and add the tomatoes, onion, and mint. Shake the dressing briefly to reemulsify, then pour over the salad and toss gently to mix.

Serve the salad on a platter or individual plates. It tastes best at room temperature but may be served lightly chilled.

ENSALADA DE JÍCAMA, MELÓN Y PEPINO

Jícama, Melon, and Cucumber Salad

Jícama, a crisp, bulbous tuber, is a favorite of street vendors in Mexico, who combine it with pineapple, cucumber, or mangos and then sprinkle the mix with lime juice and ground chile for a quick, healthful pick-me-up. This salad, with its vibrant combination of fruits and vegetables, is similar. Small orange segments or mandarin segments may be added or substituted for the melon or cucumber—only the jícama is essential.

Serve with Cochinita Pibil (page 149) or alongside Tacos de Pescado (page 64) on an informal buffet.

Serves 4 to 6

1 small jícama (about ¾ pound), peeled and cut into ¾-inch cubes

⅓ cup freshly squeezed orange juice

2 tablespoons freshly squeezed lime juice

½ teaspoon sea salt

2 chiles de árbol, toasted (page 18)

½ cup unsalted dry-roasted peanuts

½ small cantaloupe, peeled, seeded, and cut into ¾-inch cubes or balls (about 1½ cups)

2 medium cucumbers, peeled, seeded, and cut into ¾-inch cubes

2 green onions, including some of the green part, thinly sliced

2 tablespoons roughly chopped fresh cilantro, thick stem ends removed

Put the jícama in a bowl, add the orange and lime juices and the salt, and toss to mix. Cover and refrigerate, tossing occasionally, for at least 30 minutes or up to 1 hour.

Meanwhile, crumble the chiles into a spice grinder or coffee grinder, add the peanuts, and grind coarsely. (Depending on the size of your grinder, you may need to do this in batches.)

Add the cantaloupe and cucumber cubes to the marinated jícama and stir gently. Add the green onions and again mix gently.

The salad can be made several hours in advance, covered, and refrigerated. About an hour before serving, remove from the refrigerator, then right before serving, sprinkle with the cilantro and the ground nut and chile mixture.

POSTRES

Desserts

The indigenous people of what is now Mexico did not have a tradition of preparing and eating sweet snacks or desserts. Nor did the Africans who were brought there as slaves. In their native lands, they had fulfilled their craving for something sweet by eating melons; in the New World, they turned to the local pineapples, papayas, and other fruits.

It was the Spanish and French colonists who brought with them to their new homes an almost insatiable craving for sweets. Starting in the morning or later for snacks, there were churros and *buñuelos* made with the wheat soon grown in the highlands encircling Mexico City. The Spaniards' beloved bread or rice puddings, all decadently saturated in sugar syrups, frequently ended the meals.

In centuries past, egg whites were used in Spain and Mexico to glaze the gilded altars and murals inside the churches, and many desserts were created in the convents from the excess egg yolks. Simple custards or decadent flans enveloped with a coating of caramel were just some of the many ways that the frugal nuns devised to utilize the abundant yolks.

In recent years, lighter desserts have returned. Scoops of both *nieves* (ices) and *helados* (ice creams) in an incredible number of exotic flavors—one of my favorites is *nieve de leche quemada* (burnt-milk ice)—are wonderful treats when purchased from a street vendor or in a market. Nowadays, most restaurants also offer these frozen desserts, usually in duos and trios of tantalizing tropical flavors, providing a perfect ending to a meal.

GELATINA DE ROMPOPE
Eggnog Gelatin

One Christmas holiday in Oaxaca, my husband, Fredric, and I joined Pilar Cabrera's family, along with her mother, sisters, brothers, and their flock of children, for an extraordinary meal, which was to be expected from this family of talented cooks. Everyone had requested or brought a favorite dish for this celebratory *comida*, resulting in a harmonized chaos of flavors. One favorite that day was a simple *gelatina de rompope*. To know what is special about this dessert you have to realize that Mexicans do not equate gelatins with the fruit-flavored Jell-O embedded with mixed canned fruits or miniature marshmallows often found at U.S. family gatherings. In Mexico, *gelatinas* run the gambit from plastic cups filled with quivering rainbows of flavors sold by street vendors to towering pastry-shop creations that replace cakes at birthday parties. When you dine in homes, hostesses often like to show off their favorite gelatin creations, from molded vegetable and seafood gelatins to a dessert such as this one served by Pilar, flavored with rich eggnoglike *rompope*, originally a specialty of Mexican convents.

Serves 6 to 8, depending on the size of the molds

▪ FOR THE ROMPOPE
3 cups whole milk

⅓ cup sugar

2½-inch stick Mexican true cinnamon bark (page 88)

Rounded ¼ teaspoon ground cloves

Rounded ¼ teaspoon ground nutmeg

¼ teaspoon baking soda

9 egg yolks, at room temperature

1½ teaspoons pure vanilla extract

⅓ cup rum or brandy (optional)

▪ FOR THE GELATINA
3 cups whole milk

½ cup sugar

2-inch stick Mexican true cinnamon bark (page 88)

1½ cups rompope

FOR THE ROMPOPE: Mix together the milk, sugar, cinnamon, cloves, and nutmeg in a medium saucepan. Dissolve the baking soda in a large spoonful of the mixture, stir it into the pan, and place the pan over medium heat. When the liquid begins to boil, reduce the heat and simmer, stirring occasionally, for 20 minutes. Set aside to cool, then strain through a fine-mesh sieve, discarding the cinnamon.

Fill a large bowl three-fourths full with ice cubes and nest a metal bowl or pan in the ice. Using a whisk or a handheld mixer, beat the egg yolks in a medium bowl until thick and lemony, about 5 minutes. While continuing to beat, slowly pour the cooled milk mixture into the yolks. Return the mixture to the saucepan over medium

1 (¼-ounce) packet unflavored gelatin (1 tablespoon)

Canola or safflower oil for oiling the molds

▌ FOR THE TOPPING

1 cup or more rompope (optional)

½ teaspoon ground Mexican true cinnamon
(page 88), optional

2 cups raspberries or strawberries, hulled and
sliced if using strawberries (optional)

heat and simmer, stirring constantly, until
the mixture thickens and just coats the
back of a wooden spoon. Remove from
the heat and immediately pour into the
metal bowl resting in the ice. Slowly stir in
the vanilla and rum (if using). Let stand,
stirring occasionally, until completely cool.
Cover tightly and refrigerate until ready to
use. You should have about 3½ cups.

FOR THE GELATINA: Heat the milk in a medium saucepan over medium heat until hot.
Stir in the sugar and cinnamon and continue to stir until the sugar has dissolved. When
the milk starts to bubble, reduce the heat to low and gradually stir in the 1½ cups *rompope*.
Set aside to cool.

In a small bowl, sprinkle the gelatin over ½ cup water without stirring and let it soften and
absorb the liquid, about 5 minutes. Scoop the gelatin mixture into the milk mixture and
stir constantly until dissolved. Remove and discard the cinnamon bark.

Meanwhile, lightly oil a 1-quart mold or six to eight ½- to ¾-cup molds or custard cups.
Pour the mixture into the prepared mold or individual molds and refrigerate until set,
about 2 hours. If not serving right away, press plastic wrap directly onto the surface and
refrigerate until the next day.

When ready to serve, dip the filled part of the mold in a bowl of hot water for just a few
seconds. Invert a large, chilled serving plate on top of the mold and flip the mold and plate
together, shaking them gently back and forth as you turn them. As you lift the mold off, the
gelatin should slide easily out of it. If you like, pour additional *rompope* over the gelatin
and sprinkle with the cinnamon, or top with the berries. Cut into thick slices and serve at
once on chilled dessert plates. If using small, individual molds, invert directly onto chilled
plates and top as directed.

MANJAR BLANCO
White Custard Delicacy

icardo and I have tasted countless versions of this dessert made in homes throughout the states of Tabasco, Campeche, and Yucatán. For this one, we added brandy and a topping of the native chocolate of Tabasco, but another popular version uses vanilla for flavoring and shredded coconut for topping. *Manjar blanco* has an unexpected texture, the result of using cornstarch instead of eggs as a thickener.

Serves 6

4 cups whole milk

⅔ cup sugar

4-inch stick Mexican true cinnamon bark (page 88), plus 1-inch stick, ground, for garnish

1 vanilla bean

¼ cup raisins

¼ cup brandy or dark rum

¼ cup cornstarch

¼ teaspoon sea salt

¼ cup shaved bittersweet chocolate or Mexican chocolate

Pour 3½ cups of the milk into a medium saucepan, add the sugar, cinnamon stick, and vanilla bean, and heat over medium heat, stirring occasionally, until the mixture just comes to a boil, about 6 minutes.

Meanwhile, put the raisins in a small bowl, add the brandy, and let soak until plump, about 10 minutes.

Stir the cornstarch into the remaining ½ cup milk until dissolved. Dribble the diluted cornstarch into the simmering milk and cook, stirring constantly, until the mixture thickens, about 3 minutes.

Bring back to a boil and continue stirring for 1 minute, then remove from the heat.

Strain the custard through a medium-mesh sieve into a bowl. Retrieve the vanilla bean from the sieve and, using a small knife, split it lengthwise and remove the seeds with the back of the knife, adding them to the custard. (Wipe the pod halves clean and reserve for another use, such as flavoring a canister of sugar.) Discard the cinnamon.

Stir in the raisins and any brandy remaining in the bowl and the salt. Let the custard cool slightly, then pour into 6 goblets or bowls, cover with plastic wrap, and refrigerate until very cold, about 3 hours.

Just before serving, sprinkle the custard with the ground cinnamon and shaved chocolate.

DULCE DE CALABAZA
Sweet Pumpkin Puree

When the African slaves were first brought to Veracruz, most of them were put to work in the sugar plantations. The unrefined sugar became very important in their diet, giving them both extra energy and something pleasurable to eat, especially when combined with the large native squashes. It was in Veracruz that Ricardo first tasted this simple dessert, customarily served after the midday meal or for a late *cena* at the end of the day.

Although certainly atypical, this puree is also an unusual topping for vanilla ice cream with a scattering of chopped pecans. Kids, in particular, seem to love this recipe, and Dillon, the nine-year-old son of a friend, made it himself using canned pumpkin.

Serves 4 . . . .

2 pounds pumpkin, seeded and cut into large slices with rind intact (about 8 cups), or 1 (16-ounce) can unsweetened pumpkin puree

¾ cup azúcar morena or other unrefined brown cane sugar or firmly packed brown sugar (page 42)

1-inch stick Mexican true cinnamon bark (page 88), ground

If using fresh pumpkin, put the slices in a large saucepan with water to cover, place over medium heat, and cook until soft, about 45 minutes. Remove from the heat, then remove the pumpkin from the water and let cool. Reserve the water.

Scoop the cooled flesh from the pumpkin rind into a blender or food processor and process until a smooth puree forms.

Scoop the freshly made pumpkin puree or the canned pumpkin into a saucepan. Stir in the sugar and cinnamon, place over medium-low heat, and bring to a gentle simmer, stirring constantly. Cook, stirring constantly and adding some of the cooking water if the mixture gets too thick, until the mixture is smooth and has a good puree consistency. Serve in small bowls warm or at room temperature.

DULCE DE PAPAYA
Caramelized Papaya

Sunset yellow papayas cloaked in sugar syrup are a popular dessert in the indigenous communities of Tabasco and Yucatán, with each region having its own variation. In Tabasco, cooks use the local, quite small papaya known as *oreja de mico*.

According to Ricardo, the secret to this sweet is in the ripeness of the papaya. It should not be too ripe, but instead just between green and mature. The mineral lime, or *cal*, has been used in Mexico for centuries to soften dried corn before grinding it into masa, but it is also used for preparing fruits that will be put in heavy syrup so that they stay firm during the long cooking. If you have a tortilla factory nearby, this is where to get your *cal*. They will be surprised that you have asked for it, but I find they are always happy to sell some. It is also sold in drug stores as slaked lime or calcium hydroxide powder, and my local building-supply store carries it, as well.

If you will be using the small Tabascan papayas, you will need about twenty of them; if using large papayas, you will need only two or three fruits.

The chilled papaya is traditionally served with pieces of cheese. In restaurants in Yucatán, chunks of Edam are used to balance the often musky sweetness of the fruit. Gouda or Gruyère can be substituted.

Serves 8 to 10

2 pounds less-than-ripe papayas

½ cup cal (calcium hydroxide)

3½ cups sugar

2 (3-inch) sticks Mexican true cinnamon bark (page 88)

½ to ¾ pound Edam cheese, cut into thin wedges or slices

Halve the papayas lengthwise, then seed and peel each half. Cut the halves lengthwise into long segments, then slice each segment on the diagonal to form triangles about 3 inches long.

In a large bowl or other vessel, dissolve the *cal* in 3 quarts cold water, mixing well. Add the papaya pieces and let rest for 20 minutes, stirring occasionally so that the pieces do not settle on the bottom. Pick up a piece of papaya and feel it. If it is a little stiff on the surface, it is ready. If it isn't, leave it to rest several minutes longer. When the papaya is ready, drain well, then rinse several times to remove all of the *cal*.

Put the fruit in a pot, add the sugar, cinnamon, and 4 cups water, and bring to a boil, stirring occasionally. Immediately lower the heat to very low, cover, and simmer, stirring every 30 minutes or so, until the papaya becomes somewhat translucent and caramelized, 2 to 4 hours. Remove from the heat, pour into a bowl, let cool, cover, and refrigerate until well chilled. The papaya will keep indefinitely.

To serve, put 3 or 4 chilled papaya slices on each plate and spoon a little syrup over each serving. Accompany with the cheese.

HELADO DE AGUACATE
Avocado Ice Cream

At a dinner with our longtime friend Enrique Bautista at his family's Michoacán avocado ranch, we were served *truchas con salsa de macadamia* (page 168), followed by this surprising avocado ice cream for dessert. It was an inspired but natural choice: Michoacán is both the undisputed capital of Mexico's avocado production and famed throughout the country for its ice cream. When I asked for the recipe, Enrique just laughed and said to stir avocado pulp into vanilla ice cream and refreeze. One or two other ingredients can be included for a different taste or texture.

Serves 6 to 8

4 large, ripe Hass avocados

1 quart rich vanilla ice cream, slightly softened in the refrigerator

⅓ cup light rum (optional)

1 cup hazelnuts, toasted and finely chopped (optional)

Halve the avocados, remove the pits, and scoop the flesh into a blender or food processor. Process until smooth.

Put the softened ice cream in a bowl, add the pureed avocado and the rum and nuts, if using, and mix thoroughly. Transfer to an airtight container and freeze for 30 minutes.

To serve, put the ice cream in the refrigerator to soften slightly, then scoop into individual bowls to serve.

HELADO DE MANGO
Mango Ice Cream

In Mexico, a sorbet made with water is called *nieve*, or "snow," and ice cream, which is made with milk or cream, is called *helado*. Both frozen treats are a popular way to end a meal or to scoop out of a paper cup from a street vendor. This ice cream is made with the richly flavored mango, of which there are many varieties, including the most prized Manila (also known as ataulfo) cultivar that is available almost year-round in the United States. I enjoy this mango ice cream as is, but topping it with candied pecans turns it into an even more delightful end to a meal. The candied pecans are from my Texan friend Jim Peyton, who included them in his excellent border cookbook, *El Norte*.

Makes 1 quart; serves 6 to 8 . . . .

▮ FOR THE ICE CREAM
- 2 pounds very ripe mangos (2 or 3, depending on size), peeled, pitted, and cut into chunks
- 1 cup whole milk
- 1 cup heavy cream (not ultrapasteurized)
- ¼ cup granulated sugar
- 1 tablespoon dark rum (optional)

▮ FOR THE OPTIONAL CANDIED PECANS
- 1 teaspoon unsalted butter
- ½ cup heavy cream
- ½ cup whole milk
- 1 cup firmly packed light brown sugar
- 2 tablespoons light corn syrup
- 1 tablespoon pure vanilla extract
- 1 tablespoon dark rum
- 1 cup pecan halves or pieces

FOR THE ICE CREAM: Put the mangos, milk, cream, granulated sugar, and rum (if using) in a blender and process until smooth. Pour into an ice cream maker and freeze according to the manufacturer's instructions.

Transfer the ice cream to an airtight container and store in the freezer for 2 hours before serving.

FOR THE OPTIONAL CANDIED PECANS: Lightly butter a baking sheet. Mix together the cream, milk, brown sugar, corn syrup, vanilla, and rum in a heavy, medium saucepan over medium heat and stir until the sugar has dissolved. If the mixture is not at a boil, increase the heat to medium-high and bring to a boil. Stir in the pecans and cook, stirring constantly, until the mixture registers 260°F on a candy thermometer or an instant-read thermometer. Alternatively, drop a spoonful onto the prepared baking sheet; if the spoonful holds its shape, it is ready. Drop the mixture by the tablespoon onto the baking sheet, spacing the mounds evenly. Let cool to room temperature; the mounds will harden. Chop enough to measure ½ cup. To reserve the remainder for another use, pack into an airtight container and store at room temperature.

To serve, put the ice cream in the refrigerator to soften slightly, then scoop into individual bowls. Sprinkle with the candied pecans, if desired.

Mangos

Seductively aromatic and sensuously sweet, mangos (*Mangifera indica*) are native to Southeast Asia but are considered a staple by more than half of the world's population, including in Mexico, where they are grown in many sizes and shapes.

One of my most memorable Mexican eating experiences took place in the highlands of Veracruz on a sultry day. Diana Kennedy, Carmen Barnard, and I sat at a small restaurant overlooking the Río Pescadore and watched as men with their donkeys crossed back and forth over a narrow, swaying rope bridge, carrying fruits they had collected from the nearby hillsides blanketed with mango groves. Below the bridge, we could see boys scooping up *acamayas* (large freshwater crayfish) from the river's shallows. Soon, I was prying open the *acamayas,* now cooked in a heady *chile chipotle* sauce, sucking out the meat, and occasionally taking a bite of mango, the three flavors mingling gloriously in my mouth and on my fingers as I licked them clean.

Because of its large seed, a mango can be a bit awkward to cut neatly. I find the easiest way is to place the fruit horizontally on a cutting board and make a slightly off-center slice, cutting off the flesh in a single piece as close as possible to the large, flat seed. Repeat on the other side of the seed. Hold a half cut side up and score the flesh lengthwise into slices. If you want cubes, score crosswise as well, creating a lattice pattern in the size needed. Be careful not to cut through the skin. Press against the peel to fan out the slices or cubes slightly, then slice the fruit away from the peel, allowing it to drop into a bowl. Repeat with the remaining half. Any flesh remaining on the peel or the seed can be nibbled by the cook.

ENSALADA DE MANZANA
Apple Salad Dessert

Even though this dish is called an *ensalada* and it may remind you of a Waldorf salad, it is not a salad at all. Instead, it is a still-popular old-fashioned cold apple dessert eaten by Ricardo and his family during the Christmas and New Year holidays. The list of ingredients varies: Ricardo likes to add pineapple, but other variations include mandarin segments and banana slices. Let your imagination guide you. The garnish of pomegranate seeds is traditional, but if pomegranates are out of season, you can substitute cherries.

Serves 12 . . . .

▪ FOR THE SALAD
6 crisp red eating apples such as Gala, peeled, cored, and cut into ¾-inch cubes

3½ cups ¾-inch-cubed fresh pineapple

1 cup sweetened condensed milk

1 cup heavy cream (not ultrapasteurized)

¼ cup pecans, chopped

¼ cup raisins

▪ FOR THE GARNISH
Seeds from 1 pomegranate, or 12 fresh or canned Bing cherries, pitted and halved

FOR THE SALAD: In a large bowl, mix together the apples, pineapple, milk, cream, pecans, and raisins. Cover and refrigerate, stirring occasionally, for 2 hours.

When ready to serve, scoop the salad onto a large platter with a slotted spoon, allowing any excess liquid to drain off. Garnish with the pomegranate seeds and serve.

ROSCA DE PASAS
Raisin Cake Ring

María Dolores Torres Yzábal grew up in Sonora, in northern Mexico, where the food is simple, with few ingredients in a recipe. This recipe, passed down by her grandmother, is an excellent example of that simplicity, though María Dolores often dresses up the servings with sliced strawberries or other fruit for both color and taste.

Serves 8 to 10 . . . .

Butter and flour for preparing the pan

FOR THE SIMPLE SYRUP

2 cups water

1 cup roughly chopped piloncillo (2 small
cones, ½ to ¾ ounce each; page 42)

2 tablespoons unsalted butter

2 teaspoons pure vanilla extract

FOR THE CAKE

1 cup raisins

½ cup unsalted butter, at room temperature

⅔ cup granulated sugar

1 egg

1 teaspoon baking soda, dissolved in
1 tablespoon water

1½ cups sifted unbleached all-purpose flour

FOR THE GARNISH

½ cup finely chopped toasted pecans

Heat the oven to 350°F. Butter and flour a 10-inch ring mold or Bundt pan.

FOR THE SYRUP: Put the water and sugar in a saucepan and bring to a boil over medium-high heat, stirring constantly to dissolve the sugar. Lower the heat to a simmer and cook until the sugar is fully dissolved and the mixture has reduced by almost half, about 10 minutes. Add the butter and stir until melted. Remove from the heat and stir in the vanilla. Let cool.

FOR THE CAKE: Put the raisins in a heat-proof bowl, add 1 cup boiling water, and let stand until plump, about 10 minutes. Drain the raisins, reserving ½ cup of the liquid. Set the liquid aside to cool and pat the raisins dry with a towel.

Put the butter in a bowl. Using an electric mixer, beat the butter, adding the sugar a little at a time, until creamy. Add the egg and the dissolved baking soda and continue beating the mixture until light in texture.

Resift the flour into a bowl and stir in the raisins. On low speed, add the flour mixture to the butter mixture in three batches alternately with the reserved raisin water in two batches, beginning and ending with the flour mixture and beating just until combined. Pour the batter into the prepared mold.

Bake until a toothpick inserted near the center of the cake comes out clean and the cake bounces back when pressed lightly in the center, about 30 minutes. Let cool for 5 to 10 minutes on a wire rack, then run a knife around the inside edge of the pan to loosen the cake sides. Invert a serving plate on top of the pan and carefully flip the pan and plate together. Lift off the pan.

To serve, pour the syrup over the top of the warm cake and sprinkle with the pecans.

PASTEL DE ELOTE
Fresh Corn Cake

Many different kinds of cakes made from fresh corn are popular in Mexico, some of them savory and some slightly sweet and served as a simple dessert. This recipe was given to Ricardo by chef Felipe Gómez Rizo, who for the past ten years has dedicated himself to the study of Mexican pastries.

The cake can be served warm or at room temperature, either plain or lightly dusted with powdered sugar. It can also be served hot (reheated, if necessary, in a microwave oven for 2 minutes), accompanied with vanilla ice cream or slathered with butter and drizzled with orange blossom honey.

Serves 6 to 8

2 tablespoons unsalted butter

3 tablespoons fine dried bread crumbs

1⅔ cups (14½ ounces) fresh or slightly thawed frozen corn kernels

4 eggs

1 cup plus 6 tablespoons condensed milk

¾ cup plus 2 tablespoons corn oil

3 tablespoons all-purpose flour

½ tablespoon baking powder

Heat the oven to 350°F. Grease a 9-by-13-inch pan with the butter, then sprinkle evenly with the bread crumbs.

Put the corn kernels, eggs, milk, oil, flour, and baking powder in a blender or food processor and process until smooth. Pour the batter into the prepared pan.

Bake until golden brown and a toothpick inserted in the center comes out clean, 40 to 45 minutes. Let cool slightly on a wire rack, then run a knife around the inside edge of the pan to loosen the cake sides. Cut into squares to serve.

GORDITAS DE GARBANZO DULCE
Sweet Garbanzo Gorditas

Make no mistake, this is not the usual puffy gordita served as a snack with a fiery salsa. It is an anise-flavored syrupy dessert with chunks of pineapple, almost like a *buñuelo* (page 265) but made out of garbanzo beans.

This recipe comes from Fany Gerson, a talented, young pastry chef from Mexico City now living in New York City who once worked at Rosa Mexicano restaurant in Manhattan. Many other beloved versions exist, including some that use starchy fresh corn instead of garbanzos.

Piloncillo is available in most grocery stores and all Mexican markets, but finding fresh Mexican cheese may be a challenge. You can substitute a mild domestic goat cheese, or a feta cheese that has been well rinsed to remove its saltiness.

I like to serve these gorditas hot with a scoop of vanilla ice cream on the side and the remaining cooled syrup spooned over the top.

Serves 4 to 6 . . . .

FOR THE SYRUP
- 1 teaspoon aniseeds
- 2 (8- to 9-ounce) piloncillo cones (page 42), roughly chopped
- 3-inch stick Mexican true cinnamon bark (page 88)
- 1 cup diced fresh pineapple

FOR THE GORDITAS
- 1⅓ cups drained canned garbanzo beans, well rinsed
- 2 eggs
- 3 ounces queso fresco, crumbled
- 3 tablespoons all-purpose flour
- Peanut or sunflower oil for deep-frying

FOR THE SYRUP: Wrap the aniseeds in a square of cheesecloth and secure with kitchen string. Put the *piloncillo*, 2 cups water, cinnamon, and aniseed bundle in a medium-large saucepan over medium-high heat and cook, stirring occasionally, until the *piloncillo* dissolves and the water begins to boil. Add the pineapple, lower the heat to a gentle simmer, and cook until the mixture is the consistency of thick jam, about 5 minutes more. Remove from the heat and remove and discard the aniseed bundle. Set the syrup aside.

FOR THE GORDITAS: Put the garbanzo beans in a food processor or heavy-duty blender and process until pureed (tiny chunks are okay). Transfer to a bowl, add the eggs, cheese, and flour, and mix well.

Line a baking sheet with parchment paper. Divide the mixture into 10 to 12 equal portions and shape each portion into a patty about ¾ inch thick, dampening your hands if the dough is sticking too much. As each patty is formed, place it on the prepared baking sheet. Alternatively, using a small ice cream scoop, drop rounds of the mixture on the prepared baking sheet and flatten with a spatula.

Pour the oil to a depth of 1½ inches into a large, deep skillet and heat to 365° to 370°F on a deep-frying thermometer. Line a second baking sheet with several layers of absorbent paper.

Using a slotted spatula, slide 3 or 4 patties into the hot oil and fry, turning occasionally, until golden, about 2 minutes. Using the spatula, transfer the gorditas to the absorbent paper–lined baking sheet. Lightly prick both sides of each gordita with a fork. Repeat to cook the remaining patties the same way, always making sure the oil is at 365° to 370°F before adding the next batch.

Reheat the syrup to a gentle simmer, add the gorditas, and cook for 3 to 5 minutes, allowing them to absorb some of the liquid. Serve on a platter with the remaining syrup and pineapple spooned over the top.

CAPIROTADA DE LECHE
Creamy Dried Fruit and Nut Studded Bread Pudding

I've eaten many regional versions of this comforting bread pudding. The toasted bread is like a sponge, absorbing any milk, rum, or beguiling agave syrup poured over it. I have been served *capirotada* flavored with tomatoes and onions, with plantains, and with cheese, but no matter what other ingredients are included, to be traditional this dessert pudding nearly always includes some combination of nuts and raisins for taste and texture.

Pastry chef Fany Gerson shared this sweet *capirotada* recipe with me. It is from Zacatecas, where cooks like to include *acitrón*, the candied fruit of the *biznaga* cactus. It is widely available in Mexican markets in the United States. Her recipe is also embellished with unsweetened coconut, which may be hard to find in regular grocery stores but is a staple in most health-foods stores. Freshly grated coconut is even better (page 276). One year, I was fortunate to have the talented Fany, the former pastry chef of Rosa Mexicano in New York City, with me in Tlaxacala and Puebla to teach the chefs on my culinary tour. Her first book, *My Sweet Mexico,* was published in 2010.

FOR THE PASTRY CREAM FILLING

3 cups whole milk

6 egg yolks

⅔ cup sugar

⅓ cup cornstarch

   Pinch of sea salt

2 (2½-inch) sticks Mexican true cinnamon bark (page 88)

1 teaspoon pure vanilla extract

FOR THE BREAD PUDDING

4 tablespoons canola or safflower oil

1 pound day-old white, crusty French bread or baguette, cut into 1-inch-thick slices

3 tablespoons unsalted butter

1 cup raisins

1 cup skinned raw peanuts, lightly toasted

1 cup unsweetened shredded dried coconut

1 cup diced acitrón or candied pineapple

FOR THE PASTRY CREAM: In a bowl, whisk together ½ cup of the milk, the egg yolks, ⅓ cup of the sugar, the cornstarch, and the salt. Set aside.

Put the remaining 2½ cups milk and ⅓ cup sugar and the cinnamon in a heavy, medium saucepan and bring just to a boil over medium heat, stirring to dissolve the sugar. Slowly pour the hot milk mixture into the egg yolk mixture while whisking constantly. Return the combined mixtures to the saucepan, place over medium heat, and cook, whisking constantly, until the cream thickens, about 1 minute. Remove from the heat and discard the cinnamon. Add the vanilla and whisk until smooth. Transfer to a bowl and press plastic wrap directly onto the surface to prevent a skin from forming. Let cool and refrigerate until needed. (The pastry cream can be made ahead and refrigerated for up to 3 days.)

FOR THE PUDDING: Heat 2 tablespoons of the oil in a large sauté pan or skillet over medium heat. Add as many of the bread slices as will fit in a single layer and cook, turning once, until lightly golden on both sides. Remove the bread from the pan and set aside. Repeat with the remaining bread slices, adding the remaining 2 tablespoons oil to the pan as needed.

Heat the oven to 350°F. Generously butter a 9-by-13-inch baking dish.

Mix together the raisins, peanuts, coconut, and *acitrón* in a bowl. Arrange a layer of the bread slices in the bottom of the prepared baking dish. Scoop half of the cream mixture over the bread slices, spreading evenly. Sprinkle with half of the coconut mixture. Repeat the layers, finishing with the coconut mixture.

Bake until the coconut is lightly toasted, 10 to 15 minutes. Remove from the oven and let cool for 30 minutes before serving. Serve warm or at room temperature.

BUDÍN DE FRUTAS
Fruit and Bread Pudding

Unfortunately, I was not able to discover the history of this delicious bread pudding served by Malu Foglia de Blanco from the French settlement of San Rafael, Veracruz. Other combinations of fruits can be used, but it is best made with sturdy ones, both fresh and dried.

Although this pudding can be served warm, its flavor is accentuated at room temperature. If you like, top with a dollop of vanilla ice cream, brandy-laced whipped cream, or crème fraîche.

Serves 8 to 10

FOR THE FRUIT
1 large peach or nectarine, or 10 frozen peach or nectarine slices

1 Comice, Bosc, or Bartlett pear

1 Gravenstein, Rome, or Winesap apple

2 cups sugar

6 dried apricots or pitted prunes, halved

1 vanilla bean, split lengthwise

FOR THE CARAMEL
1 cup sugar

1 teaspoon freshly squeezed lemon juice

½ cup syrup from fruit

FOR THE BREAD PUDDING
1 pound French bread, crust removed, cut into ½-inch cubes, and set out to dry in a warm location for several hours

4 cups whole milk

Vanilla bean used for the fruit preparation

4 eggs, lightly whisked

¼ cup sugar

FOR THE FRUIT: Halve and pit the peach and halve and core the pear and apple. Peel the fruits and cut into ⅓-inch-thick slices.

To make a simple syrup, combine 2 cups water and the sugar in a saucepan, place over medium heat, and bring to a boil, stirring to dissolve the sugar. As the water starts to boil, add the apricots and vanilla bean, lower the heat to medium-low, and poach for 3 minutes. Add the peach, pear, and apple slices and continue simmering, stirring frequently, for 5 minutes longer. Drain the fruit into a fine-mesh sieve placed over a bowl. Set the fruit and syrup aside separately. Reserve the vanilla bean.

FOR THE CARAMEL: Ready an ice-water bath. Combine the sugar, lemon juice, and syrup in a small copper or other heavy saucepan, stir briefly with a wooden spoon, place over medium heat, and bring

6 tablespoons unsalted butter, melted

¾ teaspoon pure vanilla extract

¼ cup brandy or dark rum

1 teaspoon baking powder

to a boil. As the mixture heats, wash down the sides of the pan with a wet pastry brush to prevent sugar crystals from forming. Cook, without stirring, until the sugar dissolves fully, 5 to 6 minutes. Raise the heat to high and cook, swirling the pan to color the contents evenly, until the syrup is amber, about 5 minutes. Remove from the heat and set the bottom of the pan in the ice-water bath for no more than a few seconds to halt the cooking. Pour the hot caramel into a 2-quart baking dish or into eight 1-cup ramekins, coating the bottom(s) evenly. Set aside to cool.

FOR THE PUDDING: Heat the oven to 375°F. In a large bowl, soak the bread cubes in the milk for 10 minutes. Working over the bowl of bread and milk, remove the seeds from the vanilla bean with the back of a knife, adding them to the bowl. Gently stir the eggs, sugar, butter, and vanilla extract into the bread mixture. When the ingredients are well mixed, stir in the brandy and baking powder.

Fold the poached fruit into the bread mixture and spoon into the caramel-lined baking dish, or divide evenly among the ramekins and set the ramekins on a baking sheet. Bake until set and the top is lightly golden, about 1 hour for the large dish and 45 minutes for the ramekins. Remove from the oven and serve warm or let cool before serving. Drizzle a little of the syrup that remains from poaching the fruit over each serving.

ANTE DE COCO MARQUESOTE
Cake Layered with Coconut

ntes in a variety of flavors are classic desserts in Mexico. They are like layer cakes and are made with *marquesote,* which is similar to pound cake, saturated with syrup or some type of liquor. I have been told by Oaxacan friends that *marquesote* was named in honor of Hernán Cortés, the Marques de Valle de Oaxaca, and the traditional version of *ante,* said to have originated in the convents of Puebla, has a paste of fruits or nuts spread between the layers, which are then soaked in syrup or wine and eaten before an elaborate meal, the *ante* meaning "prior to." Somehow, at least in Mexico City, *antes* became associated with all-male *pulquerías,* where they were available for carousing men to take home to placate their wives. Whatever the origin, there is no doubt that the *ante* is a dessert with a history.

There are so many variations that it was difficult to select just one recipe, so this basic recipe for the *marquesote* is from former Oaxacan chef Iliana de la Vega, along with her addition of a coconut filling and syrup. The unsweetened coconut can be found in most health-foods stores and in some Asian grocery stores. If you can find only sweetened coconut, reduce the sugar in the coconut mixture by ¼ cup.

I am also including Mexican pastry chef Felipe Gómez Rizo's equally delicious version of *ante* soaked with *cajeta* instead of the usual syrup. *Cajeta,* or caramel, is made in many parts of Mexico, usually with goat's milk. The most famous *cajeta* comes from Celaya, Guanajuato, and is sold in thin wooden boxes, hence the name *cajeta,* or "box." Although you can buy bottled *cajeta* in Mexican markets and many grocery stores, the homemade version is better. Both store-bought and homemade *cajeta* will keep for several months in the refrigerator. It also makes a special topping for ice cream with a few chopped pecans.

Serves 8 . . . .

▌ FOR THE MARQUESOTE

2 tablespoons unsalted butter

8 eggs, at room temperature, separated

   Pinch of sea salt

½ cup sugar

1 cup cornstarch

1 cup unbleached all-purpose flour

½ teaspoon baking powder

FOR THE MARQUESOTE: Heat the oven to 350°F. Butter a 3-quart cake pan that measures 12 by 14 inches with about two-thirds of the butter. Line the bottom with parchment paper and butter the parchment with the remaining butter.

In a stand mixer fitted with the whisk attachment, or in a large bowl with a

FOR THE COCONUT MIXTURE AND SYRUP

1¾ cups unsweetened shredded dried coconut, lightly toasted

3¼ cups whole milk

3 cups sugar

2-inch stick Mexican true cinnamon bark (page 88)

¼ cup Spanish medium-sweet (oloroso) sherry or rum

½ teaspoon sea salt

FOR THE TOPPING

3 tablespoons dark raisins

3 tablespoons golden raisins

handheld mixer, beat together the egg whites and salt until soft peaks form. Using a wooden spoon, stir in the sugar until combined, then stir in the egg yolks, one at a time, mixing well after each addition.

In a small bowl, stir together the cornstarch, flour, and baking powder. Gradually add the cornstarch mixture to the egg white mixture, whisking just until incorporated.

Pour the batter into the prepared pan. Bake until a toothpick inserted in the middle of the cake comes out clean and the top is golden brown, about 20 minutes. Let cool in the pan on a wire rack.

FOR THE COCONUT MIXTURE AND SYRUP: To make the coconut mixture, put the coconut in a food processor and process until finely ground. Set aside.

In a heavy, deep saucepan, combine the milk and 1½ cups of the sugar and heat over medium heat, stirring until the sugar has dissolved. Add the ground coconut and continue to cook, stirring constantly, until the mixture thickens, about 30 minutes. The mixture should register 210°F on an instant-read thermometer. Remove from the heat and let cool completely, stirring occasionally.

To make the syrup: In another heavy, deep pan, combine the remaining 1½ cups sugar, the cinnamon, and 3 cups water over high heat and cook, stirring constantly, until the sugar has dissolved completely and the mixture coats the back of the spoon, about 5 minutes. The mixture should register 210°F on an instant-read thermometer. Remove from the heat and let sit for 5 minutes, then remove and discard the cinnamon. Stir in the sherry and salt and set aside on a rack to cool completely.

To assemble the cake: To unmold the cake, run a knife around the inside edge of the pan to loosen the cake sides. Invert the pan onto the rack, lift off the pan, and then peel off the parchment. Using a serrated knife, cut the cake in half horizontally. Place the bottom layer on a platter or tray deep enough to contain the sauce, then slowly pour half of the syrup over the cake. When the cake has absorbed the liquid, spread half of the coconut mixture over the bottom layer. Cover with the top cake layer and pour over the remaining syrup. Spread with the remaining coconut mixture, then scatter the raisins over the top. Cut into slices to serve.

Bake the *marquesote* as directed. Omit the coconut mixture and the syrup. To make the *cajeta*, combine ¼ cup water and 1 teaspoon baking soda in a small bowl and stir until the baking soda is dissolved.

Pour 4 cups goat's milk into a large saucepan, preferably copper. Stir in 1 cup sugar and bring to a boil over high heat. Reduce the heat to medium-low and pour in the baking soda mixture in a thin stream while stirring constantly. The *cajeta* should be at a low boil. Continue to cook, stirring frequently, until the mixture coats the back of a spoon and turns a caramel color, 1 to 1½ hours. Pour the *cajeta* into a bowl, stir in 1 teaspoon pure vanilla extract, and let cool.

To make the filling, reheat 1¾ cups of the *cajeta* over medium-low heat until heated through, then stir in 3 tablespoons 100 percent blue agave *tequila blanco*.

Unmold the cake and cut in half horizontally as directed. Place the bottom layer on a platter or tray deep enough to contain the sauce. Pour half of the filling over the top and sprinkle with 6 tablespoons chopped pecans. Cover with the top cake layer and then pour the remaining filling over the top, letting it spill over the edges of the cake. Sprinkle the top with 6 tablespoons chopped pecans. Cut into slices to serve. If there is extra *cajeta*, pour it into a small pitcher and pass at the table, or reserve for another use.

FLAN DE LECHE
Milk Custard

To me, this rich flan is unquestionably Spain's most important contribution to Mexico's dessert menu. I was fortunate to have been served this traditional version, an old family recipe of Ana María Lopez Landa, on a lovely crystal plate in her historical colonial home in Puebla.

The flan is best made a day in advance of serving. Almost like adorning a lily, it can be topped with a dollop of whipped cream. In Catalonia, Spain, it is sometimes sprinkled with raisins plumped in brandy and then flamed for a spectacular presentation.

Serves 6 to 8 . . . .

2 cups sugar, divided equally

4 cups whole milk

1 vanilla bean

Zest of 1 scrubbed orange, finely grated

9 eggs, lightly whisked

Heat the oven to 325°F.

Put 1 cup of the sugar and ½ cup water in a heavy skillet over medium heat and stir with a wooden spoon until the sugar dissolves. Stop stirring and let the mixture simmer until it turns amber. Be careful that it does not burn. Remove from the heat and quickly pour the caramel into an 8-cup flan mold or eight ¾-cup custard cups or ramekins, tipping the mold or cups so the entire bottom and much of the sides are lightly coated. Set aside to cool.

Pour the milk into a medium saucepan. Using a small knife, split the vanilla bean lengthwise and remove the seeds with the back of the knife, adding them to the milk along with the spent pods and the orange zest. Bring to a gentle boil over medium heat, then immediately lower the heat and simmer, stirring frequently, until creamlike and the milk has reduced by one-fourth, about 15 minutes. Stir in the remaining 1 cup sugar and bring back to a simmer, stirring until the sugar is fully dissolved. Remove from the heat and let cool.

Pour the eggs through a fine-mesh sieve into the cooled milk and stir together. Remove the vanilla bean pods and pour the custard into the prepared mold or divide evenly among the cups. Cover with aluminium foil.

Place the mold or cups in a large baking pan on the middle rack of the oven. Carefully add enough hot water to the pan to reach halfway up the side of the mold(s). Bake until a toothpick inserted into the center of the flan comes out clean, about 1 hour if using cups and 1½ hours if using the large mold. Add hot water to the pan as needed to maintain the original level. Remove the pan from the oven, and remove the mold or cups from the pan. Let cool for 1 hour, then cover and refrigerate for at least 6 hours or up to 2 days.

When ready to serve, run a knife around the inside edge of the mold to loosen the flan sides. Invert a round, deep serving platter over the mold, and holding the platter and mold firmly together, decisively invert them. Shake the mold gently, then lift it off, allowing any excess caramel to drizzle over the top. The flan should gently drop onto the platter. Cut into slices to serve, and spoon some of the caramel syrup from the platter over each serving. Unmold the custard cups the same way, inverting them onto individual plates.

VARIATION: FLAN CON LICOR DE CAFÉ Y RON (SPIRITED FLAN)
Add 1 tablespoon Kahlúa or other coffee liqueur and 1 teaspoon dark rum to the simmering milk.

ISLA FLOTANTE
Floating Island

This elegant dessert, a creamy puff of meringue, sits like an island floating in a sea of custard and has long been a favorite way to end a lavish Mexican dinner party. This recipe is from María Dolores Torres Yzábal and is quite simple to make if the directions are carefully followed.

Serves 12

FOR THE CARAMEL GLAZE

1½ cups plus 1 teaspoon sugar

Several dashes of freshly squeezed lemon juice

1 teaspoon unsalted butter, at room temperature

FOR THE MERINGUE

2½ cups egg whites (from about 18 eggs), at room temperature, separated

½ teaspoon cream of tartar

1 cup superfine sugar

½ teaspoon pure vanilla extract

FOR THE SAUCE

3 cups whole milk

18 egg yolks

½ cup sugar

Pinch of baking soda

1 vanilla bean, split lengthwise

2 tablespoons coffee liqueur (optional)

FOR THE TOPPING

¼ cup sliced almonds

Heat the oven to 350°F.

FOR THE CARAMEL GLAZE: Sprinkle 1½ cups sugar over the bottom of a 10-inch cake pan and place on the stove top over medium heat. Add the lemon juice and stir until the sugar begins to caramelize, then stop stirring and swirl the pan so that the melted and unmelted sugars combine. Continue cooking until the sugar turns amber. Lift and tilt the pan, swirling the syrup until it evenly coats the bottom and a little of the sides. Lightly brush the butter on the syrup in a thin layer, then sprinkle the remaining 1 teaspoon sugar evenly over the surface. Set aside.

FOR THE MERINGUE: In a stand mixer fitted with the whisk attachment or a large bowl with a handheld mixer, combine the egg whites and cream of tartar and beat until soft peaks form. Sprinkle in the sugar, a little at a time, and continue to beat until the mixture looks like shiny pointed mountaintops when the beater is lifted, at least 5 minutes. Beat in the vanilla.

Pour one-third of the egg whites into the cake pan (you may hear the caramel crack). Run a clean knife through the whites to eliminate any air pockets and pat down gently. Continue layering and patting down until all of the egg whites are in the pan. The whites may reach higher than the rim of the pan.

Place the cake pan in a large baking pan on the lower rack of the oven. Carefully pour very hot water into the roasting pan to reach halfway or more up the sides of the cake pan. Do not add so much that the cake pan starts to float (you might hear more cracking). Bake without opening the oven door until the puffy meringue is the color of golden sand, about 45 minutes. An instant-read thermometer inserted in the center of the meringue should register 165°F. Turn off the heat and let the meringue remain in the oven for 30 to 45 minutes. If you have a gas oven with a pilot light, leave the door open.

FOR THE SAUCE: Whisk together the milk, egg yolks, sugar, baking soda, and vanilla bean in a saucepan until a smooth sauce is created. Place over medium heat, bring to a simmer, and cook, stirring gently but continually, until lightly thickened, about 5 minutes. Be careful that you do not let the eggs curdle. Remove from the heat and stir in the coffee liqueur (if using). Let cool, then remove the vanilla bean. (Wipe the vanilla bean clean and reserve for another use, such as flavoring a canister of sugar.)

To serve, invert the cooled meringue into a wide, shallow bowl or deep platter. You may reheat the cake pan on the stove top to release more of the caramel and drizzle it over the top of the meringue just before serving. Pour most of the custard sauce around the base of the meringue and reserve the rest to pass at the table. Serve immediately or refrigerate for up to 12 hours before serving. Sprinkle the top with the almonds.

CHURROS
Crispy Fritters

Eating freshly made churros dunked into rich hot chocolate for breakfast, as I did at Churrería El Moro in the center of Mexico City, is delightful. But it was while living in northern Spain that I first became hooked on these long sugared fritters. On weekends, there were always vendors piping out fluted dough into huge vats of rippling hot oil and then lifting out the crisp-fried churros and dipping them in sugar. Purists prefer them unsweetened and dunk them immediately into cups of strong coffee mixed with hot milk.

Whether in Spain or Mexico, eating churros is an ideal way to start a day, to finish it, or to satisfy a craving for a sweet snack. To make churros similar to those found in Spain and

Mexico, it helps to have a churro maker, which can be purchased from Spanish specialty shops (see Sources). If you do not have one, you can use a pastry bag fitted with a ⅜-inch star tip. Chef Rick Bayless, who features churros in his XOCO restaurant in Chicago, suggests warming the flour before making the batter for the best result.

It is important to eat churros when they are hot, so fry just enough for everyone to have one or two and then fry more once the first batch has been eaten.

Makes 15 (4-inch) fritters . . . .

Peanut or sunflower oil for deep-frying, plus 1 tablespoon

½ teaspoon sea salt

1½ cups all-purpose flour

¾ cup sugar, preferably superfine

1-inch stick Mexican true cinnamon bark (page 88), ground, or ¼ teaspoon ground cinnamon

Pour the oil to a depth of 2 inches into a deep, heavy skillet or Dutch oven 8 to 10 inches in diameter and heat to 375°F on a deep-frying thermometer.

While the oil is heating, pour 1½ cups water into a 2-quart saucepan, add the 1 tablespoon oil and the salt, and bring to a boil over high heat. In another pan, heat the flour over medium-low for 2 to 3 minutes until just warm. When the water is boiling, remove the pan from the heat, add the warm flour to the water all at once, and stir vigorously with a wooden spoon until a ball forms.

Stir together the sugar and cinnamon in a pie pan or other shallow pan and set near the stove. To make sure the oil is hot enough, put some of the dough into the churro maker, and holding the maker over the hot oil, press out a 4- to 5-inch length of the dough into the oil, using your fingers to free it from the press. Fry the churro, rotating it as needed to color evenly, until golden on all sides, 2 to 3 minutes. Using tongs or a wire skimmer, lift out the churro, allowing the excess oil to drip back into the pan, and drain briefly on absorbent paper. The churro should be crispy on the outside and soft but not mushy on the inside. If it is, continue in the same fashion, frying 3 or 4 churros at a time and always making sure the oil is at 375°F before adding the next batch. If it isn't, adjust the temperature or the timing and test again with a little more dough.

Roll the hot churros in the cinnamon sugar just before serving.

BUÑUELOS DE VIENTO
"Puffs of Wind" Fritters

B*uñuelos* can be found throughout Spain and Mexico, but seldom in the same form. The first time I ate them was in a bustling market in Gerona, north of Barcelona, where the dough was dropped by large spoonfuls into gently bubbling oil. When the puffed, crispy fried dough was ready, it was quickly removed from the oil and lightly dusted with powdered sugar. You had to eat the *buñuelos* as soon as they were made, juggling them from hand to hand as they were extremely hot.

Soon after leaving Spain, my husband and I spent our first Christmas together in Oaxaca and experienced very different *buñuelos*. On the street outside of the city's cathedral, canopy-covered kitchens were filled with people jostling to get their clay bowls filled with a small, thin, tortilla-shaped *buñuelo* drowned in hot sugar syrup. After eating the *buñuelo*, everyone went outside, faced an austere stone facade, turned, and tossed the bowl over his or her shoulder onto the foundation wall of the historic cathedral. As they hurled their bowls, they made a wish for the coming year. Unfortunately, this long-standing tradition has been discontinued, but you can still buy these *buñuelos* here and in other places in Oaxaca during the Christmas season.

I finally got to make *buñuelos* myself in Morelia, Michoacán, but this time the *buñuelo* was large and quite fragile. My first Mexican coordinator, Carmen Barnard, introduced me to the Pulido family, who own the simple but wonderful Cenaduría Lupita, where locals come to eat on Sunday night. It is run by three sisters, one of whom, Lilia, gave us a class on making the style of *buñuelos* favored in Michoacán. What was amazing to me was how Lilia flattened the dough. Instead of rolling it out like pie dough, she put a cloth over her knee, placed the dough on it, and patted the dough, round and round, until it was paper-thin. Lilia said that any of us who were uncomfortable with this method could instead flatten the dough over an upturned large bowl. I must admit I am not very good with either technique.

In the port city of Veracruz, these lighter-than-air fritters are sold by street vendors and shaped into bracelets of dough that end up looking like crispy, crazy doughnuts. Another beautiful version of these dough puffs is a traditional treat during Ana María Lopez Landa's Christmas festivities in Puebla. She makes them with a four-inch round tin mold with a starlike design inside and a long, perpendicular handle. Her mold is similar to one I bought years ago at a street market in Tlaquepaque, outside of Guadalajara, with Sra. Landa's granddaughter, my present Mexican coordinator, Ana Elena Martínez.

All of these different versions of *buñuelo* are typically served during the Christmas holidays, but they are a fun and delicious treat any time during the year. The following simple recipe is adapted from one by Esthela Maasberg de Blanco that appears in a little cookbook from the French settlement of San Rafael, Veracruz. Be sure to dust the *buñuelos* with powdered sugar while they are still hot.

Makes 15 fritters . . . .

1 cup sifted all-purpose flour

2 tablespoons unsalted butter

1 tablespoon granulated sugar

¼ teaspoon sea salt

Grated zest of 1 scrubbed Key lime or small Persian lime

4 eggs, lightly beaten

Peanut or sunflower oil for deep-frying

½ cup sifted powdered sugar

Heat 1 cup water in a small saucepan until boiling. Immediately reduce the heat to low and stir in the flour with a wooden spoon. Add the butter, granulated sugar, salt, and lime zest and beat until smooth, 3 to 5 minutes. Remove from the heat and let cool for a few minutes. Put the dough in a food processor, add the eggs, and process until the eggs are well mixed into the dough, about 30 seconds. Transfer the dough to a medium bowl.

Pour the oil to a depth of 2 inches into a deep, wide, heavy saucepan and heat to 375°F on a deep-frying thermometer. Working in batches, add the dough by the tablespoon and fry, turning the fritters occasionally, until puffy and lightly browned, about 1 minute. Using a slotted spoon, transfer to absorbent paper to drain. Repeat with the remaining dough, always making sure the oil is at 375°F before adding the next batch.

Sprinkle the hot *buñuelos* with the powdered sugar and serve right away.

BEBIDAS

Cooling Drinks and Hot Restoratives

When hot and thirsty, a common occurrence in the sweltering, sluggish heat of Mexico's coastal areas, and even at certain times in the highlands, everyone needs a cooling drink. At the beach, an agile young girl or boy might climb up a nearby coconut palm and provide you with the liquid energy of coconut water served in its own container. Alongside the ubiquitous *refrescos,* or bottled carbonated soft drinks, offered by street or market vendors, you still happily find the traditional naturally flavored *aguas frescas*. Being offered something to drink is a sign of hospitality to be accepted with gratitude.

ALWAYS TIME FOR A BEER

For many Mexicans, beer is the more spirited thirst quencher, and a similar beverage, made from fermented corn, was drunk even before the arrival of the Europeans. By the nineteenth century, newly arrived European brewmasters, mainly from Germany, were making their familiar pilsner-style mild golden beer, which is still the favorite in Mexico. Dark amber beers eventually followed, and nowadays the entire spectrum of beer types is available, including rich, malty lagers that are good drunk with casual snack food and alongside almost any spicy dish.

I have learned that beer is vulnerable to warm temperatures, so it is best to buy it cold and keep it cold. That said, it is also best to drink it after some of the chill has lessened. Also, the ritual of serving beer with a wedge of lime is not common outside of Mexican resort areas, which means the lime wedge probably began as a marketing ploy for tourists. Apparently, for every rule there is an exception, however. Zingy *micheladas* are proof of that, breaking two rules: a hefty measure of lime juice is combined with the beer in tall glasses, and not only is the beer cold but it is also poured over ice cubes.

MICHELADAS
Icy Spicy Beer

icheladas have been a popular way to drink beer in Mexico since the 1940s. When you order one, however, you may be surprised. Usually a *michelada* is quite *picante*, but occasionally it comes seasoned with only lime juice and is more like lemonade made with beer. At some places, this milder version is called a *chelada*. I first tasted a *michelada* long ago in highland Iguala, Guerrero, where it was served as a chaser with tequila. Or, maybe the tequila was the chaser for the *michelada?* Anyway, it made for a good accompaniment to *conejo en adobo* (page 139), the sensational regional rabbit dish.

Serves 4

¼ cup sea salt

2 Key limes or 1 Persian lime, scrubbed and thickly sliced crosswise

Ice cubes

1 cup freshly squeezed lime juice (from 24 to 26 Key limes or 8 to 10 Persian limes)

4 dashes of Worcestershire or Maggi sauce

4 big dashes of bottled chile salsa such as Mexican brand Salsa Valentina or Búfalo or Tabasco sauce

2 bottles Mexican beer of choice, chilled

Spread the salt on a small, flat plate. Rub the rim of a tall beer glass with a lime slice, turn the glass over, and dip into the salt to coat the rim. Repeat with 3 more glasses, using a second lime slice if needed. Fill the glasses with ice cubes. Pour ¼ cup of the lime juice into each glass, then add a dash each of Worcestershire sauce and chile salsa.

Divide the beer among the glasses, garnish each drink with a lime slice, and serve.

A SIP OF WINE

There is an old Spanish saying, "Wine brings feelings of happiness and optimism." However, it once seemingly applied only to wines originating in Spain. No Spanish colonists were allowed to grow their own grapes in Mexico after 1699, but instead could only drink the heavily taxed wines shipped from Spain. Vineyards established around Querétaro and Aguascalientes to produce sacramental wines were the only exception.

Things changed after independence from Spain, especially in Baja California Norte, with its ideal grape-growing climate. Today, at least 90 percent of Mexico's excellent wines are bottled in the area. These wines, with their rather complex flavors, pair beautifully with Mexican dishes, even with moles and other spicy preparations. Unfortunately, most of them are taxed excessively when exported, but do try them when dining in Mexico, especially the higher-quality ones with comparable high prices. When I am in Mexico, I find both Spanish and Chilean wines are also excellent choices. At home, I am all over the map with my wine selections, and I have included some favorite pairings with many of the dishes.

⠿ THE SPIRITS OF MEXICO

It is the huge pineapple-shaped heart of the large, sword-leafed maguey plant, scientifically part of the *Agave* genus, that is the source of Mexico's best-known alcoholic beverages: pulque, *mezcal*, and tequila. More than four hundred species are found from California south to Venezuela, and in Mexico alone, some 136 different species play important roles as sources of food, fiber—and drink.

PULQUE

Long before the Spanish conquest, the indigenous people were using a scraping process to reach into the *piña* (heart) of the living maguey plant to extract a sweet liquid called *aguamiel* (honey water), which quickly fermented. This pulque was consumed primarily by the nobles, by people of advanced age, and occasionally by a woman after childbirth. Drunkenness was not acceptable, and the first time a person was found drunk, the punishment was either a severe beating or the severing of the hand that had held the pulque. The punishment for a second offense was death.

The Spanish were accustomed to drinking wine and brandy and soon began to search for local products they could use to produce alcoholic beverages. Maguey was a natural fit. It was not long before large haciendas dedicated to cultivating maguey plants and fermenting pulque were built, becoming a major source of income for the Spaniards. The labor, of course, was provided by the local indigenous people, who were often provided only meager sustenance. Many of these now-abandoned haciendas are found in the states around Mexico City; others have been restored and are again producing pulque. Because pulque is not distilled and is highly perishable, it is typically produced and consumed locally.

I enjoy this yeasty beverage drunk straight, but the less adventurous, especially when drinking it before special meals and for fiestas, often prefer it flavored with various fruits.

MEZCAL

The Spaniards then began to use the distilling process they had learned from the Moors to make *mezcal* and tequila from the crushed and roasted *piñas* of other species of maguey. It is important to note that all beverages made from the distilled liquid of the maguey plant are considered *mezcal,* including tequila. *Mezcal* is made all over Mexico, but the major producing region is the state of Oaxaca, where almost thirty thousand families derive their income from growing the maguey plant.

According to ancient legend, "A great thunderbolt struck a maguey and tore out the plant's heart, setting it alight. Astonished men saw aromatic nectar appear deep inside. They drank it without fear and ever since, accepting it as a gift of the gods." Nowadays, using this same concept, the roots and leaves are slashed off the plants growing in the fields and hillsides to expose the *piña,* a giant pineapple-shaped cone. A wood fire is built in a huge, conical pit lined with rocks, and when the fire burns down, the coals are covered with a layer of maguey fiber. The naked *piñas* are thrown on the fire and then covered with more fiber, reed mats, and, finally, soil. They are roasted for three to five days, during which time the natural starches are converted to sugar. They are then removed from the fire, hacked into smaller pieces, and tossed into a *palenque,* a circular area with a central post and giant stone wheel pulled by a horse or donkey. The animal walks endlessly round and round, grinding the roasted *piñas* into pulp, or *bagazo.* The *bagazo* is transferred to large wooden tubs, water is added, and the natural yeast ferments the mixture in about a week. The odor is tantalizingly agreeable.

The resulting liquid is distilled in small, rustic copper or ceramic stills, usually twice, and then bottled, a method almost unchanged since the sixteenth century. Making *mezcal* is still an artisanal craft, and almost all of the *mezcal* that is produced is made in homes known as *palenques,* named for the large, circular area where the roasted *piñas* are crushed. I have been privileged to have spent time in many of the *palenques* in the Oaxacan village of Matatlán and still marvel at the process.

Most non-Mexicans have long considered *mezcal* a "rotgut" drink—very macho—an image that was enhanced by the now-accepted presence in the bottle of "worms," or *gusanos,* which are thought to be a powerful aphrodisiac that improves men's chances of producing male children. They are not worms, however, but the larva of the giant skipper butterfly that perforates the lower part of the maguey plant and tunnels into the interior. In Oaxaca, they are toasted, ground with salt and chile, and used to coat the rim of glasses used for serving *mezcal* and other drinks.

Several savvy Mexican companies are now producing high-quality *mezcal* and marketing it in the United States for deservedly high prices (see Sources).

TEQUILA

In and around the little village of Tequila, in the state of Jalisco, the locals were positive that the *mezcal* made from the species of agave that proliferated in their region was superior to all others. In the late 1800s, this agave, which punctuated the hillsides in shades of blue, drew the attention of German naturalist Franz Weber, who spent time with the family who owned the largest tequila distillery. Because of his research, one variety was selected to carry the name *Agave tequilana Weber* var. *azul*.

Tequila differs in two major ways from *mezcal*. First, by law, it can only be made from this blue agave that grows in the state of Jalisco and in three adjoining states, plus the state of Tamaulipas. The other identifying characteristic is that the *piñas* are roasted in ovens or autoclaves, not wood pits, before fermenting and distilling, which means that tequila does not have the smoky flavor that distinguishes *mezcal*.

The creation of the margarita, one of the spirited drinks of choice around the world, means that tequila is now among the globe's most popular alcoholic beverages. In Mexico, tequila is usually sipped straight, with perhaps a lick of salt, a suck of lime, or the spicy chaser *sangrita*.

Be sure to purchase tequila labeled 100 percent blue agave. Other tequilas, especially some marketed as gold tequila, will include additives such as caramel color, glycerin, oak extract flavoring, and cane sugar. There are three major types of tequila:

Tequila blanco. An elegant unaged tequila, reminiscent of premium vodka, only with the assertive flavors of the agave.

Tequila reposado. "Resting" for two to twelve months in oak barrels produces a mellow tequila that is usually my choice before a meal and even during it when I am not drinking wine.

Tequila añejo. For a luxurious after-dinner sipping experience, try a good-quality *añejo* that has been aged from eighteen months to three years (to be labeled *añejo*, a tequila must be aged a minimum of one year). Its complex, mellow flavors recall Cognac.

COOLING DRINKS

Aguas frescas run the gamut from rice-white *horchata*, dusky-red *jamaica*, and molasses-brown *tamarindo* to simple melon waters, all served to revive your spirits. You will find pitchers of these same *aguas frescas* accompanying meals in homes and in restaurants.

AGUA FRESCA DE SANDIA
Watermelon Water

During the mid-1700s, João António Cavazzi de Montecúccolo, an Italian historian and missionary who visited Angola and parts of the present-day Congo, wrote that "the Blacks eat large quantities of these fruits [watermelons] . . . and are used to putting them in water in order to make it tastier."

This colorful and refreshing watermelon drink, which is popular throughout Mexico, is equally delicious made with cantaloupe or almost any fruit in season. Try using pineapple, mango, papaya, strawberries, oranges, mandarins, or limes, or a combination of fruits. I even make it with cucumbers. You can also use sparkling water instead of plain. For a party, a tipple of vodka or light rum poured into each glass will add to the merriment.

Serves 4

2 pounds seedless watermelon, rind removed and roughly chopped (about 3 cups)

1 lime

¼ cup sugar or less, depending on the sweetness of the melon

Ice cubes (optional)

1 cup watermelon balls (optional)

Put the chopped melon in a blender or food processor with 1 cup water and process until smooth. Strain through a medium-mesh sieve into a large pitcher. Halve the lime and squeeze the juice from half into the pitcher; reserve the remaining half for serving. Stir in the sugar, cover, and refrigerate until well chilled.

Just before serving, stir well. If you like, put a couple of ice cubes and a few watermelon balls into each glass, then pour in the watermelon water. Garnish each glass with a lime slice.

AGUA FRESCA DE JAMAICA
Hibiscus Water

This popular beverage is made from the dried dusky red "flowers" of a type of hibiscus (not the common garden variety). Although they look like flower blossoms, they are the sepals that cover the petals before they bloom. This refreshing *agua fresca*, the white rice drink *horchata* (page 275), and rich brown, tart *tamarindo* (page 273) are sold from large glass barrels by street vendors throughout Mexico, and are just as often the primary beverages in Mexican *fondas* and restaurants. Although it is not traditional in Mexico, I like to mix *jamaica* with an equal amount of fruity red wine for serving at informal gatherings.

Jamaica can be found in Mexican grocery stores and also in most health-foods stores, as it is high in vitamin C and is used as a diuretic.

Makes about 7 cups concentrated water; serves 8 to 10 when diluted

2 cups jamaica (about 2 ounces)

½ cup honey or sugar

Peel of 1 scrubbed orange, in strips

1 cup freshly squeezed orange juice or water, or as needed

Ice cubes

Pour 6 cups water into a large saucepan and bring to a boil over medium-high heat. Add the *jamaica*, honey, and orange zest, lower the heat to medium, and simmer, stirring frequently, for 5 minutes. Remove from the heat and let the mixture steep for 1 hour.

Strain the liquid through a fine-mesh sieve placed over a glass pitcher, pressing through as much liquid as possible with the back of a wooden spoon. Taste for sweetness and add more honey or sugar if needed, then dilute with orange juice to taste. Cover and refrigerate for several hours or for up to overnight. Serve over ice cubes in tall glasses.

AGUA FRESCA DE TAMARINDO
Tamarind Cooler

Tart and tangy tamarind water, one of Mexico's most popular *aguas frescas*, is made from the reddish brown, sticky pulp of the tamarind pod and is especially delicious served with Tinga de Cerdo (page 147) and other strong-flavored dishes. It can be made from scratch from the pulp of the pod, or you can use a paste or a concentrate, which can be purchased in Mexican, Indian, or Southeast Asian grocery stores or in some gourmet shops.

If you are traveling along the Pacific coast between Puerto Vallarta and Manzanillo, you may see tall, bushy trees smothered with red-streaked vibrant yellow blossoms. Later in the season, you may notice only the long beanlike pods dangling from the branches.

This is the tamarind tree, and although it now grows on both coasts of Mexico, the tree is originally from tropical Africa, where it still grows wild and is also cultivated. Early on the sour-sweet pulp was prized by people in India and Asia as a cooking ingredient. For example, if you examine the label on a bottle of Worcestershire sauce or a jar of chutney, tamarind extract will be listed.

You might want to double the recipe for this *agua fresca* to have enough for another time, as it is will keep in the refrigerator up to 4 days.

Serves 4 . . . .

½ pound tamarind pods (about 9), as fresh as possible

½ cup sugar

Ice cubes

To extract the pulp from each tamarind pod, pull out the stem, removing the pithy strings and tearing off the skin. You will be left with just the pulp and some big seeds. Put the tamarind pulp and seeds in a saucepan, add 3 cups water, and bring to a boil over medium-high heat. Reduce the heat to medium and simmer for 5 minutes. Pour into a plastic or glass container and let soak for 2 hours, stirring often with a wooden spoon to help break up the pulp.

While the tamarind is soaking, bring 2 cups water to a low boil, add the sugar, and stir until it dissolves. Remove from the heat and let cool.

When the pulp feels soft, using your hands, rub and squeeze the pulp to separate it from the seeds and any remaining fibers. Pour the pulp and soaking water into a fine-mesh sieve placed over a bowl. Press down hard with the back of a wooden spoon to extract the puree. Discard the solids and pour the tamarind liquid into a pitcher. Add the sweetened water and stir well. Taste and add more sugar if needed. Cover and refrigerate until well chilled. Just before serving, stir well. Serve over ice cubes in tall glasses.

NOTE

If you have purchased seedless tamarind paste, use 1 cup thick paste. Put it in a blender or food processor, add 2 cups water, and pulse until well broken up. Now follow the same directions you would use if you had started with whole pods, pressing the mixture through a sieve, adding the sweetened water, and chilling.

If you have purchased tamarind concentrate, dilute it according to the directions on the jar, then add the sweetened water and chill.

HORCHATA CON COCO
Coconut Rice Cooler

On a sun-blistering day in Mexico or Spain, nothing is more refreshing than a glass of icy-cold *horchata*. In Spain, this creamy beverage of Arabic origin was originally made from *chufa*, or tiger nuts *(Cyperus esculentes)*, small, wrinkled brown-skinned tubers with no apparent similarity to tigers or nuts, although they have a mildly nutty flavor. I first sampled this ancient Moorish drink in the province of Valencia, in eastern Spain, and became enamored, but much more common was *horchata* of rice, Valencia's most famous crop.

In Mexico, although *horchata* is usually made from rice, I've also enjoyed a delicious version in Colima that included almonds, and one in Yucatán made with melon seeds.

Ricardo likes to prepare *horchata* using fresh coconut milk, but substituting unsweetened canned coconut milk provides good flavor with much less work. If you are up to the challenge of making fresh coconut milk, the instructions follow.

Serves 6 to 8

1 cup long- or medium-grain white rice

2 (3-inch) sticks Mexican true cinnamon bark (page 88), crumbled

1 cup coconut milk

1 cup sugar

Grated zest of 1 lime

6 to 8 sprigs fresh mint

12 to 16 small cantaloupe balls or cubes (optional)

Pulverize the rice in a spice grinder or heavy-duty blender. Pour into a bowl and add the cinnamon. Stir in 3 cups hot water, cover, and let soak for at least 6 hours or preferably overnight. It does not need to be refrigerated.

The next day, working in batches, put the water with the rice and cinnamon along with the coconut milk into a blender and puree until quite smooth, about 5 minutes, making sure the mixture is not gritty.

Line a medium-mesh sieve with several layers of damp cheesecloth and place it over a large pitcher. Pour the rice mixture through the sieve, a little at a time, scraping and squeezing it into the pitcher. Combine the sugar and 3 cups water in a saucepan over low heat, add the lime zest, and stir until the sugar is completely dissolved. Set aside to cool.

Stir the cooled sweetened water into the rice mixture, cover, and refrigerate until very cold and almost slushy. Stir well, then pour into tall glasses. Garnish with the mint sprigs and cantaloupe (if using) for color contrast.

To make coconut milk from a fresh coconut, select a coconut that emits a sloshing sound when shaken. Pierce two of the three "eyes" with a nail or screwdriver and drain the liquid into a measuring cup. If needed, stir in enough water to make ¾ cup. Using a hammer, hit the sides of the coconut about one-third of the way down from the eyes. Keep tapping until it breaks open. Pry out the flesh, break into chunks, and cut away the brown skin. Grate enough flesh to total ¾ cup tightly packed. Add the coconut to the liquid to total about 1 cup. Pour the mixture into a small saucepan, bring to a boil over medium-high heat, and then remove from the heat and let cool.

Pour the cooled mixture into a blender and process until thoroughly ground. Line a fine-mesh sieve with dampened cheesecloth and place over a bowl. Pour the coconut mixture into the sieve, allowing it to drip through. Then gather the corners of the cheesecloth and squeeze the cloth to extract any remaining creamy liquid. You should have about 1 cup coconut milk. Any leftover coconut flesh can be enjoyed right away or grated and refrigerated for several days for later use. It can also be frozen in an airtight container for up to 6 months.

⋮ HOT RESTORATIVES

Coffee is a relative newcomer to Mexico—the first coffee plantations appeared in Veracruz in the early 1800s—but rich, darkly brewed coffee is almost everyone's favorite way to start and end the day.

The more traditional hot beverages, such as nourishing masa-based *atole* or frothy, comforting chocolate, are now served less often, even though both had a significant role in the history and survival of the Mexican people. If you are offered a tamal on a cold morning, however, one or the other will still be poured into a cup or bowl as part of the meal.

ATOLE AGRIO
Tangy Fresh Corn Atole

Mexicans not only eat their corn but also drink it. *Atoles,* nourishing gruel-like hot beverages usually made from masa, were an essential part of the diet of the indigenous people and they are still popular, especially to accompany tamales. Although *atole* is traditionally served plain, it is now frequently flavored with tropical fruits and sometimes even chiles. In a village in Chiapas near the archeological site of Palenque, Ricardo came across this unusual version that calls for ground fresh corn, which is intentionally left to sour. This *atole* is important to the indigenous Zoque inhabitants who still speak their native language. On a cold and dreary morning in Michoacán, a Purépecha woman served me a comforting, quite similar *atole* made from fresh blue-black corn and ground dried chiles.

Look for corn that is as starchy as possible, such as field corn, to achieve the proper consistency. Be sure to avoid supersweet corn.

Serves 5 or 6 . . . .

6 ears starchy corn, husks and silk removed

3 tablespoons chopped piloncillo (page 42), azúcar morena or other unrefined brown cane sugar, or dark brown sugar, or to taste

1½-inch stick Mexican true cinnamon bark (page 88), ground, or 2 teaspoons ground cinnamon, or to taste

With a sharp knife, slice the kernels from the ears of corn. Put the kernels in a blender, add 1 cup water, and process until smooth. Pour into a bowl, cover, and let rest at room temperature for at least 12 hours to sour the mixture.

Pour the corn mixture into a fine-mesh sieve placed over a bowl and push the starchy paste through with the back of a wooden spoon. Transfer to a saucepan, place over medium-high heat, add 2 cups water, and bring to a boil, stirring with a wooden spoon to avoid sticking. Reduce the heat to a gentle simmer and cook until the mixture is the consistency of a milk shake, about 20 minutes, adding up to 1 cup more water as needed to achieve a good consistency. Stir in the sugar and cinnamon and continue to simmer for a few minutes longer.

Skim off any foam from the surface, then pour into heavy mugs. Wait for a few minutes before serving, as *atole* can be dangerously hot to drink.

Cacao

According to my close friend and chocolate expert Elaine González, this is the tale of how cacao and chocolate were given to Mexico's inhabitants. She has told this story with great flourish many times during our trips to Tabasco and Oaxaca.

It was written in the ancient chronicles that the gods looked down with pity on the Toltecs in Tula struggling to survive in the barren land where they lived, and resolved that the God of Light, Quetzalcóatl, should assume human form and descend into their midst on a beam of starlight to teach them matters of science and the arts to help them cope with life's hardships.

Startled by his luminous arrival, unusual fair skin, and glowing white beard, the Toltecs accepted his apparition as a godly one. He was loved and admired by all and looked on as a man of virtue with high ideals and strong moral convictions. The doctrine that Quetzalcóatl preached was based on the existence of one supreme god who was not only the giver of life and death, but the creator of the sky, sea, and earth; the lesser gods were but manifestations of him. Just as this god was creative, so man should be, creating things whenever possible, not destroying them, said Quetzalcóatl. These teachings inspired among the Toltecs an artistic movement that spread throughout the central valley of Mexico.

As an act of love, Quetzalcóatl bestowed on his people a little shrub that had, until then, belonged exclusively to the gods. This *cacahuatl*, or cacao (its scientific name, *Theobroma*, meaning "food of the Gods"), was planted in the rugged fields high above Tula where Tlaloc, the rain god, saw that it was adequately nourished and Xochiquetzatl, the goddess of love and happiness, adorned it with beautiful blossoms and infused it with her spirit.

The other gods witnessed the harvesting of the fruit of this tree with increasing displeasure. A chocolate drink, *xocoatl*, prepared with the roasted beans was considered the sacred liquor of the gods but soon became an important drink among the priests and nobles of Quetzalcóatl's court as well. Cacao beans also were used as money and became symbols of a person's wealth.

Enraged by these acts of sacrilege and Quetzalcoátl's betrayal, the gods sought retribution and the ultimate destruction of the Toltec empire. They dispatched Texcatlipoca, the god of night and darkness, on a mission destined to destroy them all. Dressed as a merchant, he descended to earth on a black spider's thread to await a confrontation with his archrival, Quetzalcoátl.

Though ominous dreams of doom had forewarned him, Quetzalcoátl, an avowed abstainer, fell prey to Tezcatlipoca's evil scheme and drank the fermented juice of the *maguey*, which Tezcatlipoca offered to him as an elixir to quiet his fears of reprisal from the gods. The effect of the potent pulque was devastating, and the drunken Quetzalcoátl shouted and danced shamelessly before his scandalized people until, exhausted at last, he fell into a long, deep sleep.

It was with dismay that he discovered upon awakening that he had dishonored himself in an irreversible way with such deplorable behavior that he felt he should no longer rule the people that he loved. Grief stricken, Quetzalcoátl set out on foot on a long and perilous journey in the direction of the evening star, his home. The cacao trees that he passed along the way reflected the impending doom that prevailed throughout the land. Once green leaved and heavy with fruit, they now stood shriveled and dry, transformed into thorny mesquite trees. He scooped up a few of the remaining beans, held them tightly within his palm, and continued on his sorrowful way.

When at last he arrived at the shore of Tabasco, he cast a handful of his precious cacao beans on the beach, the god of light's parting gift to mankind. Promising to return in the year A.D. 1519, Quetzalcoátl stepped onto a beam of light from the evening star and ascended to his home.

The thorny mesquite trees still grow in the high regions surrounding Tula, painful reminders today of the demise of a great empire. But in the distant tropical land where Quetzalcoátl spent his final hours, his remarkable gift of love, the cacao tree, still flourishes, with chocolate his lasting memento.

CHOCOLATE
Cinnamon-Spiced Hot Chocolate

Mexico's cacao bean is one of its most important gifts to the world, and the comforting beverage made from it, frothy hot chocolate, is almost always served with tamales. The roasted cacao beans are ground, flavored with sugar, cinnamon, and sometimes almonds, and then formed into solid round tablets. In Oaxaca and in other states with a large indigenous population, the chocolate is often diluted with water, but throughout the rest of the country, milk is used. Mexican chocolate is readily available in most grocery stores, and more and more excellent brands are increasingly available (see Sources). Check the instructions on the package for the suggested amount of chocolate to use.

Serves 4

4 cups whole milk

4 to 5 ounces Mexican chocolate, broken into pieces

Pour the milk into a saucepan and bring to a simmer over low heat. Add the chocolate and stir continuously until the chocolate melts. With a whisk or a handheld mixer, beat until the milk has a layer of thick foam. Serve immediately in warmed mugs.

CAFÉ DE OLLA
Sweet-Spiced Coffee Brewed in a Clay Pot

The cloud-wrapped highlands of Veracruz, Oaxaca, and Chiapas provide ideal growing conditions for the shiny, green-leaved coffee plant and its bright red fruit, especially when further protected by the overhanging leaves of taller banana trees. After the fruits, or "berries," are picked and sun-dried, each of their two segments, now considered coffee beans, are roasted and then later brewed for a special cup of coffee.

In Mexico, a cup of hot *café de olla* is a tasty way to end a traditional meal. I sometimes pour in a little Kahlúa or other coffee liqueur when serving to enhance the flavors.

Serves 4

4 ounces piloncillo (page 42), chopped, or ½ cup azúcar morena or other unrefined brown cane sugar or firmly packed dark brown sugar

2 (2-inch) sticks Mexican true cinnamon bark (page 88)

3 whole cloves

Pinch of aniseeds (optional)

½ cup coarsely ground dark-roasted coffee, preferably Viennese roast

Pour 4 cups water into an earthenware pot or saucepan and bring to a boil over medium-high heat. Stir in the sugar, cinnamon, cloves, and aniseeds (if using) and continue to stir until the sugar has dissolved. Add the coffee, and when it just begins to simmer again, remove from the heat, cover, and let steep for 5 minutes.

Line a small, fine-mesh sieve with damp cheesecloth. Pour the coffee through the sieve directly into warmed mugs, or pour into a larger warm container until ready to serve.

Acknowledgments

Like my book *Cocina de la Familia,* this is more a historical culinary story than a Mexican cookbook, and it is enriched by the extensive knowledge of Mexican food, both past and present, of Ricardo Muñoz Zurita. Thank you, dear friend, for joining me.

In researching this book, I talked and cooked with many old friends and new acquaintances who shared their recipes with me, often just by letting me watch them prepare a favorite dish and eyeball the amounts. In particular, I want to thank Raquel Torres and Yolanda Ramos, both food anthropologists; Abigail Mendoza; Silvio Campos; Mónica Maestretta; Emelia Cabrera and her daughters Pilar and Aurora; and all of the other cooks and friends who openly shared their knowledge with me over the years, such as Roberto Santibañez, Elaine González, Shelley Wiseman, Carmen Ramírez Degollado, Susana Trilling, Patricia Quintana, and Iliana de la Vega. I am only sorry that I cannot list you all.

I am especially indebted to that esteemed cook of Mexico, María Dolores Torres Yzábal. I treasure her insights and her sense of humor. She is one great lady. I met María Dolores through Diana Kennedy, as she was Diana's mentor in the world of Mexican food, as Diana was mine. I thank you, Diana, for introducing us and for being my friend for so many years. You are special to me and I have absorbed many values and much knowledge from you during our times together.

For more than two decades, I have visited the diverse culinary regions of Mexico with Rick Bayless, and to him I owe a deeper understanding of how to prepare dishes that appeal even to those not familiar with Mexican food while always staying true to the sources.

I owe a special debt to Kathie Vezzani, Ana Elena Martínez, and Carmen Barnard Baca. Kathie coordinates the efforts of Culinary Adventures from Gig Harbor, Washington, and Ana Elena from Puebla, Mexico. Both have traveled and worked with me for the past thirteen years. For this book, Kathie deciphered my scribbles and tested many of the recipes with me; Ana Elena traveled with me throughout Mexico on my research trips, even venturing with me into the remote Costa Chica of Oaxaca and Guerrero; and Carmen, who was my first coordinator in Mexico, translated any recipes that I could not fathom. I could not have accomplished what I have over the past twenty years without all three of these women.

A great number of others have made my dream into a reality. First, I must thank my longtime agents, Maureen and Eric Lasher. Because of my ambition to write quite a different book, one with a historical perspective, the Lashers connected me with a new editor, Sheila Levine, at the University of California Press. Sheila saw the value of all the research I had done and with great patience and understanding worked with me to achieve my objectives. Upon Sheila's retirement, Kate Marshall became the new food and agriculture editor and Dore Brown the project editor. I owe them both a huge thank-you for their guiding wisdom and encouragement. I am also grateful to Sharon Silva for her detailed copyediting and for her patience, and to Thérèse Shere for her indexing skills.

I cannot stop here, though, as one of my dearest friends, Nacho (Ignacio) Urquiza shot the compelling photos. Melanie Ferguson, who has designed my brochures since my first culinary trip and is now an accomplished artist in Atlanta, Georgia, drew the map for this book. Sannie Osborn provided me with invaluable research material and always when it was most needed. I respect and thank you all.

Every one of these recipes was tested by me and many first by Ricardo, but I also had a volunteer group of both professional chefs and home cooks who diligently tested each recipe. I express my deepest appreciation to them for their invaluable comments: Claire Archibald, Frank Ching, Amanda Clark, Paige Delaney, Kathy FitzGerald, Leslie Garcia, Susan Goldberg, Margi Heater, Julie Hettiger, Mary Huigens, Deborah Hoy, Stephanie Maiers-Chamber, Amy McDonald-Persons, David Mitchell, Dan Osborn, Lupe Peach, Gayla Pierce, Joan Rulland, Kathy Salmonson, Sarah Schiller, Tom Siegel, CC Walthers, Kathryn Williams, and especially Susan Kay, who never said no to testing just one more complicated dish. This book is a tribute to all of you.

Finally, I am indebted to the International Association of Culinary Professionals (IACP) for the 2007 Harry A. Bell Travel Grant from IACP's Culinary Trust, which provided financial support in the beginning of this project.

∾ *Marilyn*

This book is the culmination of my many years of researching the foods of the country where I was born and of trips that I have done jointly with my friend Marilyn Tausend. I owe thanks to many of the cooks in my family who started me on this path, especially my mother, Patricia Zurita Sarracino. And I am indebted to others whom I met along the way, all of whom proudly shared their regional culinary specialties with me.

∾ *Ricardo*

Sources

Here are some places to buy items you might not be able to find locally.

Abundant Life Seeds, Cottage Grove, Oregon, has organic seeds, including purslane; www.abundantlifeseeds.com.

Aurora Exports, Susana Trilling's Seasons of My Hearts Imports, Oaxaca, Mexico, is a good source of high-quality chocolate, moles, and sea salt; www.seasonsofmyheart.com.

The CMC Company, Avalano, New Jersey, has an extensive selection of ingredients and equipment, including dried avocado leaves; www.thecmccompany.com.

Del Maguey Mezcals, Oaxaca, Mexico, and Ranchos de Taos, New Mexico, carries high-quality unblended *mezcals;* www.mezcal.com.

Frontera Kitchens, Chicago, Illinois, stocks dried and canned Mexican ingredients and cookware; www.fronterakitchens.com.

It's About Thyme, Austin Texas, is my favorite source of *hierba santa* plants, Mexican oregano, and epazote; www.itsaboutthyme.com.

Johnny's Selected Seeds, Winslow, Maine, has a good variety of Mexican herbs and vegetable seeds; www.johnnyseeds.com.

Melissa Guerra Tienda de Cocina, San Antonio, Texas, sells Mexican cookware and ingredients; www.melissaguerra.com.

Mexico By Hand, Berkeley, California, has lead-free traditional Mexican cookware and hammered copper from Michoacán; www.mexicobyhand.com.

The Mozzarella Company, Dallas, Texas, carries a great *queso fresco* and a *cacciota* that is a good substitute for *queso Chihuahua;* www.mozzco.com.

Native Seeds Search, Tucson, Arizona, stocks seeds, chiles, and various Mexican herbs; www.nativeseeds.org.

Purcell Mountain Farms, Moyie Springs, Idaho, has various types of dried corn; www.purcellmountainfarms.com.

Rancho Gordo New World Specialty Food, Napa, California, promotes many types of dried Mexican beans; www.ranchogordo.com.

Seeds of Change, Santa Fe, New Mexico, carries heirloom seeds of many essential Mexican herbs and plants; www.seedsofchange.com.

The Spanish Table is a source for churro makers and other Spanish cookware; www.spanishtable.com.

Winchester Cheese Company, Winchester, California. Born in the Netherlands, Jules Wesserlink and family make and sell traditional Dutch cheeses, including Edam and Gouda; www.sales@winchestercheese.com.

Index